WOMEN
OF THE
CLOTH

A New Opportunity for the Churches

Jackson W. Carroll, Ph.D.

Barbara Hargrove, Ph.D.

Adair T. Lummis, Ph.D.

1817

Harper & Row, Publishers, San Francisco

Cambridge, Hagerstown, New York, Philadelphia
London, Mexico City, São Paulo, Sydney

The research for this book was made possible by a grant from the Ford Foundation.

FIRST EDITION

Designer: Jim Mennick   •

Library of Congress Cataloging in Publication Data

Carroll, Jackson W.
  WOMEN OF THE CLOTH.

  1. Women clergy—United States. 2. United States—Church history—20th century. I. Hargrove, Barbara. II. Lummis, Adair T. III. Title.
BV676.C38   1982   262'.14   82-47740
ISBN 0-06-061321-1

83 84 85 86 87 10 9 8 7 6 5 4 3 2 1

Contents

List of Tables		*vi*
Preface		*ix*
1.	Women in Ministry: An Introduction	*I*
2.	American Churches and "Women's Place"	*20*
3.	The Family Font: Family Backgrounds and Life Before Seminary	*49*
4.	Entering the Male Citadel: Women Come to Seminary	*75*
5.	Experiences of Women and Men Clergy in the Job Market	*109*
6.	Clergy Effectiveness and Church Stability: A Different Equation for Men and Women?	*139*
7.	Interpersonal Relationships on the Job	*160*
8.	Personal Life and Pastoral Commitment	*188*
9.	Some Concluding Reflections: Milk, Honey, and Giants	*203*
	Appendix: Overall Individual Responses to Clergy Interview/Questionnaire	*215*
	Notes	*259*
	Index	*270*

Tables

1.1: Women in Selected Professions, 1930–1980   4

1.2: Women Clergy in Selected Denominations, 1977 and 1981   6

1.3: Women Enrolled in Master of Divinity Programs in Seminaries of Selected Denominations, Fall 1980   7

1.4: Completion Rates for the Sample of Clergywomen   15

1.5: Completion Rates for the Sample of Clergymen   17

3.1: Parental Background of Clergywomen and Clergymen   54

3.2: Original Denomination, Present Denomination, and Sex of Clergy   58

3.3: Church Activity During the Ages 18 to 22   62

3.4: Percent Making a Late Decision to Enter Seminary   63

3.5: Timing of Decision to Enter Seminary   63

3.6: Percentage of Late Deciders to Enter Seminary   65

3.7: Age Entered Seminary and Time of Decision to Enter Seminary   69

3.8: Type of Full-Time Occupation of Clergy Prior to Ordination   70

3.9: Age Upon Entering Seminary   72

4.1: Parental Background and Type of Seminary Attended   81

4.2: Motivations for Attending Seminary   83

4.3: Clergy Motivations for Being in Seminary   84

4.4: Year of Enrollment in Seminary and the Number of Women in Student Body at That Time   92

4.5: Degree to Which a Desire to Change the Sexist
Nature of the Church Was Important in
Clergywomen's Decision to Be Ordained   97
4.6: Distribution of Scores on the Organizational
Church Feminism Scale Among Women and Men
Clergy and Lay Respondents   101
4.7: Approximate Dates When Women Were First
Ordained and Percentage of Strong Feminists
Among Male Clergy   102
5.1: Perceived Ease of Getting a Parish Position
Slightly Better Than the One Now Held   117
5.2: Use and Effectiveness of Deployment Structures 120
5.3: Type of Position in Ministry   126
5.4: Position in Church and Pastoral Experience   127
5.5: Comparisons of First, Second, and Third-Plus
Parishes of Clergywomen and Clergymen as Sole
or Senior Pastors   129
5.6: Cash Salary Paid to Women and Men Clergy in
Sole or Senior Pastorates Comparing First,
Second, and Third-Plus Parishes   131
6.1: Selected Attitudes of Lay Leaders Regarding
Women Ministers   143
6.2: Lay Leaders' Responses   154
6.3: Ratings of Ministerial Effectiveness   156
6.4: Social Class and Clergy Feelings of
Accomplishment   158
7.1: Getting Along with Types of Laity   165
8.1: Spouse Resentment of Ministry   193

Preface

Cultural images do not change easily, especially those weighted with the aura of sacred tradition. This book is about changes that one such image is undergoing as increasing numbers of women enter the ordained ministry of several Protestant denominations. The image of the ordained ministry is for many people a masculine one, as we have been repeatedly reminded in sharing our findings with various audiences. But it is changing, and this book shares some of the successes and difficulties experienced by women in breaking the old stereotypes as they have entered parish ministry. Using data from interviews with samples of clergywomen, clergymen, lay leaders, and other church officials in nine Protestant denominations, we present an analysis of clergywomen, comparing them with clergymen. Our focus is on who they are and what their experiences have been in seminary, the job market, the parish, and balancing their careers with their personal lives.

We wish to emphasize the comparative perspective of the book. While the primary focus is on clergywomen, the book also gives considerable attention to clergymen. While there are unique dimensions to the experiences of clergywomen, it is important that the experiences of women pastors be seen both in their similarities as well as differences from those of men.

The book is intended for a broad audience, but especially for those interested in the ministry of the church. Clergy (both women and men), laity puzzling over whether to call a woman as pastor, denominational officials, and seminary students, faculty, and administrators will, we hope, find the book helpful. Additionally, because the entry of women into the ordained ministry is part of a larger movement of women into a variety of traditionally male occupations and professions, sociologists and others interested in these broad changes should find the book of interest.

A word about the point of view of the book is important. It is basically a descriptive work, drawing principally on sociological perspectives and methods. The authors themselves are sociologists, and one is also an ordained minister. We are likewise faculty members in theological seminaries and involved in the life of the church. These various statuses that we occupy are important in informing our work and commitments. As sociologists, we have tried to present our findings as objectively and fairly as possible, avoiding—insofar as we are aware—ideological stances in the various controversies regarding women as ordained ministers. At the same time, we would be less than candid if we did not acknowledge our fundamental sympathy for women in ordained ministry. We believe, as the subtitle suggests, that they provide a new opportunity for the churches. Nevertheless, we believe that their cause is best served by an honest telling of their story.

The study has been made possible by a generous grant from the Ford Foundation and by additional support from our respective institutions, Hartford Seminary and the Iliff School of Theology. We are particularly grateful to Mariam Chamberlain, Program Officer in Education and Public Policy at the Ford Foundation during much of the course of this study. Her concern for women in the professions, and her support and counsel in the development of this project have been very helpful.

It has also been essential to have the cooperation and assistance of the nine denominations included in the study. Official representatives of the denominations who worked with us helpfully in a variety of ways include the Rev. Faye Ignatius, American Baptist Churches in the U.S.A.; the Rev. Dr. Roger Fjeld, The American Lutheran Church; the Rev. Susan M. Robinson, Christian Church (Disciples of Christ); the Rt. Rev. Elliott L. Sorge, The Episcopal Church; the Rev. Joseph Wagner, Lutheran Church in America; the Rev. Dr. Dianne Tennis, Presbyterian Church in the United States; Marilyn Breitling, United Church of Christ; the Rev. Kathy Nickerson, The United Methodist Church; and the Rev. Ann DuBois, The United Presbyterian Church in the United States of America. We could not have completed the study without their cooperation and support.

Additionally, a number of other denominational executives, seminary faculty, clergywomen, and sociologists either served on an advisory committee or contributed insights and feedback regarding the research design and early drafts of the book. They include LaVonne Althouse, Christine Brewer, Fran Craddock, Sister Sophie Damm, Mary Sudman Donovan, Davida Foy Crabtree, Sara A. Edwards, Yoshio Fukuyama, Anne Harrison, Beverly Wildung Harrison, Suzanne Hiatt, Edward Lehman, Doris Jones, Larry Mamiya, D. Barry Menuez, Jeanne Audrey Powers, Ruth Rasche, Roddey Reid, David A. Roozen, Joan Russell, Lois Sanders, Lloyd E. Sheneman, Hilah Thomas, Kathryn Williams, Deaconess Louise Williams, and Barbara Wheeler.

A large number of other individuals also helped with the research.

While space precludes listing all of them, several are due particular thanks for their assistance in the collection, organization, and processing of the data and in preparation of the manuscript. They include Mary Jane Ross (principal research assistant), Wilhelmina Bijlefeld, Nancy and Tom Harney, Arlene Nickerson, Gilda Simpson, and Kathy D. Jansen.

Finally, we must express our deepest appreciation to the clergywomen and men, denominational officials, and seminary personnel who gave of their time in sharing insights and experiences in the interviews and questionnaires. Without their help this study would—literally—have not been possible.

Jackson W. Carroll
Barbara Hargrove
Adair T. Lummis

1

Women in Ministry: An Introduction

Census data provide little evidence for the increased professionalization of clergywomen, greater acceptance of women as clergy, [or] more use of the clergy by women as an occupational outlet. . . . In fact, the data may be interpreted to question attributing the very label of "profession" to these females. In some characteristics (e.g., educational attainment), they are more like the general labor force than like other professionals. The differences between male and female clergy in age, educational attainment, and marital status are quite conspicuous, and these distinctions suggest that clergy roles are different for females than for males or are differentially experienced by the two sexes. The opportunities for females to act as clergy are more limited than for males, and these limitations have produced a composite picture of the female clergy that at least suggests professional marginality. [1]

This assessment of the status and role of clergywomen was made by sociologist Wilbur Bock in 1967, using trend data from the U.S. Census from 1900 to 1960. We believe it to be a generally accurate assessment of the situation existing up to that time; yet, reading it in the early 1980s we become strikingly aware of changes that have occurred since he wrote.

When the history of American Protestantism during the 1970s is written, surely one of the important developments to be chronicled will be the entry of large numbers of women into the ranks of the ordained clergy, with the attendant conflicts and changes surrounding their entry. For some denominations, this dramatic increase in women clergy built on a previous history of ordaining women to the ministry. (We use the terms *clergy, ordained ministry,* and *pastor* interchangeably.) For others, notably the Episcopal Church, the decision to ordain women came only in 1977, and was preceded and followed by bitter contro-

versy. In either case, the large-scale entry of women into this traditionally male profession is an important phenomenon, one that many ap-
plaud and others decry. This growth in the number of clergywomen
has created a new situation in the ministerial profession and the
churches. The assessment made by Bock in 1967 needs to be updated
in light of the trends of the seventies. Who are these women? Why have
they chosen to become clergy? What have their experiences been in
seminary? In the job market? How are they functioning in the various
roles which ministers perform? How do they differ from their male
counterparts? How are they accepted by laity and male clergy? Are they
still marginal? What changes are they likely to bring to the ministry
and to the church? These are questions asked by many who view the
entry of women either with hope or alarm. These also are among the
questions that we attempt to answer in the following pages. We do so in
the conviction, as the title of this book suggests, that these "women of
the cloth" present "a new opportunity for the churches."

Our focus is on parish ministry in nine Protestant denominations in
the United States. The denominations include the American Baptist
Churches in the U.S.A., the American Lutheran Church, the Christian
Church (Disciples of Christ), the Episcopal Church, the Lutheran
Church in America, the Presbyterian Church in the United States, the
United Church of Christ, the United Methodist Church, and the
United Presbyterian Church in the United States of America. These
denominations are not the only ones to ordain women, nor do they
necessarily include the earliest incidence of ordaining women among
American Protestants, as we note in Chapter 2. They are, however, the
mainline Protestant denominations with the largest number of women
clergy. By "mainline," we follow Martin Marty's definition implying
religious groups that represent "the traditional, inherited, normative,
or median style of American spirituality and organization."[2] Among the
denominations with significant numbers of women clergy, these
denominations also have more formal requirements and processes for
ordaining and deploying clergy. The Roman Catholic Church and the
Orthodox Churches do not ordain women to be priests, and therefore
we do not focus on those churches in our study. The Southern Baptist
Convention, the largest Protestant denomination in the United States,
is not included here because, while it has no stated rule against ordaining women, in practice very few women are ordained as pastors by its
congregations.

We have chosen to limit our analysis to parish ministry, not only for
the sake of manageability, but because the parish is the principal and
most visible context in which clergy work. While ordained clergy, including women, work in other contexts and positions—for example, in

denominational staff positions, as campus ministers, and as chaplains and pastoral counselors—half to two-thirds of all active clergy in these denominations are in parish ministry positions. Thus the parish is the context in which clergy most frequently relate to laity and the public at large and are, thereby, the most visible.

Numbers of Women Clergy and Women Professionals

The large-scale entry of women into the ordained ministry is not an isolated phenomenon. It is part and parcel of broader changes in the attitudes and structure of American society regarding "woman's place," including her place in the work force. In 1950, for example, 29.6 percent of the American labor force was female; by 1980, the percentage increased to 42.5.[3] This growth reflects the entry of women into a variety of traditionally male occupations, including the professions. Several professions, notably nursing and elementary-school teaching, have long been regarded as "suitable" for women (requiring affective and nurturing qualities typically associated with the family and women); however, women have only recently begun to enter traditionally male-dominated professions in significant numbers. Table 1.1 shows the fifty-year trend for the percentages of clergywomen, based on the total number of clergy, men and women, in *all* religious bodies in the U.S., as reported by the Bureau of the Census and the U.S. Department of Labor. The figures include those religious traditions which do not ordain women, such as the Roman Catholic Church. This fact affects the figures for women as a percentage of total clergy and, as we shall see, somewhat obscures the sharp increases in the proportions of clergywomen in the nine Protestant denominations included in our research. This limitation notwithstanding, Table 1.1 shows a number of interesting trends.

For one thing, it shows that the long-term trend has been one of increases in women entrants into each of the three traditionally male professions. When the change in the number of women in each profession is computed, the fifty-year figures show increases of 240 percent in the overall number of clergywomen, 574 percent for women physicians, and a phenomenal 1,986 percent for women lawyers. In spite of these striking growth rates, the table reveals that women as a percentage of the total in the three professions is still rather small, more so for clergy than for the other two professions. Each is still male dominated. The table also shows the sharp increase in women entrants that occurred in each profession during the 1970s; although this rapid increase began for physicians somewhat earlier in the 1960s. The increase for women lawyers during the 1970s—over 400 percent—is especially notable. It reflects an overall substantial increase in the number of lawyers, male and

Table 1.1 Women in Selected Professions, 1930–1980
(Number and Percent of Total)

Profession	1930		1940		1950		1960		1970		1980	
	#	%	#	%	#	%	#	%	#	%	#	%
Clergy	3,276	2.2	3,148	2.3	6,777	4.1	4,272	2.3	6,314	2.9	11,130	4.2
Lawyers, judges	3,385	2.1	4,187	2.4	6,256	3.5	7,543	3.5	13,406	4.9	70,016	12.8
Physicians, surgeons, osteopaths	6,825	4.6	7,608	4.6	11,714	6.1	16,150	7.0	26,084	9.3	46,008	10.8

SOURCES: Constant H. Jacquet, Jr., *Women Ministers in 1977*, New York: Office of Research, Evaluation and Planning, National Council of Churches, March 1978, p. 5; and U.S. Department of Labor, Bureau of Labor Statistics, *Employment and Unemployment; A Report on 1980*, Special Labor Force Report 244, April 1981.

female, during the decade as the demand for legal services grew sharply and salaries for lawyers increased accordingly.[4]

The data on clergywomen in Table 1.1 include all denominations. What, more specifically, have been the trends in the mainline denominations included in this research? Unfortunately, no long-term trend data are available; however, we have figures for 1977 and 1981, a four-year trend, summarized in Table 1.2. Several points may be made.

First, only in three of the nine denominations—Disciples, United Church of Christ, and United Presbyterian—does the percentage of women clergy as a total of all clergy exceed the 4.2 percent figure for all religious bodies reported in Table 1.1. The U.C.C. with 7.8 percent has the largest proportion of clergywomen relative to total clergy. The American Lutheran Church has both the smallest number of clergywomen of the nine denominations and the lowest proportion relative to total clergy. These figures reveal that mainline denominations still have a relatively low proportion of clergywomen.

Yet, to concentrate only on the relatively small proportions of clergywomen in the nine denominations is to ignore the considerable growth, shown in Table 1.2, that has occurred in the absolute number in each denomination. (The figures for Disciples are somewhat misleading because of the way in which the denomination counts its ministers.)[5] In all of the other denominations there has been a sharp increase in the number of women clergy from 1977 to 1981. Computing the percentage change from Table 1.2, column A, we discover that the American Lutherans, who still have relatively few women clergy, nevertheless have experienced an increase of 416 percent; the number of Episcopal women priests has grown by 352 percent; and the United Methodist Church, with the largest number of clergywomen, has experienced a 312 percent increase. Not all of these women are in parish ministry; the majority no doubt are, however, and the sharp increase will continue, as seminary trends also make clear.

The number of women enrolled in seminaries in the 1980–1981 school year (the latest figures available at the time of this writing) indicates that women will make up an increasingly larger proportion of ordained ministers. In 1972, the first year for which figures on women seminarians are available, there were 1,077 women enrolled, or 4.7 percent of total seminary enrollment, in three- or four-year professional degree programs (those typically leading to ordination). In 1980–1981, there were 4,747 women in these programs, or 14.7 percent of the total. The percentage increase for women during this period was 340.8 percent, while male enrollment in the same programs grew by 25.0 percent. Thus, the rate of increase of women seminarians was over thirteen times that for men.[6]

Table 1.3 shows the 1980–1981 enrollment of women in the Master

Table 1.2 Women Clergy in Selected Denominations, 1977 and 1981
(Number and Percent of Total)

Denomination	Number of Women Clergy		Women Clergy as % of Total Clergy	
	1977	1981	1977	1981
American Baptist Churches	157	NA	1.8	NA
American Lutheran Church	18	93	0.3	1.3
Christian Church (Disciples)	388	317	5.7	4.8
Episcopal Church	94	425	0.8	3.4
Lutheran Church in America	55	210	0.7	2.6
Presbyterian Church, U.S.	75	180	1.4	3.3
United Church of Christ	400	757	4.1	7.8
United Methodist Church	319	1316	0.8	3.6
United Presbyterian Church, USA	295	630	2.1	4.5

SOURCES: 1977 data from Constant H. Jacquet, Jr., *Women Ministers in 1977*, Office of Research, Evaluation and Planning, National Council of Churches, March 1978, pp. 9–13; 1981 data supplied by the denominations listed. Data on total clergy on which percentages are computed from 1981 are from the *Yearbook of American and Canadian Churches, 1981*.

Table 1.3   Women Enrolled in Master of Divinity Programs
in Seminaries of Selected Denominations, Fall 1980

Denomination	Number of Women Enrolled	Women as % of Total
American Baptist Churches	137	24
American Lutheran Church	NA	NA
Christian Church (Disciples)	117	26
Episcopal Church	192	27
Lutheran Church in America	173	24
Presbyterian Church, U.S.	43	21
United Church of Christ	275	45
United Methodist Church	736	29
United Presbyterian Church, USA	376	32
Inter- or Nondenominational Seminaries	678	16

SOURCE: Marvin J. Taylor, ed., *Fact Book on Theological Education, 1980 – 81* (Vandalia, Ohio: Association of Theological Schools, 1981), pp. 72, 74.

of Divinity degree program. The figures probably underrepresent the actual number of women seminarians in most denominations because they are based on the denominational affiliation of the school rather than that of individual students. Many students from these denominations attend inter- or nondenominational schools and are not included in the denominational figures. Nevertheless, in 1980–1981, almost one-fourth or more of the M.Div. students in seminaries of all denominations included in the table, except the Presbyterian Church U.S., were women. The United Church of Christ topped the list with 45 percent. According to a subsequent denominational news release, the U.C.C. figure has reached 52 percent in 1981–1982.[7]

The seminary enrollment data for these denominations make clear that the numbers of women in the ranks of parish ministry will increase even more dramatically in the years ahead. If for no other reason, the sheer fact of numbers will introduce a new dynamic into this traditionally all-male profession with which both male clergy and congregations will have to deal.

Why Now?

Why are so many women choosing to enter the ordained ministry as well as other traditionally male occupations? In Chapter 2, we deal with these questions in some detail; however, several points may be made here. Considering the ordained ministry specifically, deciding to enter typically involves a sense of being called by God, whether as a special, distinctive experience or a more gradual, natural leading towards a decision. It is hard to believe that only in the 1970s did significant numbers of women feel that they were called by God to be ordained; or, even more unlikely, that God only chose to call women in the seventies. More likely, many women down through the years have experienced a call to the ministry but have found the opportunity to respond by becoming ordained blocked to them. When ordination was not possible, many of these women expressed their calling to ministry as lay volunteers or in the church-related occupations which permitted women to participate, such as deaconess programs or the religious education profession. Others perhaps did so vicariously as wives of ordained clergymen.

What made the 1970s watershed years was the occurrence of major social and cultural shifts following World War II, especially during the 1960s, making it possible for women to consider (or press for) ordained ministerial status as a way of responding to God's call. These shifts are well known and will only be briefly mentioned here.[8] For one thing, there was the existence of a strong and vocal feminist movement pushing for changes, not only in the broader society, but also within the churches. Within the broader society the success of the feminist movement was aided by the passage of a number of federal laws regarding equality of opportunity, including the 1964 Civil Rights Act's Title VII, outlawing discrimination on the basis of sex. Sex discrimination was originally included in the legislation by opponents of civil rights for black Americans in an effort to increase opposition to the entire Act. Their efforts failed and the Act was passed with considerable consequences for women's employment in traditionally male occupations. While the legislation did not extend to churches, it no doubt helped change perceptions about what constitute appropriate professions for women to enter, including the ordained ministry.

Not only has the climate changed to make it possible for women to consider these traditionally all-male professions, but there has also been a major shift in attitudes about the female role. Prior to the 1970s, especially in the fifties and sixties, a woman's role was to be a good wife and mother. As pollster Daniel Yankelovich puts it, "In the 1950s, most married women rated the housewife's job as an important, interesting and challenging task. A majority of women . . . now state that the woman who is truly fulfilling herself manages a career as well as a home."[9]

Women particularly endorsing this new perspective are those with college educations, and the increase of college-educated women has been another of the major shifts that has made it possible for women to respond to a call to the ministry and to enter other traditionally male occupations and professions. In 1950, women constituted less than 30 percent of the recipients of B.A. degrees. By 1960 the proportion rose to 35 percent, and by 1972, women constituted 45 percent of the bachelor's graduates.[10] Thus the number of persons with a requisite educational background available to become ordained clergy increased dramatically.

A final, major social shift has been the sharply declining birthrate since the early 1960s, partly reflecting the revolution in birth control methods. This decline has greatly increased the number of women with freedom to explore career options that childrearing responsibilities previously precluded. Additionally, among women who have chosen to have children, many have already fulfilled these responsibilities and have chosen to pursue a career outside the home. Indeed, many women are entering seminary to prepare for the ministry as a second career, the first career having been as mother and homemaker. A 1977 survey of Protestant seminarians probably reflects this in its finding that 19 percent of women seminarians were over thirty-five years of age as compared with 10 percent of the men.[11] A 1980 study of women seminarians in the Northeast found the *median* age of the respondents to be thirty-five.[12]

These are among the major social shifts that have affected the entry of women into the job market in traditionally male occupations, including the ordained ministry. As a result, therefore, women have been able to respond to a sense of calling into the ministry by pursuing ordination or pressing for it when it has been denied by denominational polity.

Dilemmas and Contradictions of Status

The shift that has allowed women to respond to a call to ordained ministry does not guarantee that women will be accepted into the profession by other clergy or by laity in the churches. In the quotation from Bock with which we began this chapter, women clergy were described as marginal to the profession. A central question of the research is whether professional marginality is still the case for clergywomen in light of the sharp increase in numbers. If not, why not, and what does this mean for their functioning and for the churches?

Why should women be marginal to the ministerial profession; that is, why should they not be fully accepted and integrated into it? Bock suggested that it was due to the association of maleness with the status of ministry. (Status is used here to refer to an officially defined social position.) According to Bock, the ministry "has not only been defined as masculine, but as 'sacredly' masculine. The father figure, a prominent feature of Christianity, is also a prominent ingredient in the image of the clergy."[13]

Some traditions within the Christian church uphold this sacred masculinity on theological grounds, maintaining that, since Jesus and his twelve disciples were male, so also must his priests be male. Further, some argue that the apostle Paul ruled that women should have a subordinate role in the church (I Cor. 11:1-16) and that this biblical injunction should be observed. In a more sociological vein, one might also point to the patriarchal society in which early Christianity developed and in which woman's status was inferior to that of man. Thus, it was unlikely that a chief leadership role in the churches would be given to women. These and other factors have played important roles in the identification of the clergy status with maleness and the consequent exclusion of, or resistance to, women clergy.

This identification has nevertheless been challenged, also on both theological and sociological grounds. For one thing there is a strong strain within the Christian ethic itself that challenges and relativizes ascribed distinctions (that is, distinctions defined by a person's birth), including gender. The apostle Paul can be cited in this connection as well: "There is no such thing as Jew or Greek, slave and freeman, male and female, for you are all one in Christ Jesus" (Gal. 3:38, NEB). This emphasis on freedom from bondage to traditions, including the tradition of the inferiority of women, that oppress individuals or groups is a strong one in the Christian ethic, and it provides the basis for challenge to the "sacred" masculinity of the ordained ministry. From a sociological perspective, we also note that modern professionalism (discussed in greater detail in Chapter 2) stresses norms of achievement rather than ascription. Thus, *in principle,* the capacity to perform well in a profession—an achievement norm—has superseded distinctions based on ascribed characteristics such as sex or social class. Therefore, for both theological and sociological reasons, a strong case can be made—and has been in those denominations that ordain women—that gender is not a determining criterion of the status of ordained ministry. Ministry is not an exclusively male status. There is nothing sacred about masculinity when it comes to ordained ministry. To make sex a criterion for entry into the profession is not only irrelevant and misguided, it is also inherently wrong.

Our purpose here is not to debate the merits of either side. While we personally strongly agree with the latter position, we nevertheless acknowledge that ancient traditions endure; that stereotypes of the ministry as a masculine profession persist; and that they cannot be ignored in their consequences for all concerned. The sociologist Everett C. Hughes saw this persistence of traditions and stereotypes as creating "dilemmas and contradictions of status" for professions such as the ministry.[14]

A characteristic such as gender, which may be auxiliary to a status

such as the ministry, becomes confused with determining characteristics—those essential to the status. Hughes specifically cites the ordained ministry as an example where maleness (an auxiliary
characteristic) has become confused with specifically determining traits
necessary for ministerial performance. This confusion creates dilemmas
and contradictions for those entering the status who lack the auxiliary
characteristic (women), for those already occupying the status (clergymen), and for those who interact with clergy as "clients" (lay parishioners). Therefore, even when one argues that gender ought not, in
principle, to be a relevant factor in ordained ministry, in practice it
may be.

Like one's occupation, one's sex or gender also defines a particular
status that one occupies. There are female and male statuses, with certain accompanying characteristics that people carry in their minds as
being distinctively appropriate for one or the other status. Male and
female are such powerful statuses that, even when one tries to do otherwise, it is often difficult to avoid relating to an individual as if it does
not matter whether the person is male or female. Since the ordained
ministry is also a powerful status, and since, in the minds of many, it is
associated with masculinity, a clash of expectations may occur when a
person encounters a woman minister. Should the person relate to her as
a woman? Or should the person relate to her as a minister without
regard to gender? That dilemma occurs for laity or clergy who operate
with these contradictory stereotypes in mind. A rather dramatic and, it
is hoped, dated example of this contradictory situation is contained in
an argument against ordaining women made in 1849 by a seminary
professor at Oberlin Theological School. The professor argued that,
since women are "emotional, physically delicate, illogical, weak-voiced,
vain, dependent, and most important, divinely ordained to be homemakers," they should not be ordained.[15] While extreme in his stereotypes from today's perspective, the professor's comments illustrate well
the conflict of stereotypes that some laity and clergymen may experience. Furthermore, we suspect that, even for some women, a part of
socialization into the status of ordained ministry involves having to
come to terms with their own ambivalence about occupying two statuses that have traditionally been kept separate. How is she to relate to
others in this or that situation? Primarily as a woman? Or primarily as
a minister? Or if she has no ambivalence herself, she will have to learn
how to deal with the ambivalence of others towards her.[16]

Let us be clear that we are not attempting to justify traditional
stereotypes of feminine traits. Nor do we wish to justify a masculine
stereotype of ministry. We are simply pointing to the dilemmas and
contradictions created by powerful and persisting traditions that are

part of the social fabric, in spite of efforts to declare them no longer relevant. And, as we have noted, they contribute to the professional marginality that women have often experienced in relation to ordained ministry.

But has the increased number of clergywomen begun to reduce the dilemmas and contradictions of status and also, therefore, to reduce marginality? At least two hypotheses may be put forward in this regard that receive a partial test in the chapters that follow.

One, based on the work of Rosabeth Moss Kanter, is that numbers make a difference in promoting or reducing marginality.[17] Kanter identifies four types of groups based on different proportional representation of kinds of people: (1) *uniform* groups with only one significant social type; (2) *skewed* groups in which there is a large preponderance of one type or another—for example, a ratio of 85:15; (3) *tilted* groups, with less extreme distributions—for example, 65:35; and (4) *balanced* groups with roughly proportional representation. She hypothesizes that these differences in proportion affect the attitudes and behavior of group members and their interaction with one another. Specifically, the proportion of men and women in a group or organization will affect the degree to which traditional gender stereotypes are operative and the degree of acceptance of the minority by the majority. Without going further into Kanter's theory at this point, we would hypothesize that, as the proportion of women increases in such traditionally male settings as theological seminaries and regional judicatories (regional denominational units such as presbyteries, dioceses, conferences, or synods) where clergy interact, there will be a reduction in status dilemmas and ambivalence due to contradictory stereotypes. Further, the marginality of women to the clergy profession will be reduced and eventually eliminated.

The second hypothesis is more difficult to test, at least from our data, but it also relates to the reduction of status dilemmas and contradictions and thereby also of professional marginality for women. In interviews with women seminarians, Joy Charlton found that the women were attempting to redefine the status and role of minister by adding feminine characteristics to the role definition. In contrast to a "male model of ministry," women "see themselves as bringing into the ministry 'a real affect element, a real feeling, a real nurturing element.' They are characterized as more compassionate, more sensitive, more caring. . . . In fact, those kinds of qualities are described as not only appropriate but as constituting a 'special gift' that women can bring."[18] In particular, Charlton points out, women believe they bring to the ordained ministry a style of leadership that emphasizes equalitarian rather than hierarchical patterns of decision making and exercise of authority. There was only limited support in Charlton's data for this hypothesis. However, the hypothesis supports a reduction of status contradictions between woman's status and that of clergy through a replacement of the masculine traits associated with the clergy status with feminine ones. If that were to occur, accompanied by the growing numbers of clergywomen, the professional marginality of clergywomen would also be reduced or eliminated. It is interesting to speculate whether or not this trend would lead to the professional marginality of clergymen.

Our data do not allow full tests of either of the two hypotheses; however, we are able to consider the effect of numbers in an examination of the seminary experiences of women (Chapter 4) and the relation of men and women clergy in judicatory structures (Chapter 7). The hypothesis regarding a more feminine style of ministry, especially with reference to leadership styles, is further discussed in the following chapter and tested to a limited degree in Chapter 7.

Research Design and Sample

The design of our research on clergywomen has been guided by several objectives. First and foremost is our concern to provide accurate descriptive data regarding the population of clergywomen in the nine mainline Protestant denominations. Since ours is the first major cross-denominational study of clergywomen, careful description is important. Further, we view this as a baseline study from which subsequent studies can make comparisons. Therefore, not only was a careful sample of clergywomen needed, but we have also tried to gather a broad spectrum of data on clergywomen, including their social origins and factors leading to the choice of the ministry, experiences in seminary, experiences in the clergy job market, functioning in parish ministry, and balancing career with other roles and responsibilities. This broad focus meant that we could not probe as deeply into specific areas as we would have liked. Where possible, however, we draw on findings from previous research on specific aspects of the experiences of clergywomen.

A second objective has been to provide several kinds of comparative data. In particular we wish to compare the careers of clergywomen with those of clergymen. This not only aids and sharpens our descriptive intent, but it also allows tests of hypotheses regarding differences and similarities of style, functioning, and acceptance of clergywomen. To accomplish this objective, it was necessary to sample clergymen in the nine denominations as well as clergywomen.

Denominational comparisons also were believed to be important, since denominations differ in polity and in their understanding of ministry. Therefore, denominations were selected, not only on the basis of having significant numbers of clergywomen, but also because they potentially differ in the way women are deployed, accepted, and supported within the parish ministry. In general, we have chosen to make comparisons among the nine denominations without grouping them into subtypes based on similarities of polity; however, we deal at some length with the polity subtypes in Chapter 5 in discussing the job market for clergy.

A third objective has been to view clergywomen in relation to other persons and groups within the church system who are significant to their acceptance, functioning, and support. These include not only clergymen, but also laity, seminary faculty, and denominational officials. Limits of time and research funds kept us from gathering detailed information from all of these categories of persons or from other significant persons such as spouses of married clergy. Nevertheless, in addition to the samples of clergywomen and men, we also gathered data from a sample of lay leaders nominated by a subset of the clergywomen and men from the larger sample. We also conducted interviews with women seminary faculty. Additionally, but less systematically, we interviewed denominational officials, national and regional, who relate directly to clergywomen. Several of these persons served on the project advisory committee. Data from these sources provide perspectives on clergywomen and men from those with whom they interact in their functioning in parish ministry.

A fourth objective has been to provide data that have policy relevance. That is, in our design we tried to be aware of issues of practical significance to those concerned with the recruitment, education, deployment, and support of clergy, both women and men. Some of these implications are considered in the final chapter as well as alluded to elsewhere in the book.

In designing the interview schedules and questionnaires used in the research, we drew on the work of a number of others who have engaged in studies of ministry and other professions.[19] Additionally, as a means of developing the structured interview schedule for clergywomen, we conducted two-hour, unstructured interviews with ten clergywomen from several denominations. The women were attending an international conference of clergywomen. Their responses not only helped to shape the final interview guide, but they are also included, where pertinent, in ensuing chapters.

The four primary sources of data and information regarding sampling can be briefly summarized.

First, we conducted hour-long telephone interviews with 636 clergywomen from the nine denominations included in the study. Attempts were made to secure one hundred interviews each from randomly selected clergywomen from American Baptist Churches, Christian Church (Disciples of Christ), the Episcopal Church, and United Church of Christ. From the United Methodists, who have the largest number of clergywomen, we attempted to secure two hundred interviews. From the two Lutheran (ALC and LCA) and two Presbyterian (PCUS and UPCUSA) denominations, we sought one hundred interviews total from each denominational family. This gave a total of eight hundred possible interviews; however, when each denomination selected its samples for us, they frequently included several additional names, which we used. This gave a total of 907 women contacted to request interviews. From the 907 contacted by letter (including a letter from the researchers and one from an official from the denomination of the respondent), we were able to complete 636 interviews, or a 70 percent completion rate. Approximately fifteen women declined to be interviewed; some we were unable to reach due to faulty addresses; the remainder responded too late to be included. Table 1.4 contains the distribution of responses by denomination. They range from a low of 53 percent for the Disciples to a high of 82 percent of UCC clergywomen.

As a second data source, we wanted a sample with equal numbers of clergymen for comparison with the women. Each denomination was asked to draw random samples of clergymen, according to numbers requested by the researchers. To keep costs within budget, we used mailed questionnaires rather than telephone interviews for a majority of men. The questionnaires were identical to the interview schedule. Two hundred telephone interviews with men were also attempted to enable

Table 1.4   Completion Rates for the Sample of Clergywomen

| | | Interviews | |
| | | Number | % |
Denomination	Requested	Completed	Completed
American Baptist Churches	97	67	69
American Lutheran Church	54	43	80
Christian Church (Disciples)	103	55	53
Episcopal Church	124	81	65
Lutheran Church in America	76	59	77
Presbyterian Church, U.S.	30	21	70
United Church of Christ	113	93	82
United Methodist Church	200	140	70
United Presbyterian Church, USA	110	77	70
Total	907	636	70

us to secure names of laity to be contacted and to provide a basis for comparing the quality of data gathered by telephone with that from the mailed questionnaire. The major difference in data quality seems to have been that the telephone interviews allowed for probes where necessary. The remaining men were mailed the questionnaires. The questionnaires did not ask for the respondent's name, and no follow-up reminders were sent.

Telephone interviews were completed with 120 clergymen, or 60 percent of the total. Mailed questionnaires were returned by 679 clergymen, or 59 percent of the 1,048 to whom they were mailed. We oversampled among men to ensure a sufficient return from the mailed questionnaires to make comparisons possible with clergywomen. The distribution of responses by denomination is shown in Table 1.5.

Overall responses of clergywomen and men to all interview/questionnaire items are summarized in the Appendix.[20]

The response rates for both clergywomen and men are quite good, and we believe that they allow considerable confidence to be placed in the samples. One difficulty in comparability should be mentioned. It resulted from a inability to stratify the sample by age of clergy. Since most clergywomen have entered the ministry relatively recently, they are either considerably younger overall than clergymen, or tend to have have significantly fewer years of experience as an ordained minister. Our samples reflect these age and experience differences. This necessitates controlling for age, years of experience, or the number of parishes served to make more accurate comparisons between women and men.

Characteristics of the clergywomen and men in the samples will be described in some detail later; therefore, we will forego doing so at this stage except to make one point. Because our samples of clergywomen and men were drawn on a random basis, they included too small a percentage of minority clergy to make analysis by race meaningful.

A third data source is a sample of laity. Approximately 350 clergywomen and 125 clergymen agreed to distribute questionnaires to three key lay leaders in their parishes, with instructions to include both men and women. The laity were asked to return the questionnaires directly to us. This allowed them to respond freely without concern that their pastor would see their responses; however, since we did not have the laity's names, follow-up to increase the return rate was impossible. Of the 1,383 questionnaires distributed, 737 were returned, for a return rate of 53 percent. The lay leaders are almost evenly divided by sex (52 percent are women). Also, approximately 50 percent have been members of their present congregation for fifteen or more years. Forty percent of the men and 21 percent of the women hold the position of chief lay leader in their congregations. The remainder are spread over vari-

Table 1.5 Completion Rates for the Sample of Clergymen

Denomination	Interviews			Questionnaires		
	Requested	Number Completed	% Completed	Requested	Number Completed	% Completed
American Baptist Churches	19	10	53	90	56	62
American Lutheran Church	15	10	67	59	57	97
Christian Church (Disciples)	24	16	67	105	50	48
Episcopal Church	25	19	76	152	91	60
Lutheran Church in America	19	14	74	38	32	84
Presbyterian Church, U.S.	10	7	70	23	18	78
United Church of Christ	26	12	46	168	83	49
United Methodist Church	33	14	42	251	133	53
United Presbyterian Church, USA	28	18	64	162	99	61
Total	199	120	60	1048	619	59

ous other key leadership positions, including chairpersons of the administrative boards of congregations. Just under 50 percent of both men and women are 50 years or older, with another 25 percent in the forty to fifty age bracket. Sixty-one percent of the men and 46 percent of the women have at least a four-year college degree—a generally high level of education.

Probably the major bias of this sample is that it is a sample of lay leaders (e.g., official board chairpersons, women's organization presidents, etc.), not rank and file laity. Also, we deliberately oversampled among laity who had experienced a woman as pastor. Thus, the bias is in favor of those lay leaders with direct experience of clergywomen.

The final data source included telephone interviews with women faculty teaching full-time at forty major Protestant and interdenominational seminaries. We asked the women faculty to reflect on the seminary experiences of women students, possible changes in the kinds of women entering seminaries in recent years, and possible changes in the students' orientations to feminist issues. Additionally, we asked faculty about parish ministry experiences of women graduates with whom they may have kept in touch.

Approximately one hundred faculty women were identified by telephone calls to the seminaries. The list also included several women who have administrative responsibilities for programs or services particularly related to women seminarians. Eighty interviews were completed and transcribed for content analysis.

Among the women faculty interviewed, 44 percent had been at their present seminaries three years or less, and 35 percent had been at the seminaries six years or more. Of the seventy-two women who were considered full-time faculty, 22 percent were full professors, 38 percent associate professors, 34 assistant professors, and the remaining 6 percent instructors. The other seminary women interviewed, though they worked full time at the seminary, were not considered fulltime faculty though they usually taught a course or two in addition to their administrative duties. Of all interviewed, approximately 42 percent were ordained, and 22 percent had served at least a year as parish ministers. Another 11 percent had served briefly as supply or interim clergy in parishes or as directors of music or Christian Education.

Among the seventy-five interviewed who at least taught one course a year on a regular basis, about 16 percent taught Bible, 16 percent taught church history, 19 percent taught theology or ethics, 19 percent were professors of religious education, and 18 percent taught either pastoral care or field work. Another 8 percent taught sociology or psychology of religion. The remaining three to four percent taught sacred music or Christian formation.

With the exception of about 17 percent of those interviewed, who had been at the seminaries too short a time to know graduates, the remainder were fairly active in keeping up with former women students. A fourth are very active in this regard. Such contacts primarily serve a pleasurable social function, but are also helpful to the ex-students in being able to unburden themselves on both personal or parish problems and keep abreast of new job possibilities. They are also useful to the seminary professor in knowing how helpful her teaching actually is for the ministry of her former students. Not only were these faculty and administrator seminary women able to describe the current cohort of women seminarians in various ways, but they were in most cases able to comment rather pointedly on what they perceived as important issues affecting the present and future of women in the parish ministry.

These four major samples plus the preliminary interviews constitute the principal sources of data for the report.

In the following chapters, we begin first with a look at some historical background concerning women's place in American churches, including the variety of nonordained roles played by women as well as the movement towards ordained status. Chapter 3 begins the presentation of the data collected specifically for the study and focuses on the social origins of clergywomen and men and the paths that led them into the ministry. Experiences in seminary constitute the concern of Chapter 4, including a consideration of the orientations towards feminism held by the respondents using both clergy and seminary faculty data. Chapter 5 analyzes experiences of clergymen and women in the job market: in particular, how respondents got their first and subsequent parish positions, as well as the kinds of positions and salaries received. The sixth chapter contains a description of the roles engaged in by clergymen and women in parish ministry, their assessment of their effectiveness in these roles, and a comparative assessment of their performance by lay leaders. In Chapter 7, other aspects of life in the parish are examined, using both clergy and lay leader data. There is also a consideration of how clergymen and women relate their parish ministry roles to their other roles and responsibilities. A final chapter draws together conclusions and implications that are suggested by the research.

2

American Churches and "Women's Place"

The recent large influx of women into the ranks of ordained clergy in American Protestant churches has not occurred in a vacuum, but rather as the latest episode in a continuing story of the ministry of women in those churches. The changing pattern of the place and activities of women in the churches may be seen as one of three parallel and interacting factors in the nation's history: (1) the natural history of religious movements and institutions; (2) the peculiar opportunities and strains attendant upon white settlement and expansion, including the contrapuntal development of black slavery, native American subjugation, and a mentality of conquerors; and (3) processes of modernization.

The Life Cycle of Movements in American Religion

America's denominational system is unique in that it has created, as a functional alternative to the established religions it rejected, a plurality of religious groups that can trumpet as the accepted religious wisdom, "Attend the church of your choice." In societies with formally established religions, sectarian religion can provide a deviant choice, persecuted or denigrated, but a recognizable choice against the establishment. In America, however, many of the denominations of the informal establishment were once—and not too long ago to remember—despised sects. They have passed through the normal evolution of the new religious groups quickly and recognizably.

That process may be divided into three stages that are relevant here. The first, or charismatic stage is the one in which a new vision is brought forth by a prophet or by the kind of religious ferment in which prophecy may be expected to come from anyone touched by the spirit. Usually such movements come from groups in the society for whom the old visions have been less than satisfactory or to those who in one way or another have been "disinherited" in the prevailing system. Their dissatisfaction with the patterns of the old system allow them to transcend established role definitions. Their guiding motto might well be verses from the prophet Joel, quoted by Peter on the day of Pentecost, itself a prime example of the charismatic beginnings of that new sect that was to become the Christian church:

> And it shall come to pass afterward,
>   that I will pour out my spirit on all flesh;
> your sons and your daughters shall prophesy,
>   your old men shall dream dreams,
>   and your young men shall see visions.
> Even upon menservants and maidservants
>   in those days, I will pour out my spirit.
>   (Joel 2:28–29)

This "charismatic" phase does not necessarily imply a direct relation with today's neo-pentecostals, nor should the appreciation of "gifts of the Spirit" be understood in terms only of "speaking in tongues" or other clearly identified gifts. Rather, what is implied is the freshness of a new movement which sees itself in direct contact with the divine, acting out a fresher mandate. In America as elsewhere, women have had an important place in new movements at their formative stage and have retained more formal leadership in those that continue to emphasize the importance of the "gifts of the spirit." From the beginning of their settlement in this country, for example, Quaker women had been active preachers not only at home but as itinerant speakers, a pattern they brought with them from England. Mother Ann Lee of the Shakers was considered a female messiah, and Mother Lucy Wright assumed leadership of the central Shaker ministry in 1796. Ellen White founded the Seventh-Day Adventist Church and led it for fifty years. Similarly, Mary Baker Eddy was not only founder but leader of Christian Science for a generation or more. Phoebe Palmer was only one of many women who led the Holiness movement, and has been called the "spiritual mother of sectarian bodies such as the Pilgrim Holiness Church and the Church of the Nazarene."[1] Aimee Semple McPherson was not only an internationally famous evangelist, but also founder of the International Church of the Foursquare Gospel. Alma White founded the Pillar of Fire Church. The list could be longer, but the point is clear: when a religious movement is at its charismatic phase, "women's place" is not an issue, though issues of "women's place" may have been involved in conditions that led to the formation of a new movement in the first place.

The second phase in the development of religious groups is one of consolidation and organization. It usually comes to the fore after the passing of the first generation of convert-founders. The second generation often lacks the immediate experience of the charismatic vision that impelled the first. It may also lack some of the impetus of disinheritance felt by the founders. This generation experiences the religion as an inherited tradition. If the general separation from the status system of the society remains strong, the group will probably feel it appropriate to continue to rely on the spirit and so prolong the charismatic phase. But if adherents of the movement become active participants in the status system of the wider society, organization and respectability become important goals; and the role definitions of the society at large become the natural order to which the group would grant religious legitimacy. The motto of this phase might well be Paul's caution to the Corinthians, particularly appropriate as it comes immediately after his remonstrances against women speaking in meeting: "So my brethren, earnestly desire to prophesy, and do not forbid speaking in tongues, but all things should be done decently and in order" (1 Cor. 14:39–40).

This stage possibly dominated the style of the Puritan founders who exercised such great influence over the shape of American religion, or at least those most aligned with the Separatist movement in England. The fires that had created that movement were now put to practical use in the establishment and organization of God's "New Israel in the New World." It was not time to be dreaming dreams or having visions; it was a time for putting them into action, for making all of life fit the envisioned order. It was important, also, that the new society be recognized by the rest of the world as civilized and orderly, deserving of respect in the halls of the nations. Women aspiring to prophecy were, at best, expelled. The ducking stool and witchcraft trials are potent reminders of the clarity with which those Puritan organizers defined "women's place"!

Similar processes have been repeated again and again as new sectarian groups have formed. In the earliest Baptist churches in the South, women were ordained as deaconesses, and some preached without ordination. In the eighteenth century, Separate Baptists allowed what has been described as "remarkable freedom of participation by women." After 1800, however, that freedom diminished as that body merged with the Regular Baptists. The organizational change, along with a growing number of members who were slaves, led to the restriction of leadership to white male members.[2] Similarly, in a study of one of the more recent movements to have reached the second phase, classical Pentecostalism, Barfoot and Sheppard have shown how the role of women ministers has been reduced from equality to more and more limited functions. Even in Aimee Semple McPherson's Church of the Foursquare Gospel, the percentage of ordained women had declined from 67 percent at the time of her death in 1944 to 42 percent in 1978—a loss of 25 percent.[3]

Significantly, the organizations of classical Pentecostals, in which most of Barfoot and Sheppard's study was conducted, were not joined by the largest group of black Pentecostals. Their continuing exclusion from the American system of status and rewards has encouraged a greater emphasis on the charismatic and on women's right to prophesy in the black church. But in the white churches the division of the stages could hardly be more clear: in 1924, the last racial separation of the Pentecostal church had taken place; in 1931, the General Council of the Assemblies of God had passed a resolution denying women priestly functions in the church; *and* after 1932, no other major groups in the classical Pentecostal tradition were formed.[4] The charismatic phase was over, consolidation could now begin, and that was the job of white males. Respectability demanded that women and blacks be put in their place. A similar process is already being traced in the neopentecostalism of the Catholic charismatic movement.[5]

The third phase of the development of a religious movement is that of maturity, of institutionalization, when it no longer must seek respectability, when its boundaries blur into the general social structure. No longer under the critical eye of some other "establishment," the church can now relax some of its standards and allow variations within its broader limits; it may now tolerate mildly prophetic expressions of social conscience, and attempt to lead rather than to adapt to the larger society. Its motto may be that advice offered to Timothy in the early church:

> *First of all, then, I urge that supplications, prayers, intercessions, and thanksgivings be made for all men, for kings and all who are in high positions, that we may lead a quiet and peaceable life, godly and respectful in every way. (1 Tim. 2:1–2)*

Mainline Protestantism seemed to have reached such a point, at least in the East, in the early years of the nineteenth century. The period from 1800 to 1860 has been characterized as a time of increasing "feminization" of American religion, when a loss of specific political power was accompanied by a kind of domestication of religion. Religious styles became more emotional, more accommodating, with greater emphasis on humility and Christ's sufferings. Women became more visible in the church as its organization became more complex.[6]

Within this period, women were particularly involved in the support of the local congregation, studying in Bible societies, teaching in Sunday school classes, and working in local women's societies to support the congregation's program or charitable works. Ladies' Aid societies and Altar Guilds were primarily concerned with the affairs of the local congregations, but in many of their organizations, women made use of their separation from the organizational leadership to cross congregational and denominational boundaries to join other women on many projects.

One of the primary functions performed by women in the church during this period was Sunday school teaching. Though religious education was originally expected to take place in the home or under the direction of the clergy, Americans soon found a useful combination of public education and the Sunday school as a way of training not only the poor, but the children of church members as well. In the words of one historian of the movement:

> *Converted and eager to serve, women often were the natural choices to teach children. After all, was not the Sunday school an extension of the home, and had not mothers done much of the religious teaching there? The women, not allowed to assume official responsibilities, turned to the Sunday school and other benevolent societies as significant channels of their religious zeal. As teachers in the Sunday school they became indispensable to the new movement.*[7]

That "new movement" grew to become an international force that challenged the power of denominations. Its simple creed and uniform lessons for all ages became problematic to theologians and denominational leaders, and yet the Sunday school was often the training ground out of which those very critics had come. By denying women full participation in the governance and thought of the church, church leaders had participated in their own frustration; for Sunday school teachers remained predominantly female, and the independent Sunday School Union was probably the most pervasive shaper of popular piety between its founding in 1824 and its peak in 1910.

This period of the nineteenth century also saw a new charismatic wave of the Second Great Awakening, when many new religious movements were founded, calling forth a new period of organization and consolidation after the Civil War. But the activities of women were not totally suppressed during this later period of consolidation. Rather, they were pushed to the boundaries of church structures, where tolerant males thought the women could be kept busy on unimportant projects, or into the new movements as prophets and leaders. But as women expanded their charitable concerns from children and the local poor to home and foreign missions, they moved from local to regional and national associations out of their need for a broader base to support their causes. Again, women were not particularly constrained by denominational lines, and one of the first national societies was the interdenominational Woman's Union Missionary Society, formed in 1861. Between that time and the turn of the century, denominational missionary societies were formed by the women in nearly all mainline Protestant churches, most of them independently run.

The formation of the missionary movement represents a new religious vision at its charismatic phase. Denominational leaders may have been involved in consolidation and reorganization after the trauma of the Civil War, but the great evangelical thrust of the prewar years had left converted and committed Christians across the nation with a conviction that God wanted them personally to continue to spread the Good News to all lands. Some, both men and women, had joined new religious bodies still afire with such zeal. Others, particularly women who were prevented from exercising directly their new sense of Christian responsibility, stayed within traditional patterns that aroused little opposition, but transformed those patterns into national and international networks capable of doing the work they felt called to do. In the process, many of them developed organizational and managerial skills supposed to be beyond the abilities of the "weaker sex."

Much of the emphasis on foreign missions among women focused on the need to take the Gospel to women and children in societies whose social structures male missionaries could not penetrate. Also, while many men were caught up in the enthusiasm of the missionary movement, women had additional motivation. Many of the stories they heard told of forms of severe oppression against women in non-Christian cultures, and women sought to use the liberating word of the Gospel against foot binding, bride buying, and other such practices. In addition, the sacrificial giving of women to the missionary activities they sponsored gave them a feeling that they were "a real force in the world."[8] In more than one denomination, men who were interested in supporting missions had to call upon women's groups to keep their projects afloat, and in turn women were able to exercise the power of their financial contributions to gain concessions from the all-male power structure of the denominations.[9]

The work of the Christian laywomen who supported foreign missions was also an important foundation of later movements for the ordination of women for service in home churches as well. The experience of women in the mission field gave them a sense not only of calling but also of competence, not deliberately cultivated so much as a side effect of "radical obedience." Says one historian of Methodist women in the movement:

> *The lady missionary had metamorphosed. From her first shocked gaze at a foreign race, she pursued her ideal of service into alien hamlets and cities, bush and mountains, and discovered that she was capable of heroic labors.*[10]

Not all women in missionary societies were agreed on the place of women preachers, but many of them were ready to push for clergy rights for women missionaries when it seemed likely that it would help the expansion of Christianity. And when these women returned on furlough or retired and became part of the local church, their ability and confidence as well as their wider range of experience opened doors of perception to women that made the notion of clergywomen far more accessible than it had been before.

National organizations for home missions tended to come somewhat more slowly than those for foreign missions. Part of the reason was that much of the charitable work could be done through local groups; part was the greater visibility of "meddling women" to those in structures that might be threatened by their meddling, often dominated by church leaders. The women themselves, particularly in the South, tended to prefer foreign missions support.[11] Much of the home mission emphasis of Northern women was developed around the need to provide services and education for slaves freed by the Civil War, and they were responsible for organizing many schools and services that have had a lasting impact on the region. Similarly, home mission support for Indians, mountain folk, and other isolated people was popular among the women. The home mission movement was also closely aligned with a number of reform movements, as we shall see shortly.

By the end of the nineteenth century, the charismatic phase of the missionary movement had passed in the mainline denominations, to be picked up and continued in later-developing sects. With the phase of organization and consolidation, the separate women's organizations were, one by one, absorbed into denominational structures. This process legitimated women's work in the larger organizations, and some of the women were even astute enough to have written into the merger the right to participate in decision-making bodies of the church. Disciples women, for example, retained 50 percent membership on the boards of trustees and managers of the United Christian Missionary Society.[12] Yet, even in that denomination, women have observed that reorganization has "organized them out." After forty-six years of serving as executives of the Christian Woman's Board of Missions (during which time they established homes and overseas ministries still in existence), and in more than fifty years following the reorganization, not one woman had served as top executive of any general or regional unit of the denomination.[13]

Their experience was not unique. Another denomination that has recently studied the participation of women in churchwide structures is the Lutheran Church in America. Overall, in 1980, 23.3 percent of elected positions and 24 percent of appointed ones on decision-making bodies of the denomination were held by women, up slightly over 1 percent from the figures in 1978. Women delegates to national conventions had risen in number to nearly 50 percent, but on denominational staff they were only 23 percent (almost double the 1978 figure, at that).[14] The Lutheran case, then, points to an increase in the integration of women into denominational structures only recently accelerated, and most evident in lay rather than professional involvement. Again, it is a common pattern.

The third phase of the evolution of the mission movement is probably best symbolized by the further reorganization of local and denominational women's societies in the mid-twentieth century. At that time women had been given automatic membership in the women's societies along with their church membership, regardless of their desire for involvement in these activities, and without the expectation of any call to a specific form of service by the group.

The American Experience

One of the primary conditions influencing American church life has been the high level of mobility in this country. An important force behind both the Sunday school and the home missions movements was the combination of the constant arrival of new and unassimilated immigrants on the one hand, and the expansion westward into "unchurched" areas on the other.

Immigration offered a particular challenge to the Protestant establishment, as it sought to make God-fearing, clean-living, hard-working Americans out of new arrivals through the combined agencies of the public school and the Sunday school, both of which have become part of the realm of women's work. It also brought with it another model of church women's involvement. Roman Catholic nuns began their ministry in Canada in 1639, in New Orleans in 1727. From that time on, and particularly after the mid–nineteenth century's great influx of immigrants from Roman Catholic countries, they made their mark on the society as they established hospitals, schools, churches, and orphanages. As the women who taught in public schools and Sunday schools created much of the shape of Protestant piety in several successive generations, so these sisters in the parochial schools molded popular Catholicism. Their record of service to the poor, the sick, and the outcast has made a lasting impression on the society, and the administration of their communities and services has given many of these women experiences denied others in less separate environments. Throughout the nineteenth century they worked with exceptional freedom within the areas of their ministry.[15]

Similarly, other societies with state churches and consequent strong ethnic identities produced women who came to America to minister to their people. German Lutheran deaconesses arrived in Philadelphia in 1884.[16] Others soon followed. These immigrant patterns found some indigenous development. Episcopal deaconesses were "set apart" by local bishops in the United States as early as 1885, and such actions were authorized by the General Convention in 1889. The Methodist Episcopal Church recognized deaconesses in 1888, the Methodist Episcopal Church South in 1902, and the Methodist Protestant Church in 1908. Deaconesses have also served Baptist churches, Congregational, Evangelical and Reformed, and Evangelical denominations, and are retained in the merged structure of the United Church of Christ. Their status in some denominations has been hotly debated, particularly in the Anglican tradition, where they were declared to have received Holy Orders by the 1920 Lambeth Conference, only to have the decision reversed in 1930.[17]

Given such a history, they are considered by some to be precursors of ordained women clergy. But the general definition of the deaconess in this country is that of a laywoman given special status in the church, who does full-time paid church work. Lutheran deaconesses, in addition, have been particularly likely to form communities that appear halfway between the style of Roman Catholic nuns and that of independent lay workers—a style similar to that of many Catholic sisters in this post–Vatican II era. In the United Methodist Church, most deaconesses serve in combined community service and congregational posts, in community centers, or in homes or schools of the denomination. In other denominations, the most common area of service is the hospital, though deaconesses serve in a wide range of activities. Their function often overlaps that of the home missionary. On the whole, the deaconess pattern has not gained widespread acceptance in the United States, probably because of the wider range of other options for American church women as compared with those in Europe, as well as a lack of clarity concerning the role.[18]

The home missions movement, on the other hand, was fertile ground for the involvement of American women and led to two forms of activity. In their desire to extend Christian service to the unfortunate, women became involved both in church institutions of service and in secular reform movements. It was out of their Christian concerns for black slaves that many women became involved in the abolition movement, and it was in response to not being heard in that movement that they launched the movement for women's rights that culminated in women's suffrage in 1918. It was out of their concern for the families of the poor that women built and staffed church-sponsored settlement houses and training schools. It was that same concern that launched them into the Women's Christian Temperance Union, resolved to excise the evil effects of "Demon Rum" from those suffering families.

The activities of Christian women, in church structures and out of them, were an integral part of the reform and progressive movements in post–Civil War United States. In some ways, their activities provided both the motivational seedbed and practical examples for those movements.

Another important way in which the particular history of the nation affected the involvement of women in the churches may be seen in the common history of their organizations. During the nation's formative period, women's "place" was generally in the home or the local congregation, and their primary specialized, though volunteer, involvement that of the Sunday school teacher. It is also true that during that period most attention was being given to local structures. The family was the primary economic, social, political, and educational unit; and the church, particularly as its professional leadership was so thinly spread in much of the continent, was heavily local and lay dominated. After the Civil War, as the task of nation building became a prime focus of the political and economic structures, national organizations of church women were a part of that process. One of their prime foci, foreign missions, laid the foundations of cultural expansion that brought in the twentieth century American rise to world leadership. Home missions paralleled the expansion of the nation along its western frontier, and the issues that brought about the Civil War and the problems of its aftermath were focuses of the expanding consciousness and benevolent action of women. Women's movements have affected the work of church women, not only through the interlinking of the two groups, but also as church reaction against such movements has occurred. For example, it is reported that Southern Baptist women were taking some positions of lay leadership in the churches until the women's movement began. Then they were put in their "place."[19]

The general loss of separate power by women in the reorganizations of the early twentieth century probably carried some of this negative freight along with the positive hope that the success of the movement in attaining the vote for women heralded the time when "woman's place" would be the whole area of public life. The breadth of cultural influence during that period may be seen in the fact that, even among the Quakers—that group most out of step with much of the denominational establishment—the separate Women's Meetings were abolished, and women were incorporated into the general meetings at almost the same time that other reorganizations were bringing women's missionary societies into the general structure of other denominations.[20] It was during this same period as well that the freedom of Roman Catholic nuns was severely restricted by new Vatican rules.

This does not mean that all women's organizations were suppressed. The style, however, may have become more hidden during that period. An excellent example of this more subterranean style may be found in the Episcopal Society of the Companions of the Holy Cross, organized in 1884 by a group of friends led by Emily Malbone Morgan, seeking to allow an invalid friend to participate in their good works through a network of intercessory prayer. The organization has grown to a society of about six hundred women who share a common rule and sense of vocation, though they are scattered around the world and live in quite varied circumstances. Not an "order," the society counts as members women in many professions, married or single, who claim a search "to lead a Christian life walking in the way of the Cross, sharing in intercession, thanksgiving, and simplicity of life, with special concern for social justice, Christian unity, and the mission of the Church."[21] While few people have heard of the Society, many of the leading women of the Episcopal Church, who have served as well in top positions of ecumenical agencies, are members. It includes some nuns, and now, a few priests who find in it social support for Christian activity in the society at large. Its style is indebted to religious orders, other church women's societies, and, in some ways, to organizations such as the Junior League. Its effect on the denomination or other structures will probably never be measurable; however, it should not be considered negligible. It is one of many such "pious societies."

The erosion of the expectation of full participation of women in church and society climaxed during the Cold War period following World War II, when women were firmly pushed—and often eagerly went—back into the home and the expanding local congregations of the suburbs. During this period there was a renascence of a role for women in the church first made important by the early reformers—that of the minister's wife. For generations, churches had been able to assume that when they hired a pastor they also could expect to receive the services of his wife—at no salary, of course. Ministers' wives were expected to take the lead in the women's societies as well as in the educational programs of many churches, and in addition to provide informal pastoral duties, particularly among the women and children of the congregation. In the post–World War II period, many women who felt called to serve the church in leadership roles chose to work for college and sometimes seminary degrees, then married classmates who would become the official ministers, while they provided a well-trained supportive function.

Yet it was inevitable that women who felt called in this way might also consider doing the formal jobs themselves. That period also saw the rise of pressure within many denominations to open up professional positions for women in the churches, including ordination, to clergy roles. The model on which this developed was considerably different from early forms of the pastorate for women, a factor that has been the unrecognized source of some tension within the ranks of contemporary clergywomen. The underlying influence that has created the difference is that of the process of modernization, and it is to that that we must now turn to understand this portion of the story of Protestant women in the denominational structure of the churches.

The Impact of Modernization

The use of the term "modernization" is taken from the definition of Peter Berger et al.[22] of modernization as a process based on technological production and/or bureaucracy, characterized by rationality, specialization, large-scale organization, a compartmentalizaton of various facets of the life of the individual, and a moralized anonymity that is "no respecter of persons" but only of functions. The United States has been seen as the epitome of involvement in modernization, indeed its evangelist to the rest of the world. American Protestantism in particular has been seen as a modernizing religion. The effect of modernization on women and the definitions of "women's place" within the religious institution has been particularly interesting. At stake in modernization have been definitions of work, modes of organization, and styles of leadership.

The modernization of work has largely been one defined by Marx as the alienation of labor, an alienation that has proved as intractable in socialist countries as capitalist. In essence, it involves the growing externalization of work, the loss of a sense of ownership of one's own labor. One puts in time at tasks devised by others, the final product of which may not be visible to the worker. The reward is the paycheck, not the product of one's efforts. One's value and importance thus are lodged in the paycheck, since only functional definitions of worth are appropriate, and the worth of a function in modern society is measured by the price it can command. Modern work is specialized, a small segment of a group effort, usually directed from outside the group. It is also arranged hierarchically, and a high status is granted the professional whose speciality is subject only to peer review.

Woman's work in the home has not been much touched by modernization. As homemaker, she is a generalist, not a specialist. Her reward is expected to be her perception of and participation in the happiness and welfare of her family; otherwise, her labor is unpaid. Patterns of community involvement for women have been similar. They have been largely volunteer, rewarded only by the knowledge of community betterment that has been accomplished. Traditional church work has also shared the premodern pattern, based either on demands of "radical obedience" to a transcendent call not recognized in the secular modern culture, or by the perception of "ladies" that their task in the society was one of cultural enrichment based on a traditional division of labor between the savage competition of men and the soft culture of women.

Yet the technological revolution of modernization did not leave women untouched. The new technologies freed them from much of the time-consuming drudgery of the household, and medical technology eliminated much of the risk of childbearing, along with the need to bear many children in order to have any survive. The more affluent women were, of course, the most affected by this process. It was these "ladies" who formed the mission societies and reforming crusades, these women who were free to serve and to seek avenues to act out their desire to make a difference in the world.

Even so, women who have opted for full-time church work have been largely judged by premodern values, working in generalized posts at subsistence wages on the assumption that they have other rewards. While this pattern is now more honored in those sectarian churches whose populations are less touched by modernization, it is instructive to see on the roster of missionaries of such denominations as the United Methodist a high percentage of women still listed as, simply, "missionary wife."

Organizational forms under modernization become increasingly complex and impersonal. Again, women have tended to form organizations less tinged with modernization. There is a lively contrast between the way women organized their missionary societies and the denominational boards formed by men. The women formed boards and committees that resembled (and often were) friendship groups engaged in a common task and personally supervised all the work under their care.[23] They established personal communications between missionaries and their supporters, giving the latter a sense of identification with the work which broadened their horizons and gave them an expanded sense of purpose.[24] While the men tended to publish official reports in large and expensive books, women published magazines tracts and leaflets within the financial reach of their audiences.

Again, however, women also participated in forms of modernization. When modernization is accomplished primarily through technological production, as was the case in America, task-oriented organizations like those of the mission societies are the mode. Their societies, in their work, bore some interesting characteristics of entrepreneurship.

The sociologist Max Weber has defined three types of authority exercised by leaders: the traditional, the charismatic, and the rational-legal. *Traditional* authority rests "on an established belief in the sanctity of immemorial traditions and the legitimacy of those exercising authority under them"; *charismatic* authority rests "on devotion to the exceptional sanctity, heroism, or exemplary character of an individual person, and of the normative pattern or order revealed or ordained by them"; and *rational-legal* authority rests on "a belief in the legality of enacted rules and the right of those elevated to authority under such rules to issue commands."[25] Modernization has been a process of moving toward the last of those three. We have already seen how women found places of leadership through charismatic channels. It is also evident that, while men held most of the traditional leadership posts in the churches, women came into a type of traditional leadership at the time when modernization accomplished the separation of the work place from home and community. Increasingly affluent life styles brought about by modernization were often dominated by women seeking higher status through more refined "manners." Women became the cultural mentors of men, and this often extended to religious styles as well. "Women's place" had extended to an increasingly separate private sphere of life in which were placed the home and the church. This cultural power of women "in their place" was only overthrown in the great thrust toward modernization immediately following World War II, when men took a quantum leap ahead in education with the help of the GI Bill, and women were uprooted from local communities and thrust into the new culture of suburbia where their traditional power was not legitimated. They have never since been able to build the base of status and influence held by the earlier "ladies." Instead, a bifurcation has taken place, with some women attempting to reactivate that model by emphasizing traditional women's roles, and others moving toward the roles more consistent with modern forms of leadership within the mold identified by Weber as rational-legal.

That model is best exemplified by the term "professionalization." It assumes specialization based on educational programs usually at the graduate level; yet, it also links up with definitions of the clergy role as a religious profession. Professional leadership by women in the churches has taken five primary forms, not all fully within the modern definition of the professional—religious orders, deaconesses, missionaries, lay professionals, and ordained clergy.

In American Protestantism only the Episcopal Church has had traditional religious orders. Episcopal nuns do not comprise a very large group, but there are some eighteen separate orders in the United States, maintaining forty-five or more centers and houses. The earliest of these orders was founded in 1865; the latest, in 1974. Most, however, regardless of their date of origin, emphasize, in addition to rules of religious discipline, service to church and community that is well within traditional definitions of "women's place." Many are teaching orders, and others serve children through special programs such as camps and counseling. Some give particular emphasis to serving the poor, the elderly, or the underprivileged. Some provide nursing care. Most offer their facilities and support for retreats and conferences. Only a few offer community support for women engaged in work in the secular society. Of all groups of women giving full-time work to the church, these religious sisters appear to fall most fully into traditional roles for women; yet, they have in recent years engaged in programs to update the professional competence of their members. Their position in the church tends to be peripheral to its primary formal organization, defined instead by their direct devotion to God and the service of others.

Deaconesses represent the other more traditional form of full-time involvement of women in the work of the churches. Their close relationship to religious orders is evident in the history of at least one Episcopal order, the Sisterhood of the Good Shepherd, which disbanded in 1900, allowing remaining sisters to become deaconesses.[26] However, deaconess orders usually include women living independently, including many who are married and have families. To some extent, the evolution of the deaconess role provides a model of the changes in the role of women in the church that have been brought about by modernization. The diaconate, male or female, is based on the ideal of service, and deaconesses have been characterized by the full-time service they have offered within the church or to the society at large through agencies of the church. One of the most common activities of deaconesses has been that of nursing, a position early recognized as both traditional women's work and a profession, thus a bridge from the traditional to the modern.

The nearness of the role of deaconess to that of clergy was evident in the ambivalence of the Church of England in this matter, and continues to be reflected in its American Episcopal offshoot. Suzanne Hiatt, now an ordained Episcopal clergywoman, says of this issue:

Episcopal deaconesses are a peculiar case and cannot easily be compared with other Protestant deaconesses. In the Anglican church male deacons have always been considered clergy, indeed every priest has first been ordained a deacon and remains a deacon as well as a priest. The debate at the Lambeth Conference of 1920, 1930, and 1968 was over the issue of whether deaconesses were "within the diaconate" and therefore had received Holy Orders and were clergy. (1920 said yes; 1930 said no; 1968 said yes—local option). After Lambeth, 1968, the American Episcopal Church ruled in 1970 that deaconesses who had been "set apart with the laying on of hands" had in fact been ordained into the diaconate and were to be considered clergy. That same convention stated that henceforth women deacons were to meet the same educational standards as men deacons and be subject to the same canonical requirements for ordination. The great debate in the Episcopal Church in 1964 when Bishop James Pike allegedly "ordained" a woman was over this very point. All he did in fact was to declare a deaconess, the Rev. Phyliss Edwards, to be within the diaconate and to put her in charge of a congregation.

Originally, in the mid-nineteenth century, deaconesses were revived as a low church answer to the high church party's revival of religious orders for women. With a few exceptions, such as the Sisterhood of the Good Shepherd, deaconesses did not live in community but were attached to parishes, dioceses, and missionary stations (especially in Canada where they were an enormous factor in the missions of the Northwest Territory). In the American church, however, they have been considered clergy since 1970 and are subject to the same rules and have the same privileges as male deacons. All priests, male and female, are also deacons. The office of deaconess no longer exists.[27]

While in detail Hiatt is correct in calling the Episcopal case unique, the United Methodist Church clergy shows its Anglican roots in its understanding of the deaconess role. A 1964 description of the role of deaconess in the Methodist Church defines the deaconess as:

A woman who has been led by the Holy Spirit to devote herself to Christlike service under the direction of the church. This office entitles a woman to serve the Methodist Church through any of its agencies in any capacity not requiring full clergy rights.[28]

Since at the time that definition was set out the Methodist Church was admitting women to full ordination for the ministry, it is evident that the position of deaconess was not seen as simply a substitute for the clergy position. In fact, at the present time, the United Methodist Church has instituted the Office of the Diaconal Minister as a professional position open to men and women alike, who occupy positions in the church such as the following: Director of Christian Education,

Associate in Christian Education, Church and Community Worker, Church Business Administrator or Associate, Director or Associate in Evangelism, Health and Welfare Worker, Director or Associate in Music. Again, the opening of Diaconal Ministry of this sort has not completely supplanted the position of Deaconess, but offers a slightly different position to the lay professional in the church, recognized by the denomination as necessary to the functioning of the churches, but not as part of the ordained clergy. The opposite end of the position is also blurred, since male and female clergy are first ordained deacon before they enter full elder's status as clergy and are considered ordained clergy at that diaconal stage.

The label "professional" among deaconesses is not limited to those in nursing or to the nearness of the position to that of clergy. Many deaconesses now are fully trained for a fairly wide range of professions, particularly in education and human services. In the Lutheran Church in America, deaconesses are required to meet current standards of their profession, in addition to taking required courses in theology and to serving as interns in a place of service related to their profession. They are scattered around the country; in 1978 the Lutheran Deaconess Association claimed:

> Although deaconesses in active service and fully registered students together number only about one hundred, their representation is widespread. They can be found on the territory of 26 synods. They serve or are preparing to serve in many professions as nurses, social workers, directors of Christian education, librarians, teachers, counselors, parish secretaries, institutional administrators, rehabilitation therapists, recreational directors and in other professions as well. Except for some living in retirement centers, almost every deaconess is an actively participating member of a different local congregation.[29]

Their work is placed under the direction of the denomination's Division for Professional Leadership. The Lutheran Deaconess conference defines itself as "the professional organization for deaconesses."

Yet as professionalism has increased, the number of deaconesses has declined. As one student of the movement has said:

> Why have the numbers of deaconesses been dwindling in recent years? There seem to be many reasons: the competition of many different types of vocational opportunity for work, both church and secular, is a very important one. Deaconesses have tended to have relatively poor status as church workers. This, apparently, is partly because standards for training have tended to lag behind those for other professions in the Church; partly because neither as parish workers or social workers are they ordinarily

trained for highly specialized service; partly, no doubt, because even in the Church status tends to be associated with salary. Both Methodists and United Lutherans report much greater interest in deaconess work since educational standards have been raised.[30]

In the long run, that optimistic prediction does not seem to have been accurate.

Another aspect of modernization which has had an effect on the status of deaconesses has been the principle of fairness that has been applied in modern societies, holding that separate positions for women are inappropriate. In some denominations, deaconesses have suffered the same sorts of assimilation into the wider structures of the church. We have already noted this assimilation in the establishment of the Office of Diaconal Ministry in the United Methodist Church, an office open to both women and men. In the Episcopal Church, also, the office of deaconess has been merged since 1970 into that of deacon, open to both women and men, though some deaconesses have continued to hold on to their separate designation.

There is considerable ambivalence here concerning modern values, both equality of the sexes and the nature of professionalism. The strain concerning the latter is evident in a recent statement of the Lutheran Deaconess Association:

[T]he church, the people of God, the persons in the pew, are beginning to realize that the church must always match demands for professional excellence with the need for constant pastoral concern.

The Deaconess Community has faced the same struggle to make clear that while its members are professional people, their service is motivated by deep concern for those they serve as "your servants, for Jesus' sake!" Compassion and competence must be linked together.[31]

A similar ambivalence can be found in the memoirs of many of the earliest women to achieve ordination in mainline denominations, particularly those who were missionaries. The reasons for their ordination were most often based in the work they were trying to do, rather than any demand of their own for equal status or professional recognition. Women serving in mission fields where strict separation was observed between the world of men and that of women and children were often able to make a convincing case for, and receive ordination by, churches that forbade anyone but clergy to baptize, serve communion, or perform other rites considered necessary to church life. Their motivations for having gone to the mission field were mixed, some simply following their husbands, others probably restless and feeling pinched by the limitations of the roles of women in local congregations of their time.[32]

Many were undoubtedly following what they perceived to be a divine call. But it is probable that a large percentage of them accepted the general approach stated by a Southern Methodist bishop in a 1910 debate over lay rights for women in that denomination:

> *We have reason to believe that the demand for this kind of equality is not in harmony with the general sentiment of the women of our church, who, in the main, look upon their relation to the church in the light of duties to be performed rather than of rights to be claimed.*[33]

In those days it was expected of clergymen that they also would have similar priorities, though their actual behavior in church meetings sometimes cast doubt upon it.

Modern professionalism has always been in at least some tension with the definition of clergy roles, whether held by men or by women. The clerical role, in spite of common definitions to the contrary, is probably the oldest profession, and many of its definitions and expectations arise out of pre-modern social forms. Even where clergy roles were available to women, it is doubtful that most during the pre–World War II period were understood to be professional in the modern meaning of the term. Certainly the limitations put on many women serving churches as clergy in that time show that they were not treated as self-directed professionals by the denominations they served.

Nonetheless, the 1927 Congregational Yearbook listed one hundred women ministers in full standing, many serving as pastors of local congregations. There were some 125 to 150 women ministers in the Disciples denomination at that time, and the Cumberland Presbyterians had ordained approximately fifty women between 1918 and 1928. In 1928 there were seventeen women ministers in the Unitarian Church, and twenty-five in the United Brethren. The Methodist Episcopal Church in 1920 licensed women as local preachers; and in 1924 it admitted them to a "course of study" that opened to them ordination as local deacons, authorized to preach, conduct divine worship, solemnize matrimony, administer baptism, and assist an elder (full clergy rank) in administering the Lord's Supper. After two years they could be ordained local elders, authorized to administer communion in the local congregation only. By 1928, there were 112 local deacons and sixteen local elders in this body.[34]

This stepping into professional roles tended to be, as the "local" designation of the Methodists shows, handled as positions of service to specific local congregations rather than in the full status of a minister able to serve in any pastoral appointment in the annual conference. The relation between these roles and those sought by modern women clergy is somewhat tenuous, partly because of changing definitions of professionalism in the church, as well as the clear limitations of status within the church afforded these earlier church servants. In particular, insofar as denominational judicatories may be judged professional bodies, women's role in such levels of the system was generally restricted.

In some ways, at least, the process of professionalization is best traced in the stories of women occupying other positions in the church as lay professionals, particularly in the field of religious education. An excellent example is the development of the position of Director of Christian Education, and the way in which it was handled in such denominations as the Presbyterian. In 1938, that denomination approved the status of "Commissioned Church Worker," which gave women a direct tie to the presbyteries, though no vote in them. Early standards included graduation from high school, plus at least four years of study in approved schools, two years of which involved specific training for church workers, though no degree was required. By 1949, following trends in the rest of the society, the requirement was raised to include two years of specialized study in an accredited seminary, or a master's degree or its equivalent. The upgrading of the position according to educational standards, so typical of modern professionalism, brought into existence in 1950 a lower status position of "certified church worker" for those with only undergraduate training. Many persons serving as Directors of Christian Education, however, did not seek either to be commissioned or certified. There were no denomination-wide requirements that were binding on local churches.[35]

The Methodist diaconate mentioned above is really a similar lay professional position to the Presbyterian Commissioned Church Workers. Lutherans also now have open to women and men the position of Certified Lay Professional, and other denominations likewise have on their staffs, in local congregations as well as in judicatory and national offices, numbers of lay persons, men and women, serving in professional capacities.

However, particularly at the local level, the status of lay professionals tends to be indeterminate, and the salary low. No one has better expressed the problem of the lay professional in the church than Harriet Prichard, in her reflections on the Nature of the Ministry report of the United Presbyterian Church in 1965:

> The title "Commissioned Church Worker" means a lot of things to a lot of people. To some it means professional church educator, but to others it means "church drudge," "Sunday school bracero," and many other things not worth mentioning. The title "CCW" has been given to so many different functions in the church (Director of Music, Board Staff Executive,

teacher, doctor, nurse) that the idea of educator is not singular or unique at all when connected with this ecclesiastical jargon. People in the pews do not know what it is all about! The title is in limbo—it connotes neither "clergy" nor "laity." It does not define the job being accomplished. It is a worthless specification, and The Report *does well to ask for its abolishment. Certainly better titles are not difficult to discover. . . .*

What is the "CCW" then? He or she is a competent educator (social worker, musician, or doctor) with special training in Bible and theology. The "CCW" in education has passed the Presbytery examination which allows him or her to engage in educational ministry (but many are engaged in this ministry who have not passed such an examination!) and he or she has been installed—but nothing more! There is no committee of Presbytery that continues to care about the CCW's work, that helps him or her to continue his or her education or that protects him or her from malpractice in the local church. Besides this, the CCW is without vote in the Presbytery, the body that each one is required to serve faithfully. The CCW cannot enjoy a degree of understanding, for of all tasks in the church, his or hers is the most ill-defined.[36]

Thus one factor in the growing demand for the ordination of women to full clergy status has been the need for a clarification of the status they hold in the modern church. In a society ever more specialized, in which job descriptions are expected to be explicit, professional roles for women in the church have been particularly frustrating in their generality. Yet clergy also occupy a role ill-defined by modern standards. Why should women seek this in exchange for other frustrating positions?

One reason is imbedded in another facet of the process of modernization, the division of social life into two increasingly separate spheres, the public and the private. It may be, in fact, that the division is becoming tripartite, with much of the educational institution in its own separate sphere. But what is most relevant here is the separation of church and family, as institutions of private life, from the economy and government as public institutions. In traditional societies, where the family had a more public dimension, the relegation of women to the home did not banish them from public life. Since World War II, however, and the subsequent dominance of patterns of suburban living and the role of the commuting worker, earlier trends making the sphere of the family almost invisible in the public life of the society have been exacerbated. The role of wife and mother, however honored in the tradition, is not given low status in the public dimension of life; it is given *no* status. It has no public dimension.

Much of the activity we have traced indicates the way in which church women have found a public dimension for their lives through activities of the church or parachurch groups. Yet, as modern society has tried to deal with problems of pluralism and diversification that might create tension by defining as private opinion or "life style" such potential sources of conflict as religious ideologies, the place of the church has become more and more private as well. Particularly the local congregation has become "privatized," speaking mainly to issues of home, family, and life style, and for that reason it has been understood to have become "feminized." Yet, women have been eager participants in the more public aspects of the church, particularly through social service and missionary endeavor, even if they have had to form their own social organizations to do so. Those organizations have now largely been absorbed into the denominational structures at a time when women have become more directly involved in other public structures of the society. But on the whole, as we have seen in the cases of both "amateur" and professional laity, women have not found it easy to participate in the more public portions of contemporary church life, the decision-making bodies of the denominations. These, for the most part, have been the realm of the professional clergy. Thus one motivation for seeking ordination lies in women's desire to participate in the public facets of the only institution to which they have had natural access beyond the home.

In discussing the nonordained ministries of women in the Protestant churches we have implied the boundaries set on that work by policies refusing ordination to women. In most denominations, this has indeed been stated policy, while in others it has occurred in a *de facto* way, with the limitation on women's performance of clergy roles rooted in traditions that reach far back into western history. That tradition may now even be threatening male clergy as the "privatization" of the church in modern society puts them also more and more into what has been defined as "women's place."

This is particularly true of those clergy serving local congregations. In recent years, any public voice attributed to the churches has usually come from persons occupying staff positions in denominations or ecumenical organizations, or those in specialized roles such as the campus ministry, rather than from local pulpits. For some men, the idea of an increasing number of women in those local positions of leadership becomes an attack on their already shrinking sense of masculinity, which in modern society seems so tied to involvement in the public sphere of life. Women clergy may be not only a threat as competitors in a shrinking clergy job market, but also as a symbol of the diminishing status of the profession.

The status threat extends beyond clergy to the laity as well. Women clergy are between two antagonistic forces: one based in a traditionalism that denies women clergy status simply because that has been the tradition; and another based on modern understandings of public status and power that leads people to fear a loss of both in an institution led by women. Women can share this fear, and have been known to seek male leadership in order to give their organizations status.[37]

Another fear that has affected women has been the threat posed by professional women invading the one institution in which the home-bound "amateur" has been able to have status. At a time when women are pressured to seek employment beyond the home, many for whom this message seems inappropriate or impossible to attain have found the church the one source of consolation. Having a woman in leadership in the congregation who is professionally trained and now has that kind of status, can be seen as a real threat.

Thus it has not been easy for churches to pull down barriers to women's ordination, nor is it easy to offer full acceptance to women in clergy roles once they have been ordained.

The fight for the ordination of women in the various denominations has been documented in many places. The particular details and timing in each denomination have been different. Some denominations can look back through some founding branches to one hundred or more years of the ordination of women. Some, like the Episcopal Church, still only ordain women in specific dioceses whose bishops favor the practice, and in the Roman Catholic Church the ordination of women is still a distant hope. But the modern model of the clergywomen, in most cases, is a fairly recent phenomenon, born out of social changes that occurred in the second half of the twentieth century.

Although the 1950s have been seen as a regressive decade in the area of women's roles in the society, it was also a decade during which the ordination of women to full clergy roles was opened in major denominations such as the Methodist and the Presbyterian. The great expansion of the churches during that decade created a demand for all available professional leadership. At that time professionalism developed its modern definition, as society at large began to accept the idea of leadership by a professional class. To be a professional meant that one had received specific training, usually at the graduate level, and had skills pertinent to a position somewhat autonomous yet intimately connected with the growing institutional bureaucracies of a modern society. The accent was on the training and the skills; it was inappropriate to refuse a professional position to anyone on the basis of any characteristics other than those. It was, then, a scandal to deny clergy positions to women whose training and ability had given them preparation equal to that of male clergy. ·

The push for professionalism led to the upgrading of the training for deaconesses and lay professionals in the church to a level nearly equal to that demanded of men who were becoming ordained clergy. It created a demand within the churches that opened theological seminaries to persons not planning on ordination, including women. It became evident that to refuse ordination to women simply on the basis of their sex was inappropriate in a modern system. Many of the churches that have dropped barriers to women's ordination in the past several decades have done so primarily for that reason.

However, the real rush of women to the seminaries and the pulpits did not occur when those first barriers were dropped. Rather, even in denominations in which that option had been open for a generation or longer, the rush occurred in the 1970s. Clearly there are other sociological factors at work. The timing, as well as a good deal of the rhetoric, suggests that the source of that change lies in the various movements of the mid-twentieth century, beginning with the civil rights movement and proceeding on through some of the campus causes of the 1960s and early 1970s, to current awareness of international unrest.

This observation is supported by trends in the ordination of women in denominations where it has been possible for the longest period of time. For example, there was a slow decline in the number of women ministers after World War II in the Christian Church (Disciples of Christ) and in the American Baptist denomination. It was in the early 1970s that that trend was reversed among the Disciples. In 1973, guidelines were developed for the participation of women on denominational boards, and a consultant on women in ministry was hired.[38] Similar agencies, caucuses, and other denominational structures intended to serve as advocates for women in the system were developed in other denominations during that general period.

To some extent those movements of the 1970s were protests against modernization, even while those who participated accepted it and sought places in the bureaucracy for formerly disenfranchised persons. The protest was primarily in the rhetoric, which questioned the assumption that education and proficiency are the only apparent measures of human quality. In the worldview of these movements, the contribution of women may be particularly valuable, just because of their exclusion from the modernization process. This is exemplified in the words of one of the first women ordained to the priesthood in the Episcopal Church:

As women enter into new ecclesiastical roles, with responsibilities not only for decision making and leadership in heretofore male arenas of activity, but also for new symbol-building, the present order will change. All roles, those of both men and women, will change. Nothing will remain the same. We are agents of transformation. . . .

Our transforming power is not in our gender. . . . Our power lies in our having been born, nurtured, and acculturated into a corporate symbol: a symbol not necessarily of "femininity," but rather a symbol of difference. . . .

As a woman, together with my sisters, I offer a difference—a different ethic, derived from collective exclusion, which I will help build on behalf of other "outsiders"; a different visual, audible, sensory image I will help create; a different theology I will help shape; a different priesthood into which I have been ordained; indeed, a different Episcopal Church, as one manifestation of catholic Christendom.[39]

There appear, then, to be at least three orientations of women leading to their desire to become ordained clergy. The first, which may be an element for all three but can also stand alone, is the traditional understanding of vocation, of the ministry as a "calling." In responding to their experience of God and the church, these women seek ordination simply because it is necessary for the performance of tasks they perceive to be God given. It may be easiest to see this among women to whom ordination is still closed—the many Roman Catholic women whose ministry has put them in positions of leadership in groups that, when they follow a church-encouraged tendency to celebrate their activities with the sacrament of communion, must call in an outsider, a stranger to the group, in order to have a priest authorized to perform the rite. They see this as a serious impediment to the ministry they are doing, a ministry they feel has been faithful to God's call.[40] Thus ordination is seen as the simple fulfillment of their work. Protestant women, who have for years in some denominations filled the pulpits of small churches or provided clergy services in out-of-the-way places where men could not be found or would not serve, have sought ordination for similar reasons. Many of them married, they have been willing to take advantage of a social system that allowed them the financial support of husbands, to take on ill-paid and part-time jobs that family bread winners could not afford to fill. Their professional training may have been as good as that of the men, but their understanding of the clergy role has been cast less within the modern definitions of professionalism than within traditional definitions of ministry that have carried over from premodern times.

The second orientation is that of modern professionalism, in which equality between the sexes is taken for granted among those in possession of equal training, and the role of ordained clergy considered appropriate to anyone who has the qualifications. Women coming to clergy positions in this frame of reference understand that the primary concern is one of competence, and many church people testify to the quality of ministerial performance given by many women. In a society where not all occupations are equally open to women even yet, many extremely able women have entered church professions at a time when equally qualified men have chosen among a wider range of options. The church, then, may have more than its share of able women, not only because of this, but also because of its institutional closeness to the home, and so its greater accessibility to women.

This factor may become more important in future years, as more and more older women are entering the seminaries, seeking clergy positions as second careers. For many of these women, their first career was that of homemaker, and the seminary their choice for a second career, based on experience as lay leaders in the congregation and as trained volunteers in the community. The combination of experience and ability represented by these women, when supplemented by contemporary professional theological education, may prove a powerful force in the churches in the next few decades.

Their background puts them often in a different position from that of mostly younger women whose experience is rooted in a feminism that has arisen out of the movements of the 1960s and 1970s. This third orientation toward the church, which sees it as an agency of social transformation under the leadership of women, is also a particularly powerful one in a society where we seem to hear daily demands for social transformation, for some kind of new vision.

The agenda of women seeking ordination from this orientation includes not only competence in the performance of recognized tasks of ministry, but the development of new forms of speaking, acting, and relating. They are offended by the exclusiveness of the male language about God and humankind, common in the churches, as well as by hierarchical forms of theology and church polity. Their approach is radical, not so much in the image of "radical obedience" carried by early women clergy, as in their assessment that given structures are an impediment to the gospel they preach.

A primary question for the future may be the way in which these three orientations overlap as more and more women move into the field. Will the different agendas create conflict among women clergy? Or are they, in the field, coming to some sort of synthesis that takes elements of each to build something more than the sum of the three? What are the pressures and processes of the lives of clergywomen in the church that impact upon the fulfillment of their aspirations? In entering a male-dominated occupation, will women, as one opponent of women's ordination gloomily predicted, " . . . conform to male images of priesthood and ministry, partly because of their anxiety to excel, and partly because of a desire to be accepted. They will thus be tempted to betray their vocation as women, and become carbon copies of men . . ."?[41] Or, will the influx of ordained women into church power structures, instead, revitalize these structures, in the more hopeful words of the following advocates of clergywomen, through better "yoking" of "traditional male values . . . with traditional female values as the undergirding of the administrative and institutional life of the church"?[42]

It may also be that the three orientations, though each may be stressed by different persons, tend to be present together for most. The stress may be more related to the circumstances in which women attempt to gain access to the roles to which they feel called. Barbara Brown Zikmund has noted a general pattern of the access of women to full participation in the church, which she finds falling into seven stages, and which may summarize much of what has been said here.

The first stage deals with the right of women to speak about matters of faith in the public realm, particularly in groups that include men. The second deals with the right of women to be elected and to take leadership positions in local churches. Third is the issue of female representation in upper levels of church organization, in conventions, on boards, and the like. The fourth step occurs when women seek to be recognized as valid pastoral leaders in the churches, without raising the question of ordination. The fifth is the step of ordination itself, rather than just licensing. The sixth step is that of obtaining the right to compete with men to serve the church in all ways open to men, including senior leadership in leading churches and positions of denominational leadership reserved for the ordained, such as bishop, conference minister, presbytery executive, and the like. Finally, the seventh step refers to the work of the theologian, to the right of women to think differently about the Christian faith itself.[43]

While these steps generally come in sequence, the history of each denomination shows that there has been considerable variation in the time when each reached a particular stage. All nine of the denominations in this study have reached the fifth step, at least in part. Our investigation in this chapter, while recognizing the sequence, has been concerned primarily with the working of that stage, with overtones of movement toward the sixth. It is at the sixth stage, in particular, that the professional marginality referred to in Chapter 1 begins to be put behind, and it is with the movement into this stage that the remaining chapters are concerned.

Summary

This chapter has described how the position of women in church structures of sects and denominations, particularly the mainline Protestant denominations represented in this study, has changed over time. In part, changes in the status and visibility of women in churches have been in response to internal phases within the life cycle of religious movements. In the three phases described, women have been typically permitted freedom of expression and exercise of leadership in the first early phase of the movement, or "charismatic phase." However, as the movement becomes older and larger, it enters into its "consolidation and organization phase" in which women are absorbed into a system dominated by men and not allowed much autonomy of expression, organization, or decision making. Further development of the religious movement into a well-established denomination typically creates conditions favorable for the reemergence of women as visible leaders, as the denomination and its churches become more complex and less differentiated in structure, membership, and values from the general society.

Hence, factors which are external to the denomination per se but are characteristic of general societal trends are also of great importance to women's position within churches generally and these nine denominations in particular. Modernization and its accompanying processes of specialization, bureaucratization, and professionalization have had strong impacts on religious movements, organizations, and women's position within all church structures. The increased valuing of expertise led to the upgrading of the training for deaconesses and women lay professionals. The expansion of churches in these major Protestant denominations in the fifties created a demand for professional church workers, including well-trained women. Indeed, the rationality and democratization characteristic of modernization made it appear less right and rational to exclude any because of their sex from professional church work, even that requiring ordination.

Parallel changes have occurred in the kinds of motivations women themselves have for being ordained. This chapter described three primary motivations for ordination which, though distinct, may be combined within individual women in varying degrees: (1) a traditional motivation to seek ordination as fulfillment of a calling from God; (2) a professional motivation in which individual women seek ordination as legitimate church recognition that they have achieved certain high levels of competence which would fit them to minister to others in an official capacity; (3) a desire to attain official church standing to be agents of change in order to give women influence and power in the church and society equal to that of men.

In the next chapter we will examine early life experiences which prompted clergywomen to enter seminary as compared to those important for clergymen. In the fourth chapter we will give specific attention to how these different motivations for seeking ordination seem to have been distributed among contemporary women pastors.

3

The Family Font: Family Backgrounds and Life Before Seminary

I was born in Iowa . . . an only child. My father was an inventor who placed an enormous amount of value on taking initiative . . . and always treated me as if I had good sense. . . . I think I was absolutely unsocialized in what most women my age were taught about domesticity. As I look back . . . I almost feel remorse that my mother played a very constrained role, very confined. . . . There was an undercurrent of feminism then that dealt with the male world by taking care of it and getting rid of it. And I remember feeling so close to my father that I made a very conscious decision that I wasn't going to do that, I wasn't going to make that kind of separatist covert proclamation. . . . I went to a very fancy girls' school, and I was president of everything . . . and I went to a university . . . and again I was leader. . . . My real conversion experience [to becoming an ordained minister] took place when [my parish minister] said, 'Well, it doesn't matter what women do and say anyway. Women are of no importance as far as the church and society are concerned.' He said that! . . . I had a special ministry at that point. . . . I wanted to be ordained, because to be so would perhaps change the Church in the way it treated women, because the authority still rests with the ordained person. . . . So to bring some integrity to the Church itself . . . was what I was all about, and that was absolutely clear to me at the time or I would never have gone to seminary.—CLERGYWOMAN

I was born in Hartford. . . . My parents were Welsh. My father didn't believe in educating women. Although he was very able to send me to school, he didn't feel that women should be educated for anything but home. He has his own business and he worked nights, so I was able to sneak out of the house to go to school. . . . I was in college for three years before he realized it. . . . Even though my parents weren't churchy, they

*insisted that we be brought up in the church. . . . My mother attended
church with me and my sister. The person who has had the most meaning
to me in my entire life was the pastor. . . . He was already forty when I
was a very little girl. I really learned to rely on him, and he was the
person in my life I could talk to. I don't think I would have made it as a
human being if it were not for him. Sometimes other women say that what
we need are female models, but as far as I am concerned, he was the best
model I could have had. I knew that I wanted to be a person just like
him, and even when I was a little girl I wanted to become a full-time
church worker.—*CLERGYWOMAN

Who are the women entering parish ministry today? What kinds of
influences have led them to choose this traditionally male profession?
In this chapter, we look at the social origins of women who have
become ordained ministers, comparing them with our sample of clergymen. We look at parental influences, including parents' relationships to
the church, the clergy's prior religious involvement, their college
experience, and the decision to enter seminary.

Parental Influence and Upbringing

The two women, quoted above, were among the first to enter their
seminaries; although they are from quite different backgrounds, it is
evident that, as children, each knew a man who modeled in both his
behavior and life style the kind of person she wished to become, and
gave her personal encouragement in following in his footsteps. Frequently for other women, this man was a relative (for example, several
women reported that it was a grandfather, and for one a living great-
grandfather, a Baptist preacher). Mothers were less often mentioned as
influential role models, probably because they were strictly involved in
the domestic scene. This is a confinement many of these clergywomen
volunteered in interviews that they had rejected for themselves as a life
style at an early age. A 1980 study of 183 women M.Div. students of
the Boston Theological Institute member seminaries indicated that
similar findings about the importance of a childhood male role model
hold even for those women who are entering seminary now. Often,
these women became dissatisfied after immersing themselves for some
years in the housewife and mother routines. Carole R. Bohn, who conducted this 1980 study of women seminarians, drew up a composite
portrait from her data of the typical woman seminarian, a composite
she calls "Ellen":

*. . . By the time her second child was born, Ellen was comfortably at
home with her various jobs of wife, mother and active churchwoman. As*

she passed her thirtieth birthday, Ellen began to feel restless. She was always busy, but never seemed to have enough to do. . . . Her mother, who had also been a teacher and homemaker, sympathized with Ellen's feeling, but told her it would pass. Ellen's mother had always been a strong source of emotional support, but now as she looked at her family origin, it seemed to her that it was her father's attitude toward life that she wanted to emulate. He was an active, aggressive businessman, who had always seemed to know what he wanted and how to get it. Why couldn't she approach life that way? . . . [1]

For women clergy and present seminarians, it does not appear to have been crucial that the male model during their growing-up years specifically encouraged these women to enter the ordained ministry. What was important was only that he stressed the importance to the woman of being her own person, making her own decisions, even if these were very different from those her friends made. Or, to put it another way, clergywomen were not specifically pushed toward the ministry by their fathers or father surrogates; rather, these men held the door open for the women to enter this vocation if they chose.

Having a clergyman as father was the experience of a number of women and men in our sample. Equal proportions of both men and women ordained before 1975 and after had clergy fathers. Before 1975, 15 percent of the women had clergy fathers compared to 14 percent of the men. For those ordained in 1975 or after, 12 percent of both of the women and the men had clergy fathers. These findings strongly suggest that pastor fathers modeled an occupational role and commitment just as compelling to their daughters as to their sons (perhaps regardless of whether such fathers were approving or appalled at the idea of their daughters following in their footsteps).

An important difference between the parental backgrounds of these women and men pastors is that the women were somewhat more likely than the men to be born to upper-middle class parents. One of the attributes of persons that sociologists regularly take into account is their social class. Social class is generally defined as the level or stratum which an individual (or group) occupies in a given society by virtue of his or her (or its) occupation, income, education, power, and prestige. In modern society, an individual's position on each of these attributes may very well not be consistent. For example, people of great wealth do not necessarily have a high level of education nor much prestige; or, to take a more mundane example, the pastor with the Master of Divinity or the Doctor of Ministry degree may not be making as high an annual salary as the parishioner with the high school education who is a union truck driver. Nevertheless, while the boundaries between social classes are unclear, social class background and present social position have been found regularly to be correlated with political values, lifestyles, types of mental illness, differences in patterns of friendship, participation in voluntary organizations, child rearing practices, and a host of other behaviors including occupational choice.[2] The linkages between social class indicators—typically income, education, and occupation—together or separately, and the various attitudes and behaviors is not always clear; nevertheless, the fact that these links are often present makes attention to these social class attributes important in sociological analysis.

Although there is a wide range in educational and occupational attainments of the parents of these men and women pastors, 33 percent of the clergymen had fathers who had not finished high school, compared to only 16 percent of the clergywomen. To be sure, at least part of this is due to the fact that the clergywomen in the sample are younger on the average than the men. Given the rise in the proportion of persons finishing high school over the decades, one would expect their fathers to be better educated. When we control for age, women are slightly more likely to come from families where the father was better educated than are the men. Also, women are more likely to have had fathers in professional or business executive careers than clergymen. This is especially true for those ordained in 1975 or later. Almost one-third of the women as compared with one-tenth of the men had professional or executive fathers. Having a father who is pursuing a professional or business career may be more important to women than to men in becoming parish ministers, partly since women, unlike men, are entering a non-traditional occupation for them. Because of this, women may have a greater need for a father model who is or was himself engaged in pursuing a top-level job involving considerable initiative and risk taking.

There are also alternative or additional explanations for the fact that women parish ministers tend to come from higher status family backgrounds than their male counterparts. One is that the ministry is seen as a path toward upward social mobility for the sons of lower-middle class and working class families.[3] Daughters of such families, however, would probably be actively discouraged from the ministry as a vocation, due to the tendency for lower social classes to be more theologically fundamentalist in orientation to the Bible and to women's place in religious leadership.[4] While upper-middle class parents also wish their sons to attain a high occupational and educational status, they are more likely to push their male offspring to be doctors, lawyers, or business executives like themselves. If sons of such higher socio-economic families do go into the ministry, they are more likely to aspire to positions of greater influence in the denomination or special ministries, rather than the parish.[5] Daughters in these business executive and professional families have two advantages over daughters of office workers, shopkeepers, civil service, and blue collar breadwinners. First, their families are more likely to have sufficient income to educate both sons and daughters through college and beyond. Second, parents in such families also are probably sufficiently liberal (theologically, socially, and politically) and sufficiently indulgent to support their daughters attending seminary, and even take some pride in the fact that their daughters are doing something relatively unique for women.

These general findings and associated explanations may not, however, hold for all mainline Protestant denominations ordaining women. That there are differences among denominations in the social and economic characteristics of members is a fairly well-researched phenomenon.[6] It would seem that such differences might similarly distinguish the clergy in one denomination from those in another, insofar as family background is concerned. Clergy in this present study do indeed differ in their social class origins according to denomination, as can be seen in Table 3.1. Episcopalian, Lutheran Church in America, and United Presbyterian clergy have better educated parents and fathers who are more likely to have been business executives or professionals than, for example, American Baptist, Disciples of Christ, and American Lutheran clergy.[7]

It is still true, however, that within each denomination, clergywomen are more likely to have better educated parents and fathers in higher status occupations than clergymen. Some denominations show more or less differences between the two groups than others. For example, there is little if any significant difference between the sexes in the United Church of Christ in relation to parental background, whereas the differences between the sexes in the Presbyterian Church in the U.S. are quite large.

These last two findings may bear out the place of high family status in overcoming cultural impediments to women's choice of clergy as a future occupation, since the Presbyterian Church U.S. is primarily located in the South, where greater traditionalism still applies to the role of women. It is also interesting to note that mothers of PCUS women clergy were most likely of all the denominational clergy mothers to be business executives or professionals themselves (29 percent) and have attained at least a four-year college degree (48 percent). In contrast, the more urban and northeastern geographical base of the United Church of Christ would indicate less need for women to overcome barriers to enter professions in the church or elsewhere.

The preceding analysis of why a greater proportion of clergywomen

Table 3.1 Parental Background of Clergywomen and Clergymen

	ABC W %	ABC M %	CC(D) W %	CC(D) M %	EC W %	EC M %	LCA W %	LCA M %	ALC W %	ALC M %	PCUS W %	PCUS M %	UPC W %	UPC M %	UMC W %	UMC M %	UCC W %	UCC M %
A. Father's Occupation																		
Clergy	17	11	17	8	7	13	4	11	3	14	5	15	12	12	13	14	22	22
Bus. exec. or professional	14	5	17	8	42	28	40	11	26	9	57	4	39	23	22	7	25	20
Middle mgmt., small business, civil servant, clerical worker	35	39	28	30	39	33	30	32	33	25	24	54	43	32	31	31	26	28
Blue collar or farm worker, unemployed	34	45	38	54	12	26	26	46	38	52	14	29	15	33	34	48	27	30
Total	100	100	100	100	100	100	100	100	100	100	100	100	100	100	100	100	100	100
(N)	(66)	(62)	(47)	(64)	(77)	(99)	(54)	(44)	(39)	(65)	(21)	(24)	(73)	(111)	(127)	(137)	(90)	(90)
B. Father's Highest Level of Eduction																		
Less than high school	27	43	26	33	6	17	14	34	17	46	10	40	11	30	20	40	12	26
High school graduate	25	18	16	36	19	13	27	28	33	24	14	8	17	19	24	21	19	25
Technical training or some college	15	22	16	14	20	28	13	17	21	3	33	24	15	12	15	22	19	10
College graduate	10	0	22	8	24	13	18	4	10	9	5	12	15	16	17	6	13	8
Post-graduate education	23	17	20	9	31	29	28	17	19	18	38	16	42	23	24	11	37	31
Total	100	100	100	100	100	100	100	100	100	100	100	100	100	100	100	100	100	100
(N)	(67)	(63)	(50)	(66)	(80)	(103)	(55)	(47)	(42)	(46)	(21)	(25)	(74)	(116)	(133)	(146)	(93)	(93)

Present Denomination

C. Mother's Occupation

Bus. exec. or professional (includes clergy)	11	4	16	5	15	15	17	7	14	14	29	10	18	9	16	6	14	7
Middle mgmt., small business, civil servant, clerical worker	31	20	26	14	14	14	35	17	31	12	9	8	20	12	24	19	20	10
Farm or factory worker, waitress, salesperson (clerk)	5	3	8	6	5	4	5	11	5	8	0	8	4	3	6	10	3	8
Housewife	53	71	50	75	66	67	43	65	50	66	62	64	58	76	54	65	63	75
Total	100	100	100	100	100	100	100	100	100	100	100	100	100	100	100	100	100	100
(N)	(66)	(65)	(50)	(64)	(79)	(102)	(54)	(46)	(42)	(64)	(21)	(25)	(71)	(45)	(137)	(140)	(93)	(88)

D. Mother's Highest Level of Education

Less than high school	19	23	15	23	7	19	14	23	9	12	9	24	9	24	13	30	12	21
High school graduate	29	38	27	36	30	26	33	38	33	36	24	12	20	29	28	29	26	31
Technical training or some college	30	34	33	32	26	25	25	24	38	35	19	36	35	29	34	23	29	26
College graduate	12	3	19	6	28	17	20	15	10	9	33	16	23	12	15	9	21	12
Post-graduate education	10	2	6	3	9	13	8	0	10	8	15	12	13	6	10	9	12	10
Total	100	100	100	100	100	100	100	100	100	100	100	100	100	100	100	100	100	100
(N)	(67)	(65)	(52)	(66)	(80)	(106)	(55)	(47)	(42)	(66)	(21)	(25)	(74)	(116)	(137)	(143)	(93)	(92)

come from higher social class backgrounds than do clergymen should not be construed to imply that all or even most clergywomen are from the upper-middle class. Less than half the clergywomen have (or had) fathers with college degrees or higher, and less than half have fathers who are (or were) business executives, clergy or other professionals, even though more women do so than men. Between a fourth and a third of the clergywomen over the last fifteen years, in fact, have come from what is generally known as the "working class." Economic resources of the woman's family, important as these are in facilitating her access to graduate education, were not as important probably as her own determination and the influence of a role model who encouraged her directly, or through example, to pursue the ordained ministry as a career.

We have looked primarily at the influence of father or father surrogates in the backgrounds of clergywomen. Although mothers may not have played as pivotal a role as fathers or father surrogates in impelling their daughters toward the ordained ministry, this seems probably to be primarily because the mothers were immersed in domestic duties with few aspirations to a life outside these concerns. Mothers who did not follow this typical pattern may have been more influential. Certainly, clergywomen are more likely than clergymen to have had mothers who worked outside the home when they were growing up (44 percent of the women to 30 percent of the men). Episcopal women were least likely to have mothers who worked outside the home (67 percent were housewives) and Lutheran Church in America women the most likely to have working mothers (43 percent were housewives).

Denominational differences also emerge in the type of work the mother is engaged in. As noted, both men and women in the Presbyterian Church U.S., but especially the women, were most likely to have mothers who worked as professionals or business executives. In all but two denominations, Episcopal and American Lutheran, clergywomen were slightly more likely than the men to have mothers who worked as professionals or business executives. This further suggests that having a mother in a professional or executive career may have been slightly more important to women than men in inspiring them to a career in ministry; although, simply the fact that the mothers worked outside the home at all may have been the most important influence. Or, from another vantage point, non-working mothers may have been important in showing the future clergywoman the kind of life she did *not* want to lead.

These background factors that appear important for women entering the ordained ministry may also be important for women entering other traditionally male professions. In a study of women lawyers, Cynthia

Fuchs Epstein reports that, compared to men in this profession, women tended to come from the better educated and wealthier families, who were both willing to encourage and financially support their daughters in law school. Not only were women lawyers somewhat more likely to have mothers who worked outside the home than men, but women lawyers' mothers who worked were more apt to be in professional occupations than working mothers of men lawyers. However, most mothers of women lawyers did not work in professional occupations, and Epstein reports that for many women lawyers:

> *Their mothers were negative role models in some ways. They felt that their mothers' lives had been frustrating and unfulfilling, and their talents had been subordinated to their roles as wives and mothers. Further, many mothers encouraged their daughters not to follow in their footsteps.*[8]

The similarities between the backgrounds of women pastors and women laywers are close enough that a further question has to be raised: why did these women choose the ministry over some other career? A partial answer may lie in the religious socialization of the future clergyperson.

Parental Church-Going and the Clergy's Denominational Backgrounds

Less than ten percent of the parents of these clergy were unchurched or inactive in a church when these future pastors were growing up, and about two-thirds of both these men and women had at least one parent who was active or very active in a church when the clergy were children. This is perhaps a major reason why there was very little denominational switching by the clergy. That is, 69 percent of the clergywomen and 72 percent of the clergymen were ordained in the denomination in which they were raised. Another 9 percent of both sexes were not raised in any one denomination, and eventually settled on the one in which they were ordained. About a fifth of these men and women (22 percent and 20 percent respectively) changed denominations from the one in which they were brought up. Table 3.2 shows patterns of denominational stability or switching by denomination.

The denominations which have the highest percentage of clergy who switched into another denomination are the Episcopal Church and the United Church of Christ. The Lutherans, both LCA and ALC, in contrast were the denominations most likely to have clergy who were born into them. A number of factors could account for these differences. Parental socialization may have been important; certainly the Episcopal clergy were the ones (both men and women) least likely among the

Table 3.2 Original Denomination, Present Denomination, and Sex of Clergy

Original Denomination	Present Denomination																	
	ABC		CC(D)		EC		LCA		ALC		PCUS		UPC		UMC		UCC	
	W %	M	W %	M	W %	M	W %	M	W %	M	W %	M	W %	M	W %	M	W %	M
Same	78	70	72	77	52	67	91	80	84	91	71	91	68	67	66	74	62	58
Different	22	30	28	23	48	33	9	20	16	9	29	9	32	33	34	26	38	42
Total	100	100	100	100	100	100	100	100	100	100	100	100	100	100	100	100	100	100
(N)	(65)	(63)	(50)	(66)	(79)	(107)	(56)	(44)	(38)	(65)	(21)	(22)	(72)	(116)	(137)	(144)	(86)	(92)

denominations to report that their parents were active in church when they were growing up. Episcopal clergy, therefore, may have felt freer to choose a denomination different from their parents than clergy whose parents had been very active in or committed to the denomination. Further, both the Episcopal Church and the United Church of Christ are typified as being upper-middle class. Some clergy may have transferred into either of them as a means of upward social mobility. Although analysis indicates that Episcopal men and women in particular who had switched from another denomination were less likely to have college-educated fathers than if they had been consistently Episcopalians, it is *generally* the case that those who switched denominations came from less well-educated families. However, this may be more due to lack of consistent parental religious socialization than any desire for upward social mobility. Correlations show that the lower the education and occupation of these clergy's parents, the more likely they were to be relatively inactive in the church when their children were growing up.

Religious socialization by parents and others during childhood further seems the most appropriate explanation of the relative stability of denominational commitment among the Lutheran clergy. Although approximately two-thirds of the Lutheran pastors' parents were active in the church when their children were growing up, they were not more active than parents of clergy in other denominations (with the exception of the Episcopalians). The greater stability here may have something to do not only with the fact that the Lutherans tend to have stronger ethnic ties than most other Protestant denominations; but there also may be a theological factor involved, in that the Lutheran commitment to a particular confessional or doctrinal stance may inhibit denominational change.[9]

Denominations also differ in the amount of discrepancy between men and women clergy in their degree of denominational switching. Women, as shown in Table 3.1, were 20 percent more likely than men to have switched into the Presbyterian Church, U.S., and 15 percent more likely than men to have switched into the Episcopal Church before ordination. Since the switchers in both these denominations came originally from a range of denominations and seemed to be equally divergent in other characteristics, it is probably the case that many of them were those who changed to their husbands' denomination. Men were slightly more likely than women to switch into the Lutheran Church in America, a factor which may or may not be influenced by recent unrest in a sister denomination. But overall it must be underlined again that the predominant pattern for these clergy is one of consistent and active religious socialization in one denomination.

These findings accord with earlier studies of clergy which have indicated that most were set on the path toward that profession early in life, usually in families where religion and religious practice were taken seriously.[10] The active involvement of parents in churches when these clergy were children was an important factor. Correlation analysis reveals that the more active the parents were, the more active these future clergy were in church during their young adult or college years. All told, fully 63 percent of the women and 72 percent of the men reported being active in the church as young adults, and of these, slightly under half (45 percent) of both sexes indicated that they were very active in a church between the ages of eighteen and twenty-two.

These percentages also suggest that the clergy's own involvement in a church during the college years was more important than the degree of parental activity during their childhood in predisposing them to make early decisions to enter seminary. Although by definition almost all the clergy in our sample eventually went to seminary, there is a high probability that potentially promising students who might have made good pastors decided not to because they were not involved in church during college. The college years open up many opportunities to young people; and for good students of both sexes, there are professional and academic career possibilities in occupations which are more remunerative and often have higher social prestige than ministry. Being heavily involved in a church during college would seem to be some inoculation against being lured into other professions.

College and Other Experiences Prior to Entering Seminary

Educational requirements are high for clergy in the mainline Protestant churches, and all but 3 percent of the women and 4 percent of the men earned a four-year college degree. The favorite major for both women and men was religion and/or philosophy, with 27 percent of the women and 25 percent of the men opting for this major. English and journalism followed, along with the social and behavioral sciences—anthropology, sociology, and psychology—for both men and women. It is only after these most popular majors that a division can be seen between the interests of women and men, with the women preferring speech, arts, music, and education, and men history, political science, economics, physical sciences, and mathematics.

Clergywomen and men attended different types of colleges about equally. Around half—45 percent of the women to 57 percent of the men—went to religious or church-related colleges. Private secular colleges enrolled a minority of these clergy—16 percent of the women to 15 percent of the men. Public colleges are the alma maters of about a third—39 percent of the women clergy, 28 percent of the men. Overall,

it can be seen that men were more likely than women to go to denominational colleges, whereas women were more likely to go to public colleges than men. Most of this difference between sexes in types of
colleges attended is probably due to the relatively younger age of the
clergywomen and concomitant later date of attendance. Not only were
there more church-related colleges earlier in this century, but also there
have been marked increases both in tuition costs at private institutions
and in the quality of education available at a more moderate cost at
state institutions.

Denominational differences in kinds of colleges attended by men and
women clergy indicate that Episcopal, United Presbyterian and United
Church of Christ men and women clergy were most likely (between
one-fifth and two-fifths) to attend private secular colleges. Unlike the
situation in other denominations, where more men than women attended church-related colleges, Presbyterian Church U.S. clergywomen
were more likely to attend such schools than PCUS men, 61 percent to
43 percent. This is probably due to the fact that, in the South, private
colleges are for the most part church related, and it is to private colleges
that the PCUS business executive and professional fathers are more
likely to send their daughters.[11] Disciples women were also very likely
to attend church-related colleges in equal proportions to the men (63
percent of the women, 64 percent of the men). This may be due to the
recruiting efforts of these Disciples denominational colleges for both
women and men, as well as other factors.[12] For Disciples clergy, as well
as those in all other denominations, type of college attended has
changed over the last generation and certainly in the past decade, with
those clergy (both men and women) who went to college in the sixties
much more likely to have gone to a public college than those who
received their college educations earlier than this. (Indeed among
clergy who began seminary after 1970, there is no difference between
men and women in the percent who went to public colleges—42 percent of the women and 40 percent of the men.)

One would expect to find more future clergy who were unchurched
or nominally church-related during their college years at public and
private secular colleges, and more clergy who were active and leaders in
churches as young adults at religious colleges. There is probably both
greater opportunity and social pressure for those at the latter institutions to be active in churches; in addition, those who attend religious
colleges are already likely to be active churchgoers. One study showed
that students who attended church-related colleges were as religiously
oriented as seniors as they had been as freshmen, whereas those who
attended public and private secular colleges became more secular. The
authors of this study term this the "anchoring effect" that religious

Table 3.3   Church Activity During the Ages 18 to 22
(by Type of College Attended and Sex)

Church Activity During College Years	Type of College					
	Public		Secular Private		Church Related	
	W	M	W	M	W	M
	%		%		%	
a. Unchurched to nominally church related	22	20	37	26	20	12
b. Average to active church relationship	33	34	26	34	33	41
c. Very active and a leader in a church	45	46	37	40	4	47
Total	100	100	100	100	100	100
(N)	(215)	(189)	(89)	(101)	(248)	(381)

colleges can have on students' religious beliefs "in an increasingly secularized society."[13] Religious colleges might be expected, then, to better maintain student's religious values and practices. In Table 3.3 we examine this issue for the clergymen and women in our study.

As can be seen from the table, religious colleges do *not* seem to have had a significantly greater impact on the church activity of future clergy than any other type of college. There were no consistent differences in activity attributable to college type. Possibly family background is the more important factor in predicting future clergy's involvement in a church during their college years as another study suggested.[14] However, the amount of father's education had absolutely no relationship to church involvement during college of clergymen, whether they were in public, private secular, or religious colleges. It had only a slight effect on the church involvement of clergywomen, regardless of what kind of college they attended. Women from families where the father had only a high school education or less were slightly more likely to be very active in church during college.

Church activity in college should also be associated with the time of decision to enter seminary. Table 3.4 shows this relationship. It reveals that the greater amount of church activity during college, the more likely both men and women were to make an early decision to attend seminary. The clergy who were relatively unchurched during their college years were more likely to decide after college graduation to enter seminary. This was especially true for men. Women, however, tend to make a later decision to enter seminary than men at each level of church participation during their college years.

Table 3.4 Percent Making a Late Decision to Enter Seminary
(by Church Activity During College)

Church Activity During College	W %	M %
Unchurched to nominally church related	68 (of 148)	41 (of 112)
Average to active church relationship	44 (of 192)	30 (of 276)
Very active in church	42 (of 273)	14 (of 327)
Tau Beta correlations between church activity during college and whether decision to enter seminary was made before, during, or after college	−.17 (sig. .001)	−.20 (sig. .0001)

Although the type of college attended may not have had much effect on how active future clergy were in church during their college years, it does seem to have had an effect on the timing of their decision to enter seminary, as can be observed in Table 3.5. Both clergywomen and men were most likely to decide to enter seminary before they finished college if they attended a church-related college, less likely if they attended a secular private college, and least likely if they attended a public college.

Actually, it would seem from Table 3.6 that both the amount of

Table 3.5 Timing of Decision to Enter Seminary
(by Type of College Attended and Sex)

	Type of College					
	Public		Secular Private		Church Related	
Decision to Attend Seminary	W	M	W	M	W	M
	%		%		%	
Before college	10	25	8	20	12	44
During college	30	46	47	53	49	42
After college	60	29	45	27	39	14
Total	100	100	100	100	100	100
(N)	(122)	(188)	(88)	(100)	(246)	(380)

church activity during college and the type of college attended have a somewhat independent, additive effect on men and women's decisions to enter seminary. Both men and women who go to public colleges and are relatively unchurched during their college years are least likely to decide before or during college to enter seminary; whereas, men and women who go to a religious college and are active in church during their college years are more likely to decide to enter seminary before college graduation. Consistently, and in both of these cases, women are significantly less likely than men to decide to enter seminary before they have finished college. For example, among those who had attended religious colleges and were very active in church, women were still 24 percent more likely than men to decide after college graduation to attend seminary; and among those who attended public colleges and were relatively unchurched, women were 31 percent more likely than men to decide after college graduation to attend seminary. Whatever "anchoring" effect attendance at a religious college and/or high involvement in a local church during college has on men's commitment to a ministerial vocation, it is much weaker for women. Perhaps highly religious women in *some* denominational colleges were discouraged from translating their church commitment into seminary attendance by faculty and other students at these colleges. Such women might have done better in terms of their seminary aspirations if they attended a secular college, where faculty and students would have been more indifferent to their plans to go to seminary and pursue a ministerial career. On the whole, however, as observed in Table 3.5, the atmosphere, curriculum, and people at religious colleges are conducive to both women and men making a relatively early decision to attend seminary.

Indeed, the differences between men and women in their career paths to the ministry are probably most visible in the factor of their time of decision to enter seminary. Of the total sample, only 10 percent of the women as compared to 35 percent of the men decided before college to enter seminary, and 49 percent of the women compared to only 21 percent of the men decided after college graduation. Further, this general trend holds true across denominations; women are more likely to decide to enter seminary after college than are men in every denomination. However, the strength of the relationship between church activity, type of college attended and time of decision to enter seminary varies somewhat among the denominations. For example, Disciples women were both most likely of all clergywomen to go to church-related colleges and most likely to be very active in a church during the college years, and there were no significant differences between Disciples men and women clergy in these ways (approximately

Table 3.6   Percentage of Late Deciders* to Enter Seminary
(by Amount of Church Activity During College)

Amount of Church Activity During College Years	Type of College Attended					
	Public		Secular Private		Church Related	
	W	M	W	M	W	M
	%		%		%	
Unchurched or nominally church related	77	46	73	44	57	28
	(of 47)	(of 35)	(of 33)	(of 25)	(of 49)	(of 43)
Average to active church relationship	57	39	26	18	35	14
	(of 70)	(of 64)	(of 23)	(of 34)	(of 82)	(of 155)
Very active in a church	54	15	31	24	34	10
	(of 93)	(of 87)	(of 32)	(of 41)	(of 115)	(of 180)
Tau Beta correlations between time of decision to enter seminary and clergy's church participation during college	$-.15$	$-.22$	$-.38$	$-.16$	$-.13$	$-.20$
	(sig. .006)	(.0005)	(.001)	(.04)	(.01)	(.001)

*Late deciders are those deciding after college graduation to attend seminary.

63 to 65 percent of Disciples men and women went to denominational colleges and were very active in churches during these years). In short, religious colleges proved to be an "anchoring" influence on Disciples youth of either sex. Yet the difference between Disciples women and men clergy in the time of decision to attend seminary was insignificantly different from the difference between men and women in five other denominations. For example, Disciples women were 40 percent less likely than Disciples men to decide to go to seminary before college, and 21 percent more likely than Disciples men to decide only after college graduation to attend seminary.

To take another denominational example, American Lutheran men were most likely of all clergy to attend denominational colleges (74 percent), and though a substantial number of ALC women also attended denominational colleges (54 percent), they have done so less than men. Nevertheless, slightly more ALC clergywomen than men (45 percent to 37 percent) were very active in a church during college; however, proportionately fewer ALC women than men decided before college graduation that they would go to seminary (60 percent to 74 percent). American Baptist and United Methodist men and women clergy findings closely parallel these reported for the American Lutheran.

One explanation for the finding that clergywomen overall and in each denomination were significantly more likely than men to make a late decision to enter seminary (that is, after college graduation), is surely that women receive less support from family, friends, and clergy for embarking on a seminary and ministerial career. Even though women's decisions to enter seminary were less likely than men's to be identical with decisions to enter the ordained ministry, they faced more negative and hostile reactions to this educational direction than did men. The extra time it took women to reach a firm decision to enter seminary reflects a lack of support from close associates as well as a greater uncertainty concerning how they would or could use their seminary education. Men were 17 percent more likely to feel supported by their family in their decision to enter seminary (80 percent to 63 percent of the men and women reported family support), while more women than men (24 percent to 11 percent) reported that their families were antagonistic or divided in response to the news that they intended to go to seminary. Similarly, men reported more support from their pastors (93 percent) for their intention to go to seminary than women (77 percent). However, best friends' support was more nearly equally recalled by both men (71 percent) and women (69 percent).

This discrepancy *between* sexes in the support of family members for their decision to go to seminary reported was particularly high in the United Church of Christ, United Methodist, American Baptist and the Lutheran Church in America (over 20 percentage points difference between women and men.) Little difference between the sexes was found in amount of family support reported in the Disciples of Christ and the Episcopal denominations, mainly because the clergymen in these denominations did not report as much support from family members as did the men in the other denominations. Yet, it should be noted that at least a slight majority of women in every denomination reported support from their family and from their pastors for their decision to attend seminary.

While over 90 percent of the men in all denominations except PCUS reported that their pastors supported their intentions, in no denomination were percentages of women reporting this source of support as high. Women consistently reported less support than men from pastors —particularly in the Lutheran Church in America—except in the Presbyterian Church U.S., where men and women are nearly equal in reported support from pastors (81 percent to 83 percent).

Lack of support from family and pastors may be partially compensated for by obtaining support from best friends for the decision to attend seminary. In two denominations, the Episcopal and the United Presbyterian Churches, women were ten to twelve percentage points more likely to say their best friends supported their decision. In three other denominations, however—the American Baptist, the American Lutheran and the United Methodist—men were between eleven and eighteen percentage points also more likely to say their best friends were supportive. In the remaining denominations—Disciples, Lutheran Church in America, Presbyterian Church U.S., and the United Church of Christ—there were no significant differences between clergymen and women. It may be of interest to note that higher percentages of both men and women clergy in the Presbyterian Church U.S. reported support from best friends in their intention to enter seminary than did clergy in any other denomination (86 percent of the women and 87 percent of the PCUS men).

One may choose one's friends or switch pastors, but find it more difficult to withdraw physically or psychologically from one's family. Receiving antagonistic reactions from their families when it occurred was very painful for the women, as evinced by the following women's comments on their families' reactions to their decision to enter a seminary program:

> *My family was* horrified. *My mother said, "The church is no place for a woman!"*

> *My father said, "Everyone has the prerogative to wreck their lives."*

> *My father said, "Ministry is a dead-end career"; my mother said she was afraid I would never marry.*

> *My family thought it was the most asinine thing a girl could do.*

Even the so-called supportive parents of future clergywomen were often a bit bewildered as to why their daughters should be choosing this type of graduate education.

Timing of Decision and Age on Entering Seminary: Trends for Men and Women

Another reason for the generally later decision of women to enter seminary than men may have more to do with the whole culture and place of ministry within this culture at the time women were in college, as compared to men. It seems that both men and women have been making later decisions to enter seminary in recent years. For example, among clergy ordained after 1978, compared to those ordained before 1957, women ordained more recently were considerably more likely to have made a later decision than those ordained earlier (60 percent to 23 percent). This is also true of men (31 percent of the men ordained after

1978 decided after college to attend seminary compared to 13 percent of the men ordained before 1957). Women still made later decisions in the more recent period than did men, but the difference between the sexes in time of decision making is diminishing.

This trend is also visible across denominations. In all denominations, but in varying degrees, men ordained after 1975 were more likely to have decided after college to attend seminary than men ordained before 1975 (although numbers of men in each denomination in the sample ordained after 1974 are often too few to be statistically reliable). Given the general factor of modernization, particularly its secularizing trend, it may well be that men as well as women receive less social support for a decision to enter the clergy profession. Some of this comes, not necessarily from family, friends, or church personnel, but from the broader society.

There is some indication that professions, or other occupations which have higher social prestige, have a higher proportion of students making an early decision to attend graduate professional school in the particular discipline than a profession with lower social ranking.[15] Higher social prestige makes the occupation appear more visible and attractive to youth. To assess respondents' attitudes toward the social prestige of the professional ministry, we asked them their degree of agreement/disagreement with the statement: "The ordained ministry still carries a prestige and dignity which no other profession shares." Clergywomen are 21 percent more likely than clergymen to *disagree* with the statement. Further, there is a slight but significant tendency for men to disagree with this statement the younger they are (in particular) and the later they have been ordained. (Correlations for age and year of ordination are not significant for women, probably since they are more clustered together in date of birth or ordination than are men.)

Quite apart from cultural images of ministry as a profession and personal support available for students contemplating attending a graduate level seminary, financing of a college and a seminary education may have been more problematic in the last decade than it was previously. It is possible for a young person to decide to enter seminary in high school or college without having any idea about whether or not he or she would have sufficient funds to pursue a seminary education; however, whether individuals actually enter a seminary at a relatively early age may be as much dependent on money available to them as anything else.

For whatever combination of reasons, as might be expected from the later time of women's decision to enter seminary, they do in fact enter seminary at an older age than do clergymen, with 13 percent more men

**Table 3.7   Age Entered Seminary and Time of Decision to
Enter Seminary**

Decision to Attend Seminary	Early Vocationals (Ages 20 to 22)		Delayed Vocationals (Ages 23 to 28)		Second Careerers (Age 29 and Over)	
	W	M	W	M	W	M
	%		%		%	
Before college	14	40	8	28	8	33
During college	74	53	23	42	13	21
After college	12	7	69	30	79	46
Total	100	100	100	100	100	100
(N)	(227)	(361)	(213)	(247)	(151)	(87)

entering seminary by age twenty-two (39 percent of the women, 52 percent of the men), and twice as large a proportion of women (26 percent of the women, 13 percent of the men) entering seminary at age twenty-nine or older.

While there is certainly a rough association for both men and women between the time they decide definitely to enter seminary and when they actually begin their seminary program, as Table 3.7 depicts, men are considerably more likely than women to have made a decision to enter seminary they are not able to put into effect immediately (because of finances, the draft, or some other reason). Most of the women who in fact did not enter seminary by age twenty-two did not make a decision to embark on a seminary program until sometime after they finished college.

Table 3.7 depicts a somewhat arbitrary grouping of clergy based on the ages they began seminary. Those who entered seminary by the age of 22, termed the Early Vocationals, are likely to have finished college in four years and gone directly or almost directly into seminary. Students who began seminary between the ages of 23 and 28 either took longer than four years to complete college or began seminary several years after college graduation, perhaps after working full time or trying out another field of study. At any rate, those persons, here termed the Delayed Vocationals, had probably more work and obviously more life experience before they began seminary. Students who began seminary at age 29 or later are most likely to have immersed themselves briefly or extensively in other occupations and disciplines or, in the case of many women, in the major role of full-time homemaker.

Among clergy who entered seminary before age 22, it appears that 41 percent of the women and 31 percent of the men had worked full time prior to ordination. Among those who entered seminary a little later, between the ages of 23 and 28, 72 percent of the women and 70 percent of the men had worked full time. A higher and identical proportion of men and women who entered seminary at age 29 or older had worked full time prior to ordination—86 percent of both sexes.

Although probably many of these clergy worked during seminary (as well as during and after college) the following table gives a rough indication of what other kinds of occupations clergy who entered seminary at different ages might have pursued. It shows that, of those clergy who worked full time prior to ordination and specified what this occupation was, women who worked outside the home were in higher status occupations than men who worked prior to ordination. It should be stressed that these figures are for women and men who are *now* in the parish ministry. Interviews with faculty members suggest that an increasing number of older women have not only been coming into seminary in recent years, but tend to come from a "first career" as a homemaker. However, the data on the present clergy suggest that women actually did try other occupations (often teacher, nurse, social worker, or librarian, as well as secretary—the more culturally stereotyped

Table 3.8   Type of Full-Time Occupation of Clergy Prior to Ordination
(by Age of Entering Seminary and Sex)

Type of Full-Time Occupation	Early Vocationals (Ages 20 – 22)		Delayed Vocationals (Ages 23 – 28)		Second Careerers (Age 29 and Over)	
	W	M	W	M	W	M
	%		%		%	
Professional business executives	37	14	48	22	59	15
Middle management, semi or paraprofessionals, civil service, technicians	24	25	24	24	26	47
Clerical workers, sales, owners of small businesses, police officers, military (non-officers), postal clerks	30	26	24	25	14	18
Farmers, firemen, machinists, hairstylists, skilled manual laborers	9	35	4	28	1	20
Total	100	100	100	100	100	100
(N)	(90)	(103)	(151)	(164)	(126)	(73)

"women's" occupations) before deciding to go to seminary. In spite of the influence of religious families and long activity in the church, women give evidence here of interrupted career paths toward the ministry as toward other professions.

This tendency holds across denominational lines. Only among the Disciples is there a variation from a consistent pattern of more women than men in "second careers" as clergy. There are, however, differences among the denominations. The Episcopal Church has the highest proportion of "second career" women now serving as priests than any other denomination (45 percent), with Baptists and Disciples having the lowest proportion of "second career" women among their parish clergy (15 percent). The Presbyterians, particularly the United Prebyterians, have the lowest proportion of "second career" men (5 percent). However, in none of the denominations does the number of clergymen who started seminary after age twenty-eight exceed 20 percent. Other data further indicates that there has been an increase over time, particularly in some denominations, such as the Episcopal Church and to some extent the UCC, in the proportions of both men and women who are entering seminary at age twenty-nine or older.

Actually, it is generally true that both men and women are entering seminary at later ages, although women have rather consistently made the decision to enter seminary later than men, even over time, as Table 3.9 shows. The percentage of women entering seminary by age twenty-two exceeds that of men only during the 1957 to 1969 period. This was the period immediately following the opening of ordination to women in two of the larger denominations, the United Methodist and the United Presbyterian. It was also the period following the end of the Korean War, in which veterans completed college and may have gone on to seminary. As a time of significant campus unrest, it disrupted college completion schedules of some, and probably reduced the interest in a ministerial career among other, young men. All told, however, it would seem that only under unusual circumstances are women more likely than men to enter seminary directly after college.

Because of, or despite, the greater acceptance of women in seminary, greater proportions of women have been entering seminaries at later ages than they had been. Quite probably, the greater visibility of seminaries' acceptance of women has encouraged women who had been housewives and/or in other occupations to consider a seminary education and a possible career in the ordained ministry. However, the same explanation obviously cannot be advanced to explain why men as well have been entering seminary at older ages than previously. Here, other explanations previously suggested may be apt, such as the need for work, full or part time, in a secular job to finance a seminary education,

Table 3.9   Age Upon Entering Seminary
(by Year Ordained and Sex of Clergy)

Age on First Entering Seminary	Pre-1957 W %	Pre-1957 M	1957–69 W %	1957–69 M	1970–74 W %	1970–74 M	1975–78 W %	1975–78 M	1979–81 W %	1979–81 M
Early vocationals (ages 20–22)	31	53	56	49	53	63	40	51	24	37
Delayed vocationals (ages 23–28)	50	44	28	32	25	25	36	34	42	43
Second careerers (age 29 and over)	19	3	16	19	22	14	24	15	34	20
Total	100	100	100	100	100	100	100	100	100	100
(N)	(16)	(234)	(34)	(278)	(85)	(92)	(278)	(68)	(182)	(35)

as well as the lessening attractiveness of the parish ministry as a promising vocation for young men in comparison with other professions.

The influx of more mature people into seminary training will have significant consequences for the seminaries and the churches. This new development in the ages of seminary students and potential outcomes will be explored in subsequent chapters.

Summary

The current women clergy are somewhat more likely than the men to have had working mothers. But typically most clergy mothers were homemakers. For this reason, mothers, though perhaps a source of general support, were probably not as important as fathers and father surrogates for women in modeling the kind of initiative and risk-taking behavior necessary for these women to have entered seminary and parish ministry. Clergywomen were more likely than their male counterparts to be born into families where the fathers (and often mothers) were well educated, and the father was a business executive or professional. Better financial resources of higher socio-economic class families no doubt played a large role in their willingness to underwrite in part or in full graduate education of their daughters as well as their sons. However, it is also likely that these higher social class parents are often more open to their daughters' aspiring to graduate education and an unconventional career for a woman than lower social class parents are apt to be. Too, fathers in such families would be more likely to exhibit the initiative and drive that their daughters could emulate. But, it is also true that nearly a third of these clergywomen could be described as coming from lower-middle class and working class backgrounds. It would seem that their own drive and abilities, coupled with encouragement from parents or other significant adults, obviously well compensated for whatever they lacked in the way of familial financial resources and encouragement of their ambitions.

Why these women chose the ministry over some other top professional career, such as medicine or law, may lie partially in the fact that they were typically raised in families where at least one of the parents was active in a church when they were growing up. Also, though some clergy switched denominations, the greater majority were ordained in the one in which they were raised, indicating a pattern of consistent and active religious socialization (that is, the learning of values, roles, competencies, and perspectives of a particular society, social group, or organization). The more active the parents were in a church while the clergy were growing up, the more likely the clergy were to have been active themselves in a church during their college years. Clergy who were more active in a church during their college years (because of parental upbringing, attending a religious college, or other factors) were more likely to make an early decision to enter seminary. While these findings hold true for both men and women, women were still more likely to make a later decision than men to enter seminary.

A general culture unsupportive of women attempting to enter the male-dominated vocation of parish ministry, and family and pastors less supportive of individual women's aspirations to enter ministry than they are of men's, account for the fact that women both decide to enter seminary later and in fact do enter at older ages than do men. However, men as well have been entering seminary later in more recent years than in previous ones (but still not as late as women). Perhaps this is because the attractiveness of ministry as a vocation in terms of salary, opportunities for advancement, and social prestige has been decreasing while the costs of obtaining a graduate theological degree have been increasing.

In describing effects that others—people and organizations—have had on future clergy's life before seminary and on their motivation to enter the ministry, we have undoubtedly given insufficient attention to the individual's own abilities, motivation, call, and spiritual growth which are pivotal in directing him or her to the ordained ministry. Several theorists have in fact argued that "self-initiated" socialization is more important in the long run than what the individual learns or experiences from other people. But this does not mean that other people and organizations are not also crucial in whether or not a woman or a man progresses through college and other life experiences to seminary. The sociologist Orville Brim, who, among others, argues that "in many cases the self-initiated socialization is a greater source of personality change than are the demands of other persons" is quick to point out that even in self-initiated socialization, influence of other people is not absent. He further asserts that for an individual to achieve what he or she wants, the individual "must find a supportive relationship."[16]

What the individual primarily learns from others is some idea of what to expect and how to behave as a member of the occupation or group to which he or she aspires. This is often referred to as "anticipatory socialization." Those entering any professional school—for example, a medical school, school of social work, or a seminary—come into the school with various levels of understanding and experience as to what kind of education they will be receiving at the school and what they will be doing as future practitioners. The better the fit there is between what the student expects and what the school teaches, the easier time the students will have in acquiring additional learning, as evidenced in a number of studies on professional schools.[17] While people the student knows before entering a professional school are important in anticipatory socialization, other persons in the school or in practice settings often become equally or more important in the student's continuing adaptation to the profession. In the next chapter, we examine these experiences of clergywomen and men in seminary.

4

Entering the Male Citadel:
Women Come to Seminary

The year that I began seminary, 1956, there were two other women students in the whole school. I was the only woman in my graduating class. We were not allowed to serve on the seminary council because the men students on it all went on retreats and there were no accommodations for women at campouts. I took a preaching class, and I think preached in a church once locally, but not in the seminary chapel. There was definitely that discrimination. We got along pretty well with our male colleagues, but now as we look back on it, we were kidded and teased a lot. . . . When my friend and I both walked into class, the students stood up for us. . . . Kind of stupid . . . but then it didn't seem stupid. . . . This was in the fifties . . . when a man stands up when a woman comes into a room.—CLERGYWOMAN

When I started seminary in 1970 there were three other women, and about twelve of us when I graduated. The three of us considered ourselves as the scouts for the feminist approach to theology. We were seriously considering ordination, and we wanted to go for the Master of Divinity rather than the Master of Religious Education. We were serious about that, and we let them know we were serious about that. We got the jokes—we got the stereotypes. Women had been at this seminary for many long years before, but nobody ever took them seriously, or saw them as the beginning of a potential threat. They were accepted as an abnormality. In some respects we three felt we were very pathetic and very much scouting out new territory, having more or less to chop down the trees and move the brush out of the way. . . . Most of the faculty reacted to me pretty well . . . but they would still make comments such as, "Well, if there wasn't a lady in the room, I could tell you fellows this joke!" Evidently our response and our willingness to hang in there affected some of the professors. The dean of this seminary told me a year ago that I and another woman who had come in a year or two after me had really challenged the faculty quite a bit. . . .

The idea of being a pioneer is sometimes pretty good. Kind of an adventurous thing . . . and a high morale in so far as we felt we were really scouts. . . . At least on my part, and I think on the part of the other two women, there was a tension between a sense of excitement at seeing other women coming in and a sense of "you're moving in on my territory, stay away!" Part of the reason we were troubled at seeing all these women come in is that we would say "be prepared when you go to seminary because these things are going to happen." But they didn't happen. We had already paved the way, and they didn't have to put up with some of this stuff that we had to put up with. And they could not comprehend what we had gone through and why we were so hostile and angry at certain times.—CLERGYWOMAN

What were the seminary experiences of women pastors as compared with men? Did women who entered seminaries as one of several of their sex in the whole institution encounter different treatment from faculty and others than did women entering seminaries when women students were in a definitely visible minority? What is it like for women students in seminaries now where in many institutions women comprise half the M.Div. student body? What kinds of seminary experiences are important to women seminarians who later become pastors? In this chapter, we look at the seminary experiences of women who entered the parish ministry, comparing them with the sample of ordained men who became parish ministers. We examine their reasons for selection of particular seminaries, their motivations for going to seminary, their experiences in seminary, and the influences on their decisions to become ordained.

The Seminary Scene Over the Last Decade and a Half

The two clergywomen quoted above started seminary about a generation apart. Although clearly the two women encountered quite different environments, the seminary environment for women students would change more in the five years subsequent to 1970 than it had in the fifteen years preceding this date. During the fifties and sixties some seminaries, especially interdenominational ones and those which trained missionaries, allowed women in the Bachelor of Divinity programs (precursor to the M.Div.), typically with the expectation they would teach or work along side their missionary husbands in foreign lands. Religious music and drama departments of some of the interdenominational, university-related seminaries also tended to attract women students, as did of course Christian Education programs leading to Master of Religious Education degrees or certificates in a variety of denominational seminaries. However, until the late 1960s, not only were there few women enrolled in degree programs leading to ordination, but the women who were enrolled typically were not expected to become pastors. Although the radical mood of the late 1960s and the beginnings of the women's movement brought more women into seminaries intending ordination, it was not until the early 1970s that women enrolling in the Master of Divinity program increased exponentially (for example, in the years from 1972 to 1974 the proportion of women increased 75 percent).[1] Between 1972 and 1981, as reported in Chapter 1, women's enrollment in professional degree programs had increased 340.8 percent, thirteen times the percentage for men.

Rapidly changing sex distributions in professional degree programs were accompanied by women's demands in the early seventies that, not only should seminaries admit more women, but these institutions should alter their curricular offerings and counseling procedures for women. Especially at the interdenominational, university-associated seminaries in the early seventies, seminarians pushed for more power in governance and more input into the curricular and other seminary policy decisions. Women seminarians pushed for (and typically got) courses as well as other resources (space, funds) devoted to their interests. Courses on "Women in the Church," "Women in the Bible," and the like began to be offered at many schools. Alternative approaches to theological education—for example, infusing feminist perspectives on theology and the ministry into courses, support and counseling for women seminarians including dealing with the male establishment in job seeking, advocacy for the use of inclusive language, and hiring of more women faculty—were pursued by women's coalitions inside the seminaries. Although these coalitions generally remained marginal to the total seminary program and curriculum, they nonetheless were highly visible and effective in providing support for many women seminarians and affirmation of women's right to question and overhaul the male-dominated theological perspectives that had been regnant. A recent history of the number of women's centers and coalitions; the issues they addressed; and their experiences, problems, and successes in the seventies has been written collaboratively by representatives of these programs under the name of the Cornwall Collective.[2]

Neither all the seminaries of these nine Protestant denominations nor the interdenominational seminaries where some of their students attended were equally open to women in the early 1970s. Though some substantially increased their enrollment and support of women in the latter part of this decade (notably certain of the Episcopal, LCA and ALC seminaries), a number of denominational seminaries appear to be in a kind of "culture lag" as far as acceptance of women and women's issues are concerned. As noted, those interdenominational seminaries, close to or associated with universities, were among the first to accept women in M.Div. programs and establish courses, programs, and centers especially for women. They were also centers of active feminist concerns. Union Theological Seminary in New York City, one of this group, made headlines in 1972 by its "constituency" resolution to work toward having one-half of its student body be women. This step may be one reason that, while women pastors in this present study attended over seventy different seminaries, Union Seminary was represented by more M.Div. graduates than any other: a total of 36 women. The next most frequently mentioned seminaries by women pastors, Yale Divinity School and Princeton Theological Seminary (a denominational school), were named by 29 women each. The pluralism in types of students in university related schools, their diversity in curricula,[3] and their heritage of theological and social liberalism, predisposed them to accept women into the professional degree program and provide a forum for feminist concerns. However, as will be considered below, these interdenominational, university seminaries have become less attractive to all students planning to be pastors, as denominations have begun to put pressure on their students to attend seminaries of their own denomination. Also, by the latter part of the 1970s, many of the denominational seminaries were openly recruiting women and taking some care to insure that women seminarians had good experiences, or at least as good an experience overall as did men among the student body. To be sure, this openness to admitting ever increasing numbers of women in the M.Div. programs indicates some degree of value change toward the benefits of having women in the ordained ministry. There are cynics, however, who suggest that acceptance of women by these seminaries was occasioned to considerable degree by their drive to survive falling enrollments of academically qualified men.

Although the number of full-time women faculty in mainline Protestant seminaries has increased very slowly over the last decade—from about seventy in 1971 to a little over one hundred in 1981—the use of adjunct and part-time women lecturers and tutors has helped increase the number of women faculty. The sexism of some tenured male faculty may be a factor behind the relatively few women in tenured faculty positions or even in full-time seminary faculty positions at all; however, it is also the case that there are very few tenured positions opening each year for anyone, and the projections for creating many new faculty positions in the near future are dismal.[4]

Overall, then, the climate of most seminaries with reference to women is better reflected in their provision for women students than in their record of hiring women as faculty. Interviews with the eighty women seminary faculty and administrators, conducted for this study in 1981, indicate that the climate for women seminarians is comfortable in at least two-thirds of the seminaries (and in the opinion of three-fourths of the women faculty). Inclusive language is the norm, and faculty treat women and their concerns seriously. Too, in most of these seminaries nearly half of the student body are women. Of the remaining schools, several denominational seminaries not on the east coast or above the Mason-Dixon line may be comfortable for women with traditional or professional orientations, but are either too paternalistic or too male dominated in structure and perspective to be comfortable for students who are active feminists. A half-dozen seminaries were generally comfortable for women, but had one or two male professors in key positions who were antagonistic to women and their concerns. Yet, in the main, by 1981 the seminaries serving these nine mainline Protestant denominations had become pleasant and stimulating institutions of higher education for women students, which represents a rather dramatic change within these institutions in the last decade.

Selection of Particular Seminary and Motivations for Attending Seminary

Although the interdenominational, university-related seminaries were among the first to enroll women, the distribution of women and men pastors in this present study indicates quite clearly that the great majority of persons who are now parish ministers graduated from denominational seminaries. Only 13 percent of the women (a total of 83) and 9 percent of the men (a total of 66) got their first professional degrees from one of the interdenominational, university seminaries. While these seminaries have enrolled women, they have not concentrated on training for parish ministry to the same extent as denominational seminaries and are typically not considered by denominational officials as offering as good a preparation for the parish ministry as denominational schools.[5] Studies in 1964 and 1974 of Union Seminary in New York City, one of the university seminaries most dedicated to educating students for the parish ministry, show that only about a third of the students in the M.Div. program both enter and leave with the firm intention of being a parish minister.[6] The data for this present study also indicate that there is a decline overall in the proportion of women and men graduates of university schools who became pastors. In the period from 1961-65, 27 percent of the women and 9 percent of the men in our study attended university seminaries for their first professional degree (B.D. or M.Div.), but only 12 percent of the women and 5 percent of the men who had attended seminary since 1973 attended a university seminary for this degree.

Results from a Presbyterian study of seminary selection showed that the candidates (men and women) who had chosen to go to these university-related seminaries were different from those who chose a denominational seminary in that they were more interested in teaching and counseling than in preaching, not as sure of what kind of ministry they would like to do, and more liberal ideologically and theologically. They were more interested in the academic reputation of the seminary than those students who chose denominational seminaries, and more likely to travel far from home to attend one of these interdenominational, university seminaries.[7] Although probably a third of these students attending university seminaries will go into and remain in the parish ministry, it suggests that there may be a difference between students who chose to attend them and those choosing denominational seminaries, as well as differences students may encounter between the schools themselves.

Among the parish ministers in our study, it appears in Table 4.1 that those who went to interdenominational, university-related seminaries tended to come from higher social class families than those who went to the denominational seminaries. Both women and men clergy from families where their fathers were well educated and/or held professional or executive positions were more likely to be an interdenominational, university seminary graduates than graduates of a denominational seminary. However, because there were proportionately more women than men whose fathers had been well educated and were employed in high level occupations, the women at university seminaries were also more likely than the men at these seminaries to come from higher social class families.

Clergy were asked why they had gone to their particular seminary. Twenty-two different types of reasons for seminary selection were coded from their open-ended responses. Geographical location was the most frequently given kind of reason for choosing to go to a particular seminary, though this was slightly more often given by women. For example, 22 percent of the women to 18 percent of the men chose their seminary at least partly because it was near where they or their family lived. Another 20 percent of the women compared with 16 percent of the men chose the seminary because of the area of the country it was in (which may or may not have been near their family), but was where they wanted to live for graduate work. For example, "I like an urban setting"; "I love California"; "I'd always wanted to go East."

There were a few denominational differences in these reasons given. The American Lutheran women were most likely of all clergy to choose a seminary because it was near home (41 percent). They are also the youngest clergywomen on average of all the denominations (43 percent of the ALC women compared to 20 percent of the total women were

Table 4.1   Parental Background and Type of Seminary Attended

	Interdenominational University Seminary		All Other	
	W	M	W	M
	%		%	
A. *Father's Education* (Highest Level Attained)				
High school graduation and technical school	25	42	45	61
Some college and college graduation	32	29	28	20
Graduate education or graduate degree	43	29	27	19
Total	100	100	100	100
(N)	(82)	(66)	(533)	(659)

Tau Beta correlation between father's education and whether clergy went to a university seminary or other: women, $-.14$ (sig. .0002); men, $-.11$ (sig. .001)

	W	M	W	M
B. *Father's Occupation*				
Clergy	17	16	12	13
Professionals and business executives	43	32	27	13
Middle-management, shop owners, salespersons, clerical, civil service	24	27	33	33
Farm workers and blue collar, waiters, barbers, skilled workers	16	25	28	41
Total	100	100	100	100
(N)	(79)	(63)	(515)	(633)

Tau Beta correlation between father's occupation and whether clergy went to a university seminary or not: women, .12 (sig. .0006); men, .11 (sig. .001)

under thirty-one at the time of this study), and somewhat more likely to be married (63 percent of the ALC women to a 55 percent of all clergywomen in this study). Possibly these two factors made a nearby seminary attractive. ALC women (as well as ALC men to some extent) were also more likely than clergy in other denominations to cite a third generally popular reason for choice of seminary: the seminary was denominational.

ALC clergy were no more likely than any other, however, to mention another related reason for going to a particular seminary: that it had been attended or recommended by their home pastor or their denominational executive. Among the total sample, 15 percent of the women and 21 percent of the men pastors gave this as one reason for going to a particular seminary. Other characteristics of a seminary were also important reasons why clergy selected one or another, such as the kind of curriculum offered, the academic soundness of the program, and the whole tone of the seminary. As might be expected, while going to a university-associated seminary was not often mentioned as a reason in itself for attending a particular seminary, those who chose university seminaries were somewhat more likely to cite the academic reputation and well-known faculty than those who chose denominational seminaries.

Type of seminary attended was not related in the present study to what these pastors' motivations were for attending seminary when they first arrived on campus. There were, however, major differences between men and women clergy regarding their motivations for attending seminary. Clergy were asked whether each of three possible motivations was "primary," "secondary," or "not a reason" for their being at seminary. The three were: "personal spiritual growth and faith development," "discovering in which ways to best serve Christ in the church and world," and "preparing to be a parish minister." Looking at those clergy who selected each as a "primary" reason for entering a seminary degree program (see Table 4.2), it is clear that men were considerably more likely than women to have entered seminary because they wanted to be parish ministers, while women were more likely than men to come to seminary to develop spiritually and/or to find out how they might best use their faith and abilities in the work of the church.

Table 4.2 shows clearly that, while all three motivations were at least a secondary reason for most of the clergymen, for nearly two-fifths of the clergywomen, preparing to be a parish minister was not a reason at all for attending seminary. Proportionately, twice as many clergymen as women were primarily motivated on entering seminary to prepare for the parish ministry. In other words, not only were women who eventually became parish ministers more likely to make a later decision to enter seminary than men who entered the pastorate, and actually enter seminary at a later age than men; they were also more likely to take longer than men to decide finally on the ministerial specialty of parish ministry. This makes sense in light of the discussion in the preceding chapter of the lack of cultural and personal support for women to enter seminary as reason for their generally later decisions than men to pursue a seminary degree.

A number of these women further explained, as other reasons or motivations for attending seminary, that they had couched their ambi-

Table 4.2 Motivations for Attending Seminary

	Women %	Men %
1. Personal Spiritual Growth and Faith Development		
Primary reason	60	40
Secondary reason	30	47
Not a reason	10	13
Total	100	100
(N)	(613)	(693)
2. Discovering in Which Ways to Best Serve Christ in the Church or World		
Primary reason	64	51
Secondary reason	26	38
Not a reason	10	11
Total	100	100
(N)	(613)	(690)
3. Preparing to Be a Parish Minister		
Primary reason	35	73
Secondary reason	26	19
Not a reason	39	8
Total	100	100
(N)	(612)	(696)

tions to others and themselves in more acceptable terms for women. As one woman said, "I told others that my ambition is to prepare for Christian Education work. I would have liked to be preparing to be a pastor, but I didn't have the guts." More volunteered that they explicitly came to seminary to learn theology, whether that was true because of a theological and intellectual "curiosity"; to be "able to have a theological basis for what I was doing"; to "gain a better understanding of my faith through academic biblical and theological studies"; or to teach theology in a college. Most of the women who said they came initially primarily to study theology also indicated that they hoped this study would give some direction to their lives; for example, "Theology was always a major interest, but I also wanted to discover what my gifts were for ministry and how I could use them in a church vocation."

Several women, especially those who entered seminary when only a few women of their denomination were enrolled in professional degree programs, indicated they did so to support the ministry of their hus-

Table 4.3   Clergy Motivations for Being in Seminary*
(by Year Entered Seminary and Sex)

Year Began Seminary	Women	%	Men
Before 1960	30 (of 59)		79 (of 358)
1960 – 1969	31 (of 100)		68 (of 195)
1970 – 1973	25 (of 191)		61 (of 71)
1974 and later	45 (of 242)		65 (of 55)

*% = percent saying "preparing to be a parish minister" as a primary motivation on first entering seminary.

bands; for example, "I entered seminary intending to be a better pastor's wife, to polish up my skills, and to be supportive of his ministry." Several men and women indicated that a primary reason they came to seminary was to test whether their own faith, values, and social commitments could be fulfilled though the institutional church, or, as one put it: "[I had] a post–World War II humanitarian urge to work for a better world through the church."

With the greater prevalence and acceptance of women parish ministers, one might expect that there to be a parallel increase in the proportion of women who enter seminary primarily because they want to be pastors rather than for the other kinds of reasons described. Indeed, this seems to be the case, as Table 4.3 shows. After the 50 percent increase in women in seminaries between 1972 and 1974, a higher proportion of women entered seminary with the firm intention of being a parish minister.

Time of decision to enter seminary and age on actually entering seminary are also important in whether or not clergy had primary commitment to preparing for the parish ministry on first entering seminary. It may be recalled that time of decision to enter seminary (before, during, and after college) and age on first entering seminary are positively and significantly correlated (.30 for women and .21 for men). Both men and women who made an early decision (before college) to enter seminary were more likely than those who made a later decision to have decided, at the time of entering seminary, to be a parish minister. But women who actually entered seminary at an older age than the majority were more likely to have had parish ministry as a priority than those who entered young. (Age on entering seminary was not related to desire to study for the parish ministry among clergymen.) Among clergywomen, for example, 56 percent of the 62 women who decided before entering college to attend seminary, compared to only 31 percent of those 298 who decided after college to attend, actually entered seminary with the priority goal of preparing for the parish ministry. But 33 percent of those 155 who entered seminary at age twenty-nine or older entered primarily because they wanted to prepare for the parish ministry. These data indicate the existence of two patterns through which women decide on parish ministry as a ministerial specialty. First, for any combination of reasons, there are some women who, in their teens or earlier, develop a conviction that they are called to be pastors and pursue this goal with a single-minded devotion. Second, there are other women who may or may not have decided before they were adults that they wanted to specialize in parish ministry, but probably did look at other forms of ministry and other careers (including marriage and beginning a family). In the course of doing this, they became convinced that they should and could become good pastors and then entered seminary to prepare themselves for this vocation.

Obviously, since so many of these women entered seminary without much or any intention of becoming pastors, there is at least another pattern of women's decision-making that leads them to the parish ministry. Although a few will enter the pastorate after some years as a denominational staff member, chaplain, professor, and the like, the bulk of the remainder will probably, like these present women pastors, come to the decision that they want to be pastors as a result of experiences they have while they are seminarians.

Seminary Experiences of Women and Men Pastors

In the last chapter, we noted the importance of "anticipatory socialization"—knowing something about what the requirements, life style, and expectations for a pastor are before an individual comes to seminary—in aiding the student in actively seeking out those educational experiences which best meet his or her vocational goals. But, as also suggested, having experienced a high degree of anticipatory socialization for seminary or parish ministry may not be sufficient for the seminarian to obtain these desired opportunities and experiences. There may, for example, be a lack of opportunity to take the kinds of courses or field work experiences that the student feels he or she needs. Also, faculty members' values and preferences may lead them to interact differently with various kinds of students. One socialization theorist points out that it may be as much what the student "learns about the values and competencies he/she is defined as having that is most important in terms of individual level socialization consequences, rather than his/her own values or own feelings of competence."[8] Don-

ald Ploch's 1971 study of faculty values concerning desired emphases
for Protestant seminaries indicated that there were no "generally agreed
on norms to legitimate the content of the curriculum as a whole. . . .
Education is individualized because no one vision of seminary education is strong enough to master the field."[9]

This situation makes it important to investigate how faculty are in
fact communicating their own particular values to different kinds of
students, and what impact (if any) faculty have on seminarians' attitudinal change about themselves, their faith, and the kind of ministerial career they should enter. "Individualized" curricula and faculty
treatment of seminarians carry with them the strong possibility that,
within a single seminary program in a single year (let alone over time),
seminarians encounter quite different experiences.

Nevertheless, as previously noted, most seminary faculty and environments have changed positively and drastically within the last ten to
fifteen years with respect to women seminarians. Can it be inferred
from recollections of their seminary experience how these present clergywomen and clergymen assess their treatment by faculty and recall
how influential faculty were (or tried to be) on their decisions to be
ordained and enter the parish ministry?

First, it appears that these clergy have relatively pleasant memories
of their seminary years. Despite the fact that 75 percent of the women
attended seminary after 1968, in contrast to an equal proportion of men
who began seminary before 1968, there is surprisingly little difference
between the sexes. Both men and women pastors generally enjoyed
their seminary years. Further, two-thirds of both sexes reported that
they have since found their seminary education "quite valuable" for
their work in parish ministry. Three other denominational studies done
in 1978 with UCC, Lutheran, and United Presbyterian clergywomen
also report a majority of women remembering their seminary experiences as pleasant and attributing value to their M.Div. education in
preparing them for ministry.[10]

While the majority of both men and women pastors recall being
treated either warmly or "like any other student" by faculty when they
were seminarians, women were slightly more likely to note warm treatment from faculty. Nonetheless, women were also more likely than
men to recall faculty treating them as a "curiosity," holding them at
arm's length, pretending that they did not exist (for example, by addressing all students as "gentlemen"), or worse, refusing to recognize
women when calling on students in classroom discussion. About 10
percent of the women clergy remember faculty members as being
friendly toward them, but not taking them seriously as students or as
candidates for ordained ministry. Apparently, a number of faculty pre-

sumed that the women seminarians were "there to marry a future clergyman," as one woman pastor recalled who entered seminary in 1973. And another entering about that time similarly reported that faculty "treated us with care because they saw us as 'preparing' to be ministers' wives."

But what if they were already minister's wives and did not appear content to confine themselves to that ministerial role, or what if they were older than the general run of women in seminaries? Some clergywomen's descriptions paint a rather hostile or awkward reaction from their seminary professors under these circumstances. One clergywoman, who entered seminary at age forty-one, recalled that her faculty:

> treated me very peculiarly, partly due to my age, partly due to the fact that I was female. Not many faculty were at ease with me, able to hold a common conversation with me. Some thought I was looking for a man. In general—awkward!

Another second-career woman entering seminary in 1972 gave in the following description of her reception:

> Because of my age and sex, faculty were both polite and indifferent, acting as if they hoped I would disappear. Several actively tried to discourage me from entering the parish ministry, saying I had "the best of all possible worlds—as a pastor's wife!"

A few women noted that their older age was an advantage, especially perhaps when combined with experiences in a professional status, as indicated by the following reflections: "I was a thirty-five year old college professor when I went to seminary. The faculty treated me like a peer."

From numerous other comments made by women it is clear that seminary faculty were more inclined to treat women seriously (at least as students) if such women were in fact academically superior. Eleven percent of the women to 8 percent of the men noted that they actually received "preferential treatment" from faculty. Most of these women explained that this was because they were indeed outstanding students, and that, as one put it, the faculty "liked my brain!" Some women also attributed their preferential treatment by seminary faculty to the fact that they were so unique at the time; for example, "I was spoiled rotten because of being the only woman."

The women who began in visible numbers to go into professional degree programs leading to ordination at seminaries in the early 1970s were typically academically superior to many of their male classmates. There is some indication that this situation led at the time to an alternating, ambivalent treatment of women seminarians by faculty: valuing them as students but still uncomfortable with the thought that they might try to be ordained. A study of Lutheran women seminarians in M.Div. programs in 1975 (only five years after it was "legal" for Lutheran women to be ordained in the LCA and ALC denominations) depicted faculty as often very aware that their women seminary students were highly motivated to do well academically and trying to adjust their language to include women and their ears to hear the women's perspective; however, they were exceedingly slow to act on women seminarians' suggestions for change in curriculum and programs, if they acted at all.[11] Another study of an interdenominational university seminary in 1973 also showed a faculty quite aware of women's academic competence. Most professors were attempting on some level to teach well the growing number of women students. However, it was similarly the case that professors tended to treat men, both in and outside of class, as junior colleagues or at least as potentially promising parish ministers if the students were academically above average. They did not, however, appear to be able at that time (with minor exceptions) to extend this treatment to academically above average women.[12]

Recall of their interaction with seminary professors by clergywomen who attended seminary at different times indicates that, the later they began seminary, the better experiences they had with seminary faculty. For example, among the clergy who attended seminary between 1961 and 1965, 61 percent of the women to 92 percent of the men reported that the faculty gave them preferential, warm, or at least impartial treatment. But among those who began seminary in 1974 or later, the difference between sexes disappears, as 83 percent of the women and 88 percent of the men reported that faculty treated them well in this fashion. Furthermore, the data suggest that, while this increase was true for women pastors who attended both interdenominational and denominational seminaries, the increase over time was even greater in the interdenominational university schools.

One of the reasons given by our respondents for this last finding is that the university seminaries began to increase the proportion of women seminarians and women faculty more rapidly than did the denominational seminaries. As indicated in the opening section of this chapter, this is probably an accurate depiction. Comparing men and women pastors who began seminary before and after 1970, it seems from their recall that university seminaries not only had more women students earlier than the denominational and independent seminaries, but increased the proportion of women in their student bodies faster than did the other seminaries. For example, among those attending seminary before 1970, 20 percent of the women at university seminaries compared to 9 percent of those at denominational seminaries reported there had been over thirty women seminarians at their seminary at that time. Among clergywomen who attended seminary after 1970, 64 percent of those attending university seminaries compared to 27 percent of those attending denominational seminaries reported there were thirty or more other women there at the time. (Men who attended these different types of seminaries confirm this relatively greater number of women and growth in numbers of women at the university seminaries.)

Similar findings obtain for numbers of women faculty. For a third of the women pastors who attended interdenominational university seminaries before 1970, there were no women faculty, compared to 50 percent of the women who attended denominational seminaries reporting this absence of female professors. But after 1970, only one woman and no men pastors who attended an interdenominational university seminary reported that women faculty were nonexistent on campus, compared to about 40 percent of both sexes who reported this was the case at the denominational seminaries they had attended. Fully 50 percent of the women pastors who attended university seminaries after 1970 said they had three or more women professors at their seminary, compared to only 10 percent of the clergywomen who attended denominational seminaries after 1970. The presence of women professors may indicate why women students at university seminaries had a better chance on the average of being treated seriously as students, though this factor may not necessarily have led faculty to encourage them to be pastors. Indeed, the far greater faculty emphasis on preparation for parish ministry at denominational seminaries[13] indicates that there may be little relationship at the university seminaries between faculty acceptance of women as serious students and encouragement for them to enter the parish ministry.

Among the total sample, there was no significant difference between men and women pastors in their recollection of whether seminary faculty had "clearly encouraged" them to enter the parish ministry. Fifty-three percent of the women and 51 percent of the men indicated that they had received such vocational encouragement. Similarly, there was little difference between men and women in their recall of whether any professors had discouraged them from entering the parish ministry. A minority of both, 16 percent of the women and 8 percent of the men, said that some professors had tried to dissuade them from becoming pastors. Although we cannot tell from our survey of present parish ministers how many seminarians of either sex were successfully turned away from pursuing a career in parish ministry, those that attended interdenominational, university seminaries and became pastors were no more likely to report that faculty tried to discourage or encourage them to enter the parish ministry than those who went to denominational seminaries. Women who entered seminary before 1970 were even slightly *less* likely to report attempts by faculty to discourage them from becoming parish ministers if they attended university, interdenominational seminaries than if they attended a denominational or independent seminary—11 percent at the university related to 21 percent at the other seminaries. No significant difference is found between women attending the two different types of seminary after that date. This data accords with previous description of the university seminaries as being early leaders in openness of their doors and programs to women.

Lehman's 1978–79 study of American Baptist men and women third-year seminarians and those already ordained and in ministry,[14] from whose study the questions of faculty encouragement/discouragement were derived, suggests that there may well be some denominational differences in this regard. This proved to be the case. Generally the American Baptist, Episcopal, LCA, and United Presbyterian samples were the highest in proportion of women indicating that some faculty had attempted to discourage them from entering the parish ministry when they were seminarians. These were a minority of about 20 percent in each of these denominations. However, there were really no significant differences among denominations on this question and hardly any on the question of faculty encouragement to enter the parish ministry. Most faculty encouragement was reported by American Lutheran women pastors (63 percent) and least by United Presbyterian women pastors (43 percent).

Whether or not faculty were remembered as specifically encouraging or discouraging these pastors' aspirations as seminarians to become parish ministers, not all pastors remembered faculty as actually being of much influence on their decisions to be ordained. While only about a fourth of these men and women pastors could say definitely that their seminary faculty and other seminary personnel were *not* important in their own decision to be ordained, at the same time, no more than 37 percent of the women and 25 percent of the men said that these seminary faculty and administrators were as much as "quite important." For both men and women, there was a significant positive correlation (.34 for women, .30 for men) between their attribution of influence on ordination by seminary professors and their reports that some seminary faculty had encouraged them specifically to go into the parish ministry. However, it is also obvious from these correlations that there were many clergy of both sexes who were encouraged by faculty to enter the parish ministry, but really do not feel faculty at the seminary had much influence on their decision to be ordained. Of course, some of these men and women entered seminary already firmly intending to be ordained and become parish ministers. Hence, their early decision precluded much, if any, later influence from in-seminary persons or experiences.

As indicated in the above percentages, somewhat more women (about 12 percent more) than men cited faculty in seminary as being influential on their decision to be ordained. This may be because, as noted, women pastors on entering seminary were more likely than men to be unsure of what their eventual career in ministry might be. They were also more inclined to see seminary as a place where they might grow spiritually. In short, it is likely that women seminarians in the 1970s were more open to in-seminary influences than were men. Indeed, women were considerably more likely than men to mention their clergy field work or intern supervisors as quite important influences on their decisions to be ordained (34 percent of the women to 19 percent of the men); they were also more likely to mention other in-seminary or seminary-associated learning experiences that would particularly prepare them for the practice of ministry, such as field work and interns (70 percent of the women to 57 percent of the men saying this was quite important in their decisions to be ordained). Also, more women than men said their friends (who were typically classmates in seminary) were quite important in their decisions to be ordained (48 percent of the women to 25 percent of the men). Men, on the other hand, were more inclined to say that clergy of churches they attended were quite important in their decision to be ordained (51 percent of the men to 40 percent of the women); but for most of these men, this influence came prior to entering seminary. Just a third of the clergywomen said that other women pastors were quite important in their own decisions to be ordained. But most women, when they were seminarians, knew no clergywomen (34 percent) or did not know them well enough to obtain modeling clues or even support from women pastors.

The presence of other women students on campus provided perhaps a greater opportunity for women to make friends and share their experiences with other women undergoing the same kind of educational experience; however, the absolute numbers of women students on campus at the time these women clergy were there had no effect on how much influence they attributed to friends or professors on their decision to be ordained. Although there have been greater numbers of women present in seminary in recent years, both women and men in this study were not likely to have attended seminary when even a third of the student body were women, as is evident in Table 4.4.

Interview data of a qualitative variety suggests that women pastors who entered seminary when the number of women had increased had a

Table 4.4 Year of Enrollment in Seminary and the Number of Women in Student Body at That Time

Number of Women in Student Body	Before 1961 %		1961–1965 %		1966–1969 %		1970–1973 %		1974–1979 %	
	W	M	W	M	W	M	W	M	W	M
0–3	29	44	24	36	6	23	10	8	4	5
4–10	25	27	20	29	31	57	33	36	18	26
11–30	36	22	46	29	51	13	40	40	39	40
31 and more	10	7	10	6	12	7	17	16	39	29
Total	100	100	100	100	100	100	100	100	100	100
(N)	(48)	(299)	(41)	(100)	(51)	(74)	(161)	(62)	(191)	(42)

more comfortable experience than those who attended when women students comprised a handful in the entire institution. Nevertheless, the actual numbers of women seminarians present when these pastors attended had no relationship to other in-seminary experiences and influences with one exception—motivation to be ordained. As noted in the first chapter, the proportional representation of women in a group has at least to get toward a "tilted" distribution (say perhaps 65 percent men to 35 percent women), according to Kanter's theory, before their "token" status is reduced. Although there was certainly an increase over time in women's enrollments, and although they were a decided presence in the classrooms, never or seldom does the proportion of women get out of Kanter's "skewed" category where women are apt to be treated as tokens.[15]

Although sheer numbers of other women students present appeared to have little discernible effect on the ministry of these women pastors after leaving seminary, this was not true for men. We asked how many clergywomen our respondents talked with regularly in an average month. The year in which men (or women) attended seminary had no relationship to how many women clergy they were now talking with regularly. However, for clergymen (but not clergywomen), the more women in the student body when they attended seminary, the more likely they are now to talk to more clergywomen regularly. For example, 49 percent of the 177 clergymen who went to a seminary where there were no more than three women in the total student body said they presently talked to no clergywomen regularly. But only 22 percent of those clergymen who went to seminary when there were over thirty women seminarians said they did not talk regularly to any clergywomen now. So men seem to have learned something from having women around them as fellow seminarians: the value of continuing collegial relationships with women clergy after ordination.

Motivations for Being Ordained

Why do clergy, both men and women, seek ordination, or official authorization to enter the clergy status, and engage in its functions? Do men and women differ in their motivation? The most important reason that these clergy, especially women, wanted to be ordained was simply that they felt called by God to ordained ministry. Seventy seven percent of the women to 67 percent of the men said this was "quite important" in their decision to be ordained. Less than 10 percent of these clergy said that a "conviction that God wished you to be ordained" was unimportant in their own decision to seek ordination. Among them was one iconoclastic clergyman who said, "Niebuhr taught me to be more modest about what God wanted me to do!"

Clearly less important for most clergy, but still of some importance for three-fourths as a motivation for being ordained, were: (1) "greater acceptance of my ministry by having official church legitimation as an ordained person"; and (2) a "desire to administer the sacraments and perform other priestly acts." Both reasons were somewhat more important to women pastors for ordination. For the first, 58 percent of the women to 47 percent of the men said this was "quite important." Or they said that that ordained status gave them a legitimacy with laypersons, hospital personnel and others which facilitated their entry into difficult situations as well as their attempts to engage in ministry.

To some extent being ordained to full ministerial status is parallel to licensing in the professions of law, medicine, and other service professions. By passing exams after completing graduate professional school, the would-be practitioner is certified by the licensing board of the particular profession as having the requisite moral character, basic knowledge of the discipline, and skills to help clients effectively. The more prestigious professions have acquired the legal right to control entry into the occupation, to accredit schools of the profession, and to certify practitioners or revoke their certification. They are granted this right because they successfully pressed their claim that extended training of practitioners is essential for the good of society, and the corollary claim that the professional governing body alone can judge the appropriateness of the standards it sets and the degree to which they are met.[16] An individual who needs help in solving a problem can go to the appropriate certified practitioner and be relatively confident that professional is competent and ethical. Similarly, individuals who are ordained by their denomination as having the requisite moral character, commitment, knowledge, and skills to be clergy will be seen by lay officials as having the legitimate right to be in places not open to the general public (for example, in hospitals and prisons after visiting hours); they are also more likely than laity to be viewed by parishioners and non-parishioners as official representatives of the church. Also, because they are ordained, they will be more readily accepted than lay members by those who do not know them personally as competent to counsel, advise, and otherwise aid them.

In Chapter 1, we referred to the traditional image of the clergy status as "sacredly masculine." Because of this, women are likely to have more difficulty in being seen as legitimate representatives of the church or as having the skills to minister to others by many public officials and parishioners. Indeed, a good number of women may have tried to minister as laypersons with notable lack of success in having these attempts accepted. For this reason, it is not surprising that slightly more women than men cite their desire "to have official church legitimation as an ordained minister" as an important reason for their being ordained. A number of the women were very aware that, as laywomen, they would have little authority within congregations or denominational structures, and their reasons for getting ordained were quite honestly to get the respect and "clout" they saw the ordained men in their denomination as having. This point is clear in the following quotations from clergy-women:

The knowledge that I couldn't work in the church as a first class citizen if I weren't ordained was the major reason. [It was] pragmatic.

First and most important in my seeking ordination was that I did not want to be a second class citizen.

In Chapter 2, we suggested at least three orientations to ministry held by clergywomen. Several of the statements regarding motivation for ordination to which women were asked to respond reflect these orientations. For example, a good proportion of both clergywomen and men who cited their desire for official church legitimation as a reason for seeking ordination may be those who have the "professional orienta-tion" to ministry. Those with this orientation see ministry as partly an occupational role which requires that the practitioner have certain lev-els of competence in specified areas. This orientation does not exclude a feeling of divine call; rather it also includes an emphasis on having psychological, academic, and skill qualifications as important.

Clergywomen are even more likely than men to say they got ordained at least partly so thay they could "administer the sacraments and per-form other priestly acts." Fifty-six of the women cited this as a quite important reason compared to 35 percent of the men. In part, re-sponses to this item are denominationally related, since denominations vary in their sacramental emphases and practices. For example, there are relatively few sacramental and priestly acts restricted to clergy in the American Baptist Churches, but a relatively large number of activi-ties are restricted to clergy in the Episcopal and Lutheran denomina-tions. Accordingly, less than a third of the American Baptists (31 percent of the women and 17 percent of the men) said "desire to ad-minister the sacraments and perform other priestly acts" was quite im-portant in their decision to be ordained, while approximately three-fourths of the Episcopal and Lutheran clergywomen and half the men said this factor was "quite important."

It is especially in those denominations with a strong sacramental em-phasis that the difference between clergywomen and men is most pro-nounced. The Episcopal and the two Lutheran denominations are also those which were the latest to ordain women; hence, women had longer to observe men alone leading key parts of the worship service and to dream of also being permitted to do so. On the other hand, American Baptists were the first to ordain women. This denomination also has less of a sacramental tradition; thus, administering the sacraments and leading worship are not as likely to be the same male-stereotyped activities as in the former denominations. Therefore, participation in them is not as strong a motivating factor for American Baptist women in seeking ordination.

Apart from these denominational differences regarding a sacramental emphasis, some clergywomen and men in all denominations may desire ordination in order to act as a priest liturgically because of a nontraditional orientation to ministry as a "calling." In this orientation, preaching and sacramental acts are central expressions of the worship of God who has called them and set them apart for this.

A third orientation to ministry discussed in Chapter 2 is a desire to transform the church, a desire often rooted in feminism of one kind or another. Of the three orientations, this was clearly less important for the clergywomen in this study than other reasons mentioned for becoming ordained. Over a third of the women pastors (36 percent) said that "a desire to change the sexist nature of the church" was not important in their decision to seek ordination. Only 27 percent said it was "quite important." The United Church of Christ women were most apt to see this as quite important (38 percent) and the Lutheran Church in America clergywomen least likely (18 percent indicating quite important). Apart from these two extremes, denominational differences were slight.

Women who attended university, interdenominational seminaries were slightly more likely than those who attended denominational and independent seminaries to wish to become ordained in order to change the sexist nature of the church (36 percent of the women attending university seminaries to 26 percent at all other seminaries). This difference occurs in large part because university seminaries were first to enroll larger numbers of women seminarians; and the more women seminarians at a seminary when these clergywomen attended, the more likely they were to give changing the sexist nature of their denomination as an important reason for seeking ordination, as Table 4.5 indicates.

Although there has been a rise over time in the proportion of women seminarians who say that a desire to change the sexist nature of the church was of at least some importance in their decision to be ordained, it is also clear from Table 4.5 that the number of other women in the seminary was helpful in raising or maintaining a consciousness about the prevalence of sexism in the church. Earlier, in the late 1960s and early 1970s, the culture on many campuses, including some seminaries,

Table 4.5 Degree to Which a Desire to Change the Sexist Nature of the Church Was Important in Clergywomen's Decision to Be Ordained*
(by the Number of Women Seminarians When Clergywomen Began Seminary and the Year of Enrollment)

Year Enrolled in Seminary	Number of Women in Student Body When Clergywomen Began Seminary			
	0 – 3 %	4 – 10 %	11 – 30 %	31 and more %
1960 and before	15	36	31	40
Tau beta − .22, sig. .04	(of 13)	(of 11)	(of 16)	(of 5)
1961 to 1965	44	72	48	100
Tau beta − .19, not sig.	(of 9)	(of 7)	(of 19)	(of 4)
1966 to 1969	33	40	52	50
Tau beta − .07, not sig.	(of 3)	(of 15)	(of 26)	(of 6)
1970 to 1973	69	63	52	65
Tau beta − .02, not sig.	(of 16)	(of 54)	(of 64)	(of 27)
1974 and later	43	38	58	64
Tau beta − .19, sig. .001	(of 7)	(of 34)	(of 74)	(of 75)

*% = percent saying "desire to change the sexist nature of the church" at least somewhat important in their decision to be ordained.

was sufficiently supportive of working for racial and sexual justice, that support from other women seminarians was not necessary in order to convince many women seminarians that church attitudes toward women needed changing, and that they might help do this by entering the ordained ministry. When campus radicalism began to die down after 1973, the presence of women seminarians in sufficient number became increasingly important in supporting a desire to change the sexist nature of the church through ordained ministry.

It is important to reiterate that of all three orientations toward the ordained ministry, the feminist one, as reflected in a desire to transform the church, was least important. Further, even for those to whom it was of some or major importance, a conviction that God wanted them to be ordained was of at least equal importance. Also, while definitely contributing to opening seminaries and ordained ministry to women, the feminist movement was not the perceived reason that most women gave for entering seminary or the ordained ministry. Once in seminary or the parish, women became more aware of the degree to which women have been discriminated against within church structures, including the clergy job market and attitudes of laity and male clergy. A good number of the women clergy in this study who entered seminary when there were few women in their seminaries (or in any seminary) are also likely to have developed a feminist orientation regarding church structures and other aspects of church life. A recent UCC study of clergywomen and another of United Methodist clergywomen make a similar point,[17] as does a study of the clergy job market in general.[18] Similar findings probably obtain for women studying for the rabbinate. One interviewer reports the comments of a woman rabbi to the effect that she did not enter seminary *because* she was feminist, but became so during her study of the Jewish heritage and the way in which it had kept women as second-class citizens.[19]

Decision to seek ordination is not the same as getting ordained, especially for clergywomen who attempted this feat in places and times when ordination of women was frowned upon by local powers-that-be in their denominations. In the total sample, although slightly over half the women (54 percent) said it was quite easy for them to get ordained to full ministerial status after seminary, over three-fourths (78 percent) of the men indicated that getting ordained had been easy for them. Denominational differences do occur here, Episcopal and United Presbyterian women note the most difficulty; Disciples and United Church of Christ women note the least.

Although a feminist concern to change church structures was not a primary reason for the majority of women seeking ordination, feminist concerns are important to many clergywomen. We turn now to a consideration of these concerns in relation to church structures.

Feminism in Seminaries and the Formation of the Church Feminism Scale

The history of feminism in denominations and of the response of churches to the women's movement in the nineteenth and early twentieth centuries is in one sense an account of how churches subverted the radical feminist vision of full equality with men into an emphasis on the "special virtue" of women. Beverly Harrison has documented this point forcefully.[20] Although the churches were not successful in destroying the spirit of feminism, they were able to channel it. As Harrison expresses it, "To stay in the church, one had to become a 'soft feminist,' one who accepted woman's 'special virtue.' "[21]

The feminist movement, which grew in the late 1960s and 1970s outside the churches, initially took on a harder or more radical feminist thrust, that is, attempting to change structures to incorporate women fully and equally in positions of authority. After the initial phase, it became more inclusive in its emphasis, stressing the liberation of men as well as women by denying the status of gender as a determinant either of activities or of occupations.[22] Also, elements of the "soft feminism" orientation were present—not surprisingly, since ideologies of social movements as rapidly ascendant as the women's movement was in the early seventies often tend to incorporate contradictory elements. They become differentiated, as various groups within the movement emphasize different aspects of the ideology. In the secular feminist movement, a kind of "soft feminism," which emphasized feminine strengths that women alone could bring to organizations and activities, tended to lead away from a focus on changing structures. These feminists who stressed the "particular gifts of women" were often in ideological if not actual conflict with other feminists who stressed androgynous abilities needed for successful performance in occupations.[23]

By the mid 1970s, the feminist movement in religious organizations (congregations, seminaries, and denominational headquarters), also exhibited these various emphases and strains. Elements of the "soft feminism" were present, but the focus on changing church structures also was emphasized. Questions of who was included and excluded from the feminist movement; issues of power, race, and sexuality; and the concern of what should be the primary focuses of feminist attention arose among the women's groups and centers at many Protestant seminaries.[24] Although the same kinds of diverse focuses which were manifesting themselves in the secular feminist movement also appeared in the feminist movement in the seminaries and denominations, there seemed to be a convergence of opinion among feminist seminarians, faculty, clergy, and lay leaders, as Zikmund expressed it, that women should have "not only equality of opportunity and the right to compete with men for ecclesiastical power . . . but the right to think differently about the Christian faith itself . . . and translate the tradition into non sexist words and concepts."[25]

As a legacy of the activist, secular feminist movement, the goals of equal access to positions of power and professional occupations, equal pay for equal work, and inclusive language, though not fully realized in practice, have come to be accepted by most socially and politically liberal persons as just and necessary to pursue. Ideological success perhaps is indicated in that both women and men can generally espouse all major goals of the women's movement without considering themselves "feminists."[26] This situation, along with the varying focuses among self-defined feminists, however, does create ambiguities in what the term "feminist" means in any given situation.

In this study, our interest was to determine to what extent individuals, both male and female, lay and clergy, espoused values specifically relating to the right of women to enter ordained and nonordained church leadership positions and the use of inclusive language in churches and church-related publications. We were not so much concerned whether or not these individuals would label themselves as "feminists." Accordingly, a number of questionnaire/interview items were examined as possible indicators of advocacy of these positions. Statistically, we found that the following four items fit together best in this regard:[27]

(1) More women should be ordained to full ministerial status in denomination.
(2) There should be more women in executive staff positions in regional and national offices of my denomination.
(3) My congregation should appoint or elect an equal number of laywomen to laymen on the parish governing board.
(4) Inclusive language should be used in church publications and services.

These items, asked of all clergy and lay leaders in this study, were combined to create an index of what we call Organizational Church Feminism. The individual items will be given greater discussion in Chapter 6, especially in terms of lay leaders' responses. Those who agreed with each question were given a score of one; those with mixed responses a score of two; and those who disagreed a score of three. When responses for the four items are summed, it is possible to achieve a score ranging from four to twelve. It should be pointed out that secular radical feminists without any church leaning probably would not find ready identification with this scale because of its church focus and relative "mildness." Nevertheless, clergy and lay leaders of both sexes who agree with the items are defined here as "strong church feminists," regardless of whether they would define themselves as "feminists" or whether they put their private convictions into practice in decision making or advocacy. The distribution of female and male lay leaders and clergy on the scale of Organizational Church Feminism can be seen in Table 4.6.

We have labelled a score of 4 on this scale as indicating a "strong feminist" orientation. If the respondent has given more negative than ambivalent responses he or she has been labelled "anti-feminist." However, in this analysis we will typically use the scale without reference to particular arbitrary dividing points, with the exception of the "strong feminists" who are sometimes highlighted in their positions on other items of interest.

From Table 4.6, it can be seen that slightly over half the clergywomen (56 percent) and slightly under a fourth of the clergymen (24 percent) are "strong feminists" according to the scale. Proportionately fewer of the lay leaders, but still more women than men, are classified

Table 4.6   Distribution of Scores on the Organizational Church Feminism Scale Among Women and Men Clergy and Lay Respondents

	Clergy		Lay	
	W	M	W	M
	%		%	
Strong feminists (score 4)	56	24	27	17
Feminist (score 5)	19	17	21	23
Moderate feminists (score 6)	13	17	19	14
Nonfeminist (score 7 and 8)	9	24	19	29
Antifeminist (score 9 to 12)	3	18	14	17
Total	100	100	100	100
(N)	(615)	(704)	(334)	(332)

as "strong feminist." While a minority of both clergy and laity are in the "non-feminist" or "anti-feminist" categories, it follows popular thinking that laity are more likely to fall into these categories than clergy (laymen being the most likely to be "non" or "anti-feminist" and clergywomen the least). This last finding holds across all denominations, except Episcopal and American Lutheran Churches, where clergymen, especially, are more likely to be "anti-feminist" than laity. But as might be expected, among clergy within each denomination, clergywomen were more likely to be "strong feminists" than clergymen. Interestingly, when we take into account the approximate date in which women were first ordained to full ministerial status in the denomination (see Table 4.7), it appears that the longer women have been ordained, the greater the proportion of strong feminists among male clergy. This suggests a favorable prognosis for the eventual elimination of this divergence of opinion between the sexes on women's place in ecclesiastical structures.

Until this perspective changes, however, clergywomen are likely to perceive a sexist orientation among many of their male colleagues and denominational officials. Women who said they became ordained partly to change the sexist nature of the church are also, overall, likely to be strong feminists by the Organizational Church Feminism Scale. However, this correlation is only statistically significant for those women who began seminary since 1970, especially for those who began since

**Table 4.7   Approximate Dates When Women Were First Ordained
and Percentage of Strong Feminists Among Male Clergy**

Denomination	Approximate Date Women First Ordained	% Strong Feminists Among Clergy
United Church of Christ	1853	39
American Baptist Churches	(100 plus years)	29
Disciples of Christ	1888	30
United Presbyterian	1956	29
United Methodist	1956	19
Presbyterian, US	1964	21
Lutheran Church in America	1970	20
American Lutheran Church	1970	16
Episcopal	1977	15

1973. In other words, many of the women ordained in the 1960s, who did not initially pursue ordination to change the sexist nature of the church, have nonetheless come to espouse eradicating sexist barriers to women's entry into power positions in the church *after* having some experience in ministry. For example, two-thirds of the fifteen women who began seminary in the period of 1961–65 and said they did not become ordained to change the sexist nature of the church are now "strong feminists" by the Church Feminism Scale. By contrast, only a third of those seventy-eight women who began seminary in 1974 or later and said they did not become ordained to change the sexist nature of the church have since become "strong feminists." The experience of their predecessors however, indicates that another few years in the ministry may change their opinion. As noted previously, those women pastors attending seminary most recently were more likely than those attending in earlier years to seek to be ordained in order to change the sexist nature of the church. More recent graduates (since 1970) are also now likely to be "strong feminists" in their endorsement of the items making up the Church Feminism Scale. For example, almost 85 percent of those beginning seminary in the 1970s are affirmative on all items.

Since the time that most of our respondents graduated from seminary, the proportion of women has doubled and tripled at many of the seminaries they attended. Furthermore, the average age of the student body in the M.Div. programs has typically risen. What effect might these developments have on women's experience in seminaries, on their motivations to get ordained, on their endorsement of feminist concerns in changing church structures and language, and on their ministry in the parishes? In order to get some idea of how women seminarians now differ from those women who went through seminary three, five, and ten years ago, we asked approximately eighty women seminary faculty and administrators to describe the current situation.

Characteristics of Current Women Seminarians According to Women Faculty

The rise in the average age of all students entering seminary, and especially women, which we noted in the last chapter, was commented on by most of the faculty women interviewed. Although we were not able to get hard statistics, it seems that, in many seminaries, half or more of the student body is age twenty nine or older, and several reported an *average* age of thirty-five in their entering M.Div. classes.

Most of the women seminary faculty interviewed noted clear differences between second-career women and those women coming right out of college or seminary. Faculty women most often noted that the older women tended to be more dedicated to studying in seminary and becoming pastors than were first-career women. However, the older women were also likely to be far less self-confident about their academic abilities than were the younger women. Faculty members typically enjoyed working with second-career women, not only because they eventually turned out to be very good students on the whole, but also because they tended to be much more realistic about life in general and particularly about the parish ministry than most first-career women.

Within this broad generalization about second-career women, especially those at seminaries with a large proportion of older women seminarians, faculty women found they could discern different types of second career students. One obvious difference is that some second-career women seminarians have had a first career of housewife-mother, while others have worked as professionals or in the business world. According to many faculty, the former full-time homemaker who comes to seminary typically takes a little longer to adjust to the seminary academic routine and may need more personal support from faculty for the first year or so than do those women who have worked outside the home. There also appears now to be a group of second-career women who are coming to seminary more for personal and spiritual "healing" than with the clear vocational goals that are more characteristic of older women students.

The faculty women did not typically know nearly as many second-career men as they did women, partly because there simply were not as many second-career men in the seminaries and partly because they did not have as much contact with these students as they did with the women. The few faculty women who felt they could comment on the differences between second-career women and men had divergent impressions of what the average second-career man was like. Some characterized them as "losers" who, unlike the second-career women, could not make it in their first career. Others characterized them in the opposite fashion as self-confident and devout Christians who, though successful in their first careers, felt that something was missing in their lives. It may of course be that different types of seminaries attract different types of second-career men and women.

The most outstanding and frequently mentioned characteristic of current second-career women in seminaries was that they tend to have been actively involved in parishes as lay persons for some years before entering seminary. To quote one woman faculty member who expressed the feelings of a number of others:

> *The second-career students are the most exciting population of seminary students . . . and this is because most of the women have been deeply involved as volunteers and laypersons in their congregations. . . . Never before in the history of the church have we had leadership of people who have come out of the rank and file in such numbers. . . . We have never had pastors who have been in the pew for twenty or thirty years!*

Faculty women had different opinions on whether or not the second-career women tended to be more or less feminist than the first-career women. Again, this may indicate two different groups at least of second-career women self-selecting themselves into different seminaries in varying proportion. In the present sample of clergywomen, for example, there is *no* relationship between the age at which women entered seminary and whether a desire to change the sexist nature of their denomination was important in their decision to be ordained, or whether they are strong feminists now (on the scale of Church Feminism).

Another change among current women seminarians noted by half of the women faculty is, however, a decrease in women students actively espousing feminist causes and concerns. Varying definitions of feminism are to some extent operative here, in that these women faculty do differ among themselves in how they define feminism. For example, some stress the "unique gifts that women bring to ministry" and others emphasize more women's equality with men and the need for correcting structural oppression and organizational sexism. But most were in accord that women students are less aware of, or interested in, women's struggles for recognition and position in church and society historically. Perhaps worse, the students are perceived as lacking any apprehension that they themselves might encounter problems in pursuing an ordained ministry in parishes and chaplaincies because they are women.

Just over half (51 percent) of the faculty women interviewed believed that feminism had declined among women seminarians. Nineteen percent believed feminism instead has changed its nature and form of expression but not actually declined. Only 7 percent believed feminism had increased among women students at their seminaries in the last few years. The remaining faculty women described women seminarians as being heterogeneous in response to feminism—a mixture of pro, con, and ambivalent—or unchanged. Some faculty women could not answer the question.

Those who noted a decline in expression of feminist concerns among women students on campus attributed it to two main factors: the increase of women to the point where they are no longer a small minority in the student body (or a minority at all); and the substantial gains women have made in being accepted and well-treated at seminaries, hearing inclusive language used by most professors and male students, and seeing more women in parish positions. Women students are also aware that graduating M.Div. women are getting first parishes with relative ease. These gains are feared by some faculty as lulling women seminarians to sleep, assuming the problems of sexism in the ministry to have disappeared.

Another factor for a decrease in the expression of feminist concerns on seminary campuses is that increased numbers of women bring greater diversity among the women and an accompanying lack of cohesiveness. It becomes more difficult to form groups that speak with one voice. Additionally, 10 percent of the faculty mentioned the generally greater conservative mood of the country and of the families from which these women seminarians were being recruited. A few felt that the quality of women seminarians had declined, that they were neither as bright nor as given to taking initiative as women in previous seminary classes have been. The following quotes are illustrative of some of these points made by faculty women:

The gains of the feminists have been enough so that the inequities are not as salient. Also, there has been a swing to the right. There is still so much resistance from men to women in ministry, and women are scared of asserting themselves. In the middle to late sixties, very bright and adventurous women went into seminary and tried to get ordained. Now, a more average kind of woman goes to seminary.

Women students don't recognize the struggle that went on to get them here, do not align themselves primarily with women or with the concerns of women. They are much more highly individualistic now. All of these students who come in today see women faculty, see language that is inclusive, see at least surface openings for them, and so they assume that the

*problem isn't there anymore. I also think this generation of students re-
flects a general movement toward highly indiviualistic satisfactions for
themselves.*

Those one-fifth or so of the women faculty who felt feminism had
changed in nature rather than actually decreased, gave some of the
following explanations:

*Women are about as feminist as they were a few years ago. Any changes
in feminism are in the direction of it becoming more complex, that is,
people are realizing that the issues are more complicated and less simplistic
black-white as first supposed.*

*Feminism has changed among the women students. They are not as mili-
tant or strident. They are more settled down and determined to make it.
But they are willing to speak up when they see a problem.*

The comfortable climate for most women seminarians in these mainline Protestant seminaries currently noted by the faculty women may
indeed be an unrealistic preparation for what confronts the new woman
graduate once she arrives in the parish. As one faculty woman put it,
although "the official church structure has been shamed into being less
overtly sexist, oppression is coming out in much more subtle forms,"
and the women students' naivete will work against their being able to
confront this sexism effectively.

However, it may also be that women seminarians are increasingly
coming into seminaries and the parish ministry with a professional
orientation, incorporating the feminist objectives of increasing women's
entry into ecclesiastial power structures and the clergy, but focusing
more on acquiring and exercising professional expertise and spiritual
insight in the practice of ministry.

Summary

Seminary environments for women students have changed more in
the last ten years than they changed during the preceding twenty years.
Women who entered the degree program typically leading to ordination
in the fifties and sixties would seldom have seen more than one or two
other women students, if that, and no women faculty. By the turn of
the decade, two or three women were beginning to appear in most
seminary classes of the mainline Protestant seminaries, but particularly
those interdenominational seminaries associated with universities. In
the early 1970s the numbers of women began to double and triple at
most seminaries every year, until by the mid-seventies they had become
at least a fourth of most entering junior classes. By the end of the
1970s, this proportion had increased until women made up about half

of the seminarians in the M.Div. programs at most of the mainline Protestant seminaries.

The women who eventually became pastors in this study were not, however, as likely as were the men to enter seminary with any firm plan to prepare themselves for the parish ministry. Nearly two-fifths of the women had no intention on entering seminary of becoming pastors. Women entering seminary more recently were more likely than those who entered seminary earlier to have come intending to be parish ministers. Women enjoyed their seminary experiences and have found the education they received valuable for their ministry, even though they may have had a few disagreeable experiences with some male professors or students. Seminary environments improved steadily for women over the decade, and recent women graduates are more likely to report good treatment by faculty than those who graduated earlier.

Probably because women are less likely than men to have come to seminary already firmly committed to the parish ministry, they were more open to in-seminary influences. Women were particularly apt to say their thinking about ordination and a ministerial career were influenced by their field work or intern experiences and their friends on campus. The strongest factor in women's decisions to be ordained was their belief that they had a call from God to the ordained ministry, similar to men. Among other reasons, over half the women also were motivated to seek ordination because they perceived that this official recognition from the church would facilitate their ministries. Approximately the same percentage of women desired ordination because they wanted to be able "legally" to perform certain sacramental functions reserved for clergy (possibly reflecting a more traditional orientation to ministry as a calling reserved for those set apart by ordination). Less than a third of the women were seeking ordination in order to change the sexist nature of their denominations, although overall this reason was at least somewhat important to about half of the women who became pastors. Evidently, the third orientation leading women to ordination—a desire to transform the church from a feminist perspective —was not as important for present women pastors as the other two orientations, although it certainly played a part. Interviews with current faculty women in seminaries indicate that fewer women on campus desire to enter the ordained ministry in order to transform the church. Rather they seem more interested in acquiring professional competencies which would enable them to be successful in the parish.

Women pastors typically came to espouse original feminist goals of inclusive language, as well as increasing the proportion of women in the clergy and of all women in the local church and denominational power structures. On a scale of Organizational Church Feminism formed from question items used in this present study, women and men clergy and laity were classified according to their agreement with these goals.

More women than men experienced difficulty in becoming ordained. Although ordination is now more open to women, in most denominations ease in getting ordained is tied very closely to whether or not the seminary graduate is able to get a first parish call. We will explore this question and other aspects of the clergy job situation in the next chapter.

5

Experiences of Women and Men
Clergy in the Job Market

In the early 1970s the battle for the acceptance of women was in the seminaries. By the late 1970s, the seminary fight had mostly been won. It has shifted to the judicatories as women seek to get jobs.—SEMINARY FACULTY WOMAN

I don't think it makes any difference in finding a parish if a woman is single. Because if you are single, they wonder why. If you are married to another minister, that causes problems in how you are placed. If you are married to someone who is not a minister, then you have the question, "Well, is he going to move with you?" There are only three options, and all three of them cause problems with the hierarchy. What it boils down to is that they don't want to deal with women!—CLERGYWOMAN

Women pastors in my area have done outstanding jobs so that district executives are screaming for more women.—CLERGYWOMAN

Far too many men and women will only serve in certain areas or in the city. They are unwilling to go where they are needed. They are serving themselves, not the Lord, the Church or its people.—DENOMINATIONAL EXECUTIVE

These comments reveal differing perspectives on the job situation for clergywomen and raise several issues that make it difficult to give a simple answer to the question of how clergywomen are faring in the job market. In this chapter we explore this question, looking at a variety of concerns about the employment of clergywomen and men: ease of getting a first job; use and perceived helpfulness of the denominations' placement systems, including the advocacy of judicatory officials; types of parish jobs and parishes, and salary levels. We also consider the experiences of clergy couples in the job market. We are especially fortunate not only to have our own data but also that from two studies of particular denominations[1] that focused mainly on job placement of women and therefore treated the issues in more depth than we were able to do.

How Clergy Get Jobs

To understand how women are faring in the clergy job market, we consider first how clergy get jobs. While it may seem incongruous to think of clergy, who typically understand themselves as responding to a divine call, negotiating in a market for jobs, it is nevertheless necessary to do so. Each denomination has established its own internal labor market in which clergy find employment in congregations or other church-related employers. Because these "internal markets" differ, and because these differences affect the way clergywomen and men find employment, we will describe them briefly, noting both their similarities and differences.

Following Carroll and Wilson's distinctions in *Too Many Pastors?*[2] three major formal methods of deploying pastors are used by the denominations in our study. First, there is what may be called an open method of deployment, used by those denominations that give primary emphasis to local congregational autonomy, for example the American Baptist Churches, the Christian Church (Disciples of Christ), and the United Church of Christ. In the extreme form of the *open* method, the congregation is free to secure and employ whomever it wishes to have as pastor. The person selected is ordained (certified) by the congregation. The candidate is free to negotiate whatever terms he or she chooses and to accept or reject any offer the congregation may make. The adequacy of the candidate's professional training is determined by the congregation.[3] The denominations mentioned above do not completely reflect this extreme form; however, in each, the final authority in clergy deployment is the congregation. The denominational deployment structures exist primarily to facilitate congregational decision-making.

A second method is a variant of the open method and may be called *restricted open*. Used by the Episcopal Church, the two Presbyterian bodies (UPCUSA and PCUS), and the two Lutheran denominations (ALC and LCA), this method allows considerable congregational choice in securing a minister, while at the same time restricting the pool of persons who are eligible for consideration. A denominational body or official determines criteria for ministry in the denomination and admits (approves for ordination) only those persons who meet the criteria. They are judged on such matters as the adequacy of their training, their theological orthodoxy in relation to the denomination's position, and various personal attributes. Once approved they become a pool of candidates from which congregations may select. While laity are often involved in the examination of candidates, clergy tend to dominate and function as gatekeepers into the denomination's ministry.

The third method is distinctively different and is practiced only by the United Methodists among the denominations in our study. It may be called a *closed* method in that the denominational body (as distinct from the congregation) has virtually complete control of both the admission of candidates and their deployment in churches. Committees made up entirely of clergy (Boards of Ordained Ministry in the United Methodist system) screen and admit candidates based on denominationally established criteria. Deployment is carried out by bishops who appoint clergy to churches on the advice of district superintendents. Congregations and clergy must be consulted in the appointive process; however, ultimate authority for appointment belongs to the bishop. Under current United Methodist practices, every clergyperson (once admitted and ordained into the ministry) is guaranteed an appointment by the annual conference (regional body) of which he or she is a member. The appointment may be in a local church or in some other position approved by the bishop.

This overview of the three major methods of deployment calls attention to important historic differences in the labor markets of differing denominations; however, there are common features.

For one thing, all of the denominations in our study, with the exception of United Methodist, have developed some formal structures for deployment that operate denomination-wide. These include some type of national clearinghouse, often computerized, whereby clergy seeking a change of positions may have a résumé on file for distribution to local churches or other church agencies that have a job opening. Likewise, such a clearinghouse usually makes available to clergy a list of available positions in congregations and other church agencies. There is no requirement that clergy or congregations in any of these denominations use the national offices; however, they are available for use, and as we shall note, it seems to be important that clergywomen in particular use their denomination's services.

Parenthetically, we note that the development of national deployment services is an example of the way in which modernization, mentioned in Chapter 2, has affected churches and clergy. It is an attempt to bring rational methods and universalistic selection criteria to bear on clergy placement. Or, in other words, it reflects an effort to develop efficient methods of matching available jobs and job seekers throughout the denomination and to give everyone a fair chance of being considered.

A second common feature is the use of regional judicatory officials (bishops, conference or executive ministers, executive presbyters) to assist clergy and congregations in the placement process. Moving from the open, through restricted open, to closed methods, there is increasing formal authority granted to the regional executive vis-à-vis the clergy and congregation; however, it is safe to say that in all cases the regional executive plays a key role in the process, whether by using formal authority or informal (but powerful) personal influence. He or she is the linking person through whom most clergy and congregations make initial contact. In both the United Methodist Church and those denominations that fall in the restricted open type, the judicatory official (or a regional judicatory committee) must approve an appointment or call of a clergyperson to a particular congregation in his or her judicatory; however, there is variation in the degree to which some officials in restricted open denominations actually exercise this perogative. As we shall see, regional judicatory officials are usually crucial in the success or failure that clergy, especially clergywomen, meet in the job market.

A final similarity in the three methods is the growth of congregational power in the selection of ministers, even in a denomination such as the United Methodist Church with its essentially closed-method deployment. The consultation between United Methodist congregations and bishops that is now mandatory is an example. The bishop may ignore the congregation's wishes, but the "marriage" between a minister and reluctant congregation is unlikely to be happy. In all denominations, not simply those in the congregational (open) tradition, congregations have considerable voice in who their minister will be.

The various methods that operate in clergy labor markets reflect primarily the formal process of deployment. Obviously, too, there are informal networks—"old boy" networks or "cousin" systems as they are sometimes called in the denominations. These consist of friends, relatives, former college or seminary classmates, who may inform a clergyperson of a vacancy (often before it is public information in the formal system), or who may suggest to a congregation that a particular clergyperson should be considered seriously as a candidate. Such systems are especially powerful and effective in smaller denominations that have familistic characteristics.

It is possible for a clergyperson seeking a job to ignore both formal and informal systems and to apply directly to a congregation with a job opening. We suspect, however, that most clergy and churches that are a part of a denomination would not choose to use this method. Not only do some denominational polities prohibit it, but there is so much at stake in the selection of the right person for the congregation that congregations are unlikely to bypass the various formal and informal structures available to them in selecting a clergyperson.

Entering the Job Market

We turn now to the data from our survey, beginning with a look at how women, as compared with men, have fared as they entered the job market. In doing so, we must repeat our caution that our data include only those women and men who have succeeded in securing a parish call or appointment. Most people knowledgeable about the clergy job market believe that it is not too difficult for women or men to secure a first placement or appointment in parish. The difficulty is more likely to arise in subsequent moves.

We asked the clergy how long it took them to obtain a first parish position.[4] Eighty-five percent of the women and 95 percent of the men were able to find a position within six months. The percentages rose to 91 percent of the women and 97 percent of the men who found positions within a year. While the figures for most denominations followed this pattern, United Methodist and United Presbyterian women were most likely to have received a parish appointment or call within six months (90 percent). Presbyterian Church U.S. women had the lowest percent getting called within six months, but that figure was a rather respectable 76 percent. The guarantee of an appointment for United Methodists no doubt explains the ease most women experience in that denomination. United Presbyterians have an active program of advocacy for the placement and support of women.

In general, then, neither women nor men in our sample report having had great difficulty in their first placement. What kinds of first positions clergy find and how they fare in subsequent placements are also important and will be considered later in the chapter.

First, however, we consider how our respondents view the current prospects for clergy entering the job market. This question is important, not only because our respondents are close to the situation and able to give an assessment; their perceptions also are often communicated to seminary students and to others contemplating a ministerial career and may have a bearing on career decisions.

Respondents were asked for their perceptions about the job market for seminarians graduating in 1981 (the year the data were gathered). Women were asked only about the situation for women graduates, while men were asked about all graduates. There were significant differences that do not seem explicable by different question wording. Only 5 percent of the men believed that new graduates would have an easier time than they did; however, 31 percent of women believed this would be the case. Almost 60 percent of the men and over one-third of the women thought the situation for new graduates would be more difficult.

When asked why they responded as they did, women who believed new graduates would have an easier time most frequently gave as their reason that the increased exposure of women has made them more acceptable. Also, they believed that, because women have proved themselves in ministerial positions, there will be less apprehension that they will lead the church into ruin. Others cited improved denominational support as making first placements easier.

Men, on the other hand, tended to compare the current placement situation with the time of their own entry into the job market when there was a shortage of clergy. The current job market, as a recent study has shown,[5] is one of a surplus of clergy in several mainline Protestant denominations (e.g., especially Episcopal, United Presbyterian, and United Church of Christ) and a relatively balanced situation in others (e.g., the Lutheran Church in America). Thus when clergymen view the prospects for new entrants, they compare it with their situation and are more pessimistic than women. Both the men and women are seeing the same job market, but they are viewing it from different perspectives. To use a sociological concept, their reference groups are different, and they perceive the job market differently as a result.

Even if there are jobs available, a number of men and women respondents believe the positions will probably be relatively unattractive to new graduates. That is, the positions are likely to be in marginal situations; for example, churches with poor salaries or in isolated locations.

These varying perceptions from men and women concerning the job market show further differences when the year the respondent was ordained is considered. Clergywomen ordained prior to 1970, and men ordained prior to 1975, are likely to believe the current situation will be more difficult for new entrants. The differences in perceived difficulty almost disappear for men and women ordained after 1974, with approximately one-third of each group saying the situation will be more difficult. Women, however, remain more optimistic, regardless of year of ordination.

When we compared denominational variations in perceptions of the job market for new clergy in 1981, less than 15 percent of the clergymen in all denominations believed that new clergy would have an easier time than they had. The greatest pessimism among clergymen—that new entrants will have a more difficult time—comes from UCC (80 percent), Episcopal (79 percent), and United Presbyterian (77 percent), the denominations with the most difficult current job markets. Least pessimistic among men (at approximately 30 percent each) were Disciples and United Methodists. Over half to two-thirds of the men in the remaining denominations are pessimistic, led by American Baptists at 67 percent.

Women clergy in all denominations are significantly more optimistic than men, but there are also denominational differences in optimism and pessimism. For example, only 14 percent of the Presbyterian Church U.S. women believe new women entrants will have an easier time, as compared with four out of ten LCA women. There is in fact considerable pessimism about the job market for new entrants among women in several denominations: American Baptist, Disciples, Episcopal, and Presbyterian U.S. women are all somewhat pessimistic (between 47 and 57 percent). Only United Methodist women show little pessimism (17 percent saying that the job market would be more difficult in 1981).

In summary, (1) women are typically more optimistic than men about prospects for new entrants as compared with the situation when they were ordained; (2) with minor exceptions, the longer clergypersons, either men or women, have been ordained, the more pessimism they express about the situation for new entrants; and (3) there are significant denominational differences for both men and women in their perceptions of the 1981 job market for new clergy. Several of those differences seem to reflect the job situation for clergy in particular denominations; others may reflect denominational deployment practices.

Changing Parishes

Many seminary faculty and judicatory officials whom we interviewed expressed the opinion that entry level jobs are really not too problematic—if entering clergy are willing to accept what is available. Their fears, rather, are with second, third, and subsequent calls or placements. Not only does this fear reflect recognition of the present oversupplied job market, but also a suspicion regarding women that they may not be accepted as sole or senior pastors in larger, high-status churches as easily as men. One United Methodist official said, "The jury is still out on second and third appointments. Will these appointments be horizontal or will [women] in fact be moving in their careers to more responsibility and more opportunity?" A faculty member at an interdenominational seminary echoes this apprehension:

> . . . For a lot of women, it is time to move. They've been in parishes for three or four years. A lot of parishes that were initially open to women have sort of said, "Well, we've done that; we've had our woman," and so second level positions are becoming very difficult. And a lot of my friends are now looking for secular work. They never had any intention of

doing that. . . . One of the things that needs to be raised with women who are in seminary now is to say, "Hey, look, it ain't all cake out there." It is really going to be difficult, and in terms of having a career that grows and develops within parish ministry, . . . women are going to have to be prepared. I think women going into the ministry today need to be prepared in two professions. That's tragic but I think it is true.

References to "career" and upward mobility in both comments articulate the expectation shared by many clergy that each successive move to a new position within the church should be a move *up* the career ladder. Such an expectation is obviously not unique to ordained ministry; it affects many occupations, especially professional and managerial ones. But will it be possible for clergy, especially women clergy, to move upward in the current job market?

To assess how clergy themselves perceive the possibilities for upward mobility, we asked about plans to leave their current position for another job within the next couple of years. Just over half of all clergy say that such a move is likely, with seven out of ten of both men and women anticipating a move to another parish. The majority of women not wishing another parish expressed a desire to serve in a hospital or other type of chaplaincy situation. Male clergy not interested in continuing in the parish were considerably more likely to express interest in a denominational staff position.

Respondents were also asked whether they thought it would be easy or difficult to obtain a position slightly better than the one now held; that is, how likely is it that they will be able to climb the career ladder? Table 5.1 shows the responses broken down by gender. Sixty percent of the women and 55 percent of the men anticipate some degree of difficulty in upward mobility; although that leaves 40 and 45 percent of the women and men, respectively, who are relatively optimistic about their chances, in spite of the difficult job market. What are some of the factors that affect these perceptions?

Age is one contributor to differences. Men under age forty are especially optimistic, with six out of ten believing that there will be relative ease of upward mobility. There are only slight differences among women, with older and younger women both falling near 40 percent in perception of relative ease. Men who are currently fifty years or older are least likely to believe upward mobility will be easy (34 percent indicating "somewhat" or "very easy"). Their responses may reflect that these men are already at the "top" churches on the career ladder and have nowhere else to go that can be defined as "slightly better." Women over fifty, on the other hand, are not typically at the top of the ladder, as reflected in their slightly more optimistic responses (38 per-

Table 5.1   Perceived Ease of Getting a Parish Position Slightly Better Than the One Now Held

	Women %	Men %
Very easy	12	9
Somewhat easy	28	35
Somewhat difficult	38	41
Very difficult	22	15
Total	100	100
(N)	(600)	(705)

cent indicating relative ease). The pessimism of older men may, however, support findings from previous research that older clergy are especially vulnerable in a difficult job market; that is, they are among those most likely to find mobility difficult.[6] An American Lutheran official told us that older clergymen in that denomination are having more difficulty finding calls than are women.

There are also denominational differences in perceptions of ease of mobility if the person were to try to get a slightly better parish position than the one now held. United Methodists are most likely to be optimistic, with just under two-thirds of men and women believing an upward move will be relatively easy. The United Methodist closed method of placement with its guarantee of an appointment is clearly behind this assessment. The optimism about *upward* mobility probably reflects the fact that United Methodist bishops attempt to move clergy to relatively "better" or at least comparable situations where possible. This, however, is not guaranteed. Episcopal clergy, especially clergy-women, and American Baptist clergymen, are the least optimistic about upward mobility. The response of the Episcopal clergy is interpretable in terms of the current oversupply of clergy in that denomination. Evidently American Baptist clergy also find upward mobility difficult. Approximately one-third to one-half of the clergy in the remaining denominations expressed optimism.

Large differences in optimism over upward mobility exist between men and women in several denominations, especially among Disciples and in the Lutheran Church of America, where men are 22 percent higher in optimism than women. Disciples and Presbyterian Church U.S. women (18 and 27 percent respectively) are also much more likely than men to believe that it will be very difficult to better their current position in a move. Explanations for these differences are not readily apparent. Some may reflect differences in denominational structure and practice; others may reflect regional variations.

While such factors are important, characteristics pertaining more to individual clergymen and women may also affect their perceptions of the chance for obtaining a better move. In addition to age, which has already been suggested as important, a clergy's experience of success or failure in his or her current parish makes a difference in perceptions about mobility. In Chapter 6, we examine these various measures of success in some detail. Here let us simply note that clergy—both men and women—who are experiencing a degree of success in their present parish are more likely to believe moving to a better parish will be relatively easy. Indicators of success include positive self-evaluations of a variety of clergy roles, getting ideas accepted by parish governing boards, feeling satisfaction with their current position, and finding that their present position maximizes the use of their talents. Such success breeds confidence in both men and women that they will also be successful in obtaining better parishes in future moves.

Getting Jobs: Factors That Help or Hinder

Earlier we noted the different denominational methods by which clergy find church positions and churches find clergy. How do these various methods work for women and men? Additionally, how do various *personal* attributes of the clergy themselves help or hinder the process of job seeking? To answer these questions we use both our own data and findings from Edward C. Lehman Jr.'s studies of American Baptist and United Presbyterian clergywomen.

As Lehman's analysis suggests, there is a sequence which many clergy follow in job seeking, particularly in denominations using open or restricted-open methods. The formal placement structures, especially the national denominational deployment offices, are consulted first to discover job openings. Informal contacts also are consulted. Once contacts have been established with local congregational search committees, the importance of the national structure is diminished and regional or local factors become more important in helping a clergyperson secure an interview with a congregation. These regional or local "gatekeepers" include regional judicatory leaders who may have to give official approval, seminary officials and faculty, and clergy or lay friends who are known to the congregation and can vouch for the candidate. At this point, personal attributes of the clergyperson come strongly into play and become paramount in the final stage, the interview itself.

We asked clergy general questions about their use of the formal deployment structures. Approximately six out of ten clergy indicate that they have adequate information about vacancies. When responses are compared by denomination and sex (Table 5.2), there are two significant differences within denominations by sex: Episcopal women are less likely than men (by 13 percent) to report having adequate information, while the opposite is true for United Church of Christ clergy where women are 16 percent more likely to answer affirmatively. Overall, no more than half of the clergy, male and female, in the American Baptist, Lutheran Church in America and the United Methodist Church report having adequate information.

Three-fifths of the women and men (excluding United Methodists for whom the question does not apply) reported using the national deployment services and have a current profile or dossier on file with the national office. However, as Table 5.2 reveals, there is considerable variation by denomination and sex. Some of the denominational variation reflects differences in how denominational systems function. Some, for example, encourage all clergy to keep current profiles on record; in others, clergy use the service only when looking for a change. Half of the men and 60 percent of the women are not currently looking. Thus, we will ignore overall denominational differences in Table 5.2 and consider variations by sex within denominations.

In four denominations, women were significantly less likely than men to report using the national system. These include Disciples (31 percent fewer women than men), Presbyterian U.S. (21 percent), American Lutheran (14 percent) and UCC (12 percent). While the differences may result from fewer women looking for a change of positions, it is also probable that fewer women than men in these denominations choose to use the national system.

We asked those currently using the national system how helpful they have found it to be in getting interviews or actual positions. Approximately one-third of the women and men express some dissatisfaction. Table 5.2 shows responses by denomination and sex. Denominational differences are evident regardless of sex, with Disciples most satisfied and Presbyterian U.S. clergy least satisfied. Because the latter denomination is comparatively small, regional, and often described in familistic terms—its informal placement network is called the "cousin system"—these factors may make the denomination's formal system less important for placement. Nevertheless, when sex is taken into account, PCUS men are significantly more satisfied with the denomination's formal system than are women (a 24 percent difference). American Baptist and Episcopal women are also less satisfied than men with their denominations' systems.

When those not using the national system were asked why they were not doing so, the major reason given, other than that they were not

Table 5.2 Use and Effectiveness of Deployment Structures
(by Sex and Denomination)

Percent Saying:	ABC W %	ABC M %	CC(D) W %	CC(D) M %	EC W %	EC M %	LCA W %	LCA M %	ALC W %	ALC M %	PCUS W %	PCUS M %	UPC W %	UPC M %	UMC W %	UMC M %	UCC W %	UCC M %
Presently using placement services of the national denomination office.	90	89	47	78	80	88	63	62	56	70	37	58	24	35	Not Applicable		45	57
(N)	(63)	(62)	(49)	(64)	(79)	(103)	(54)	(42)	(39)	(64)	(19)	(24)	(70)	(108)			(89)	(88)
National Office helpful at least in getting interviews at churches	38	56	65	68	26	40	47	35	52	49	20	44	52	49	Not Applicable		58	63
(N)	(55)	(54)	(23)	(53)	(57)	(96)	(35)	(31)	(25)	(47)	(5)	(16)	(27)	(59)			(41)	(60)
Have adequate information about all church related vacancies.	44	46	58	50	56	69	51	50	67	64	75	84	75	81	49	52	80	64
(N)	(64)	(59)	(52)	(64)	(77)	(100)	(53)	(46)	(42)	(63)	(20)	(25)	(78)	(110)	(127)	(133)	(93)	(87)

currently looking, was that regional and personal ties are also necessary and seem more important. Some women indicated that they were restricted, for family reasons, from moving to other regions and, thus, did not believe the national system to be helpful. Others, both men and women, indicated that they do not trust the national office or the processes used.

Regional denominational officials are a key link in the effectiveness of the denominational deployment system, regardless of denomination. In all but the United Methodist Church these persons receive resumes of available clergy from the national office, often consult directly with congregations in the choice of their pastors, and confer wth clergy regarding available jobs. They frequently use executive discretion in agreeing or refusing to accept a given minister into the judictory. For example, Episcopal bishops have the right to refuse a particular clergy-person entry into a position in the diocese, and other denominational officials can informally withhold their endorsement of the clergy, which is often tantamount to a veto.

Clergy were asked to what extent they anticipated their own regional officials might affect their placement or mobility negatively. Less than 10 percent of either sex would go so far as to say that they anticipated a great deal of trouble; however, 45 percent of the women and 39 percent of the men anticipated at least some possibility of a negative influence by their regional officials. When responses were compared by denomination and sex, United Presbyterian women and men were least likely of all denominations to anticipate any difficulty (18 and 14 percent respectively). Episcopal women were the most likely to anticipate problems, with two-thirds indicating some degree of difficulty. Over half of the American Baptist women and 40 percent of the Disciples, Lutheran (both), and Methodist women also anticipated some or much difficulty.

In giving reasons for anticipated problems, women were most likely to cite officials' reluctance to be advocates for clergywomen in the churches under their jurisdiction. A comment by one women, typical of many others, is that executives in her denomination are "more neutral than negative; but nevertheless the result becomes negative." An American Baptist woman said, "Even the [denominational] executives who are open to women have other priorities. For example [securing employment for] blacks." A Lutheran woman anticipated difficulty "because, since most of the districts have their two or three token women, bishops feel that they don't have to help the advancement of women." Or again, "In the United Presbyterian Church no one officially badmouths women, but. . . ." Or finally, a Methodist woman commented that "Unless the bishop is forceful in placing women and encourages district superintendents to support them, we're in a lot of trouble."

What these quite typical comments highlight is that for women to be placed it is necessary for judicatory officials of all denominations to be more than pleasant but inactive in support of women clergy; rather, they need to be active advocates if women are to find jobs. One large United Methodist annual conference was cited to the researchers as a case in point. The conference has very few women clergy, and several women have transferred out in recent years. Neighboring conferences, in contrast, have significant numbers of women. The difference is in the attitude of the bishops.

The fear of negative recommendations from denominational officials is not restricted to women. A comment by UCC clergymen is very typical: "Our present executives are on the inner circle [of the denomination] and can casually pass prejudicial judgment that can harm or help, *and the parish minister never knows*" (emphasis supplied). Other comments from clergymen indicated that they were perceived as being "too independent" or as "not playing ball," and were thus not helped in job seeking by their denominational officials.

By no means are all comments about denominational officials negative. Many women praise the efforts of their regional officials. Said one United Methodist, "My bishop leans over backwards for women and thinks they are better than men. I have also proved myself quite highly to my bishop." Her last comment is echoed by a number of men and women. Both sexes, but especially men, are apt to cite their personal competence as a reason why they expect support from denominational officials in their regions.

It would be inappropriate to place all blame or praise regarding clergy job seeking and mobility on denominational placement systems or regional judicatory officials. In denominations which call clergy, vacancy or search committees of lay members of the congregation play a major role. Indeed the congregation as a whole typically has the final "say" regarding the pastoral call. Even United Methodists, as noted, make consultation with congregational leaders regarding appointments mandatory. We asked both clergy and lay leaders a number of questions regarding their congregations' preferences for men or women clergy. Much of this material will be dealt with in the next chapter; however, several findings are pertinent here.

We should repeat the caution that our lay leader sample is biased in favor of those who have experienced having a woman as pastor. While this may lead those with experience to be more favorable to women, it may also, in fact, make them favor a man as their next pastor. They may wish to avoid being typed as a congregation with women pastors.

(We treat this "alternation" hypothesis more fully in the following chapter.) These possibilities need to be kept in mind in interpreting the data.

Earlier, we suggested that personal attributes of clergy are more critical for congregational choice by the time the job search process has reached the interview stage. Thus, we listed a number of personal attributes and asked both laity and clergy what would be the likely gender preference for a new minister for each attribute listed. Clergy were asked to respond on behalf of the congregation as a whole. Laity were asked to express their personal preference. Attributes listed included the following: single person in mid-twenties; about sixty years old and widowed; divorced; widowed with children under ten years; obese; and physically very attractive. Two-thirds or more of the clergymen responding believe their churches would prefer the male candidate regardless of the attribute listed. Six percent or fewer believe their church would prefer a woman. Approximately two-fifths (ranging from 38 to 47 percent depending on the listed attribute) of the clergywomen also believe their church would prefer a man, with only 11 percent or fewer indicating preference for a woman on any attribute. Clergywomen are much more likely than men to believe that gender would make no difference with reference to the attributes.

Lay leaders are considerably more likely than clergy to say that the sex of the clergy makes no difference. Regardless of the attributes listed, 60 percent or more of the laymen and women give this response. Where preference is expressed, laymen are consistently more likely to prefer a man; however, fewer than 10 percent of the men or women would prefer a woman candidate.

The differences between clergy and lay leader perceptions are striking. The probable explanation for them is that clergy are responding in terms of their perceptions of the likely preference of the congregation as a whole. Laity are responding for themselves; however, they are leaders in their congregations and describe themselves as theologically more liberal than rank-and-file members. Thus they probably are not entirely representative of their congregations.

With reference to the attributes themselves, there were generally such insufficient differences in how each attribute would affect gender preferences for a new minister that we have not commented on the differences. However, in interviews, many respondents believed that being divorced and being over age sixty and widowed would likely disqualify a candidate regardless of sex.

Also pertinent to congregational preference for clergy is a question asked both clergy and lay leaders. "If a ministerial vacancy should occur in my congregation (or finances permit an additional minister to be hired), the search committee should actively seek a woman candidate." Responses to this question will be considered more fully in Chapter 6; however, here we note that laity and clergy, men and women, are relatively evenly distributed across the three possible responses: agree, have mixed feelings, disagree. Slightly more clergymen agree than clergywomen (40 to 34 percent respectively) with the reverse direction being true for laity (34 percent of the women agreeing and 20 percent of the men). Evidently, a large majority of clergy and lay leaders are mixed at best or negative in their attitudes toward affirmative hiring for women. Given the stronger preference expressed for male clergy rather than female, we believe that someone of influence, more likely the judicatory executive, will have to give at least a subtle push for women if they are to be placed.

As a way of both concluding this section on deployment practices and adding additional insights into the process, we note several findings from Lehman's studies of American Baptist and United Presbyterian clergy. Lehman focuses in greater detail than we have on deployment practices in these two denominations. Both of his studies confirm the importance for women of using the formal placement structures and procedures. This is necessary to provide legitimation for the women as bona fide candidates to regional judicatory officials and congregations.[7] Lehman's Baptist data indicate that the greater the number of formal structures used by a woman, the more her formal identity as a minister is likely to be legitimated. If she ignores the formal structures and relies on informal networks or direct contact with parishes, she is likely to be viewed as "not playing by the rules." The same findings do not hold for Baptist clergymen, for whom personal attributes were more important in final placement outcomes.[8]

In Lehman's study of United Presbyterian women the findings are similar to those for Baptist women;[9] however, the Presbyterian study does not include clergymen. The findings once more show the relevance of formal structures and informal networks for early stages of the placement process, especially for legitimation of the clergywoman, and the increasing importance of personal attributes of the clergywoman during the interview stage.

In addition, Lehman documents how the number of "special needs" restricts chances for satisfactory placement and salary level for the candidate. Respondents were given a list of factors that might limit the location and nature of a church job. They included restrictions such as their spouse's job, needs of their children, or their own educational needs. The greater the number of needs specified, the fewer the number of interviews the candidate had, the fewer the calls she received, and the lower her salary.[10]

Types of Parishes and Parish Positions

Thus far, we have primarily considered perceptions about the job market and mobility within it. What kinds of parishes do the clergy in our sample actually serve? Are there differences between the parishes and types of parish positions available to men and women clergy? Do kinds of parishes and types of positions available differ for men and women as they move through their careers? Answers to these questions are critical in determining whether women are overcoming professional marginality in the ordained ministry.

Women apparently are likely to experience more limited opportunities than men as they move into second and subsequent parish positions. Lehman also has hypothesized that churches experiencing decline or difficulty will be more receptive to women than those experiencing some degree of success. The latter are likely to view clergywomen as a drastic deviation from tradition and consequently as an organizational threat.[11] Hence clergywomen by default have an increased chance of being hired by declining churches. Lehman cites data from a study of American Baptists to support the hypothesis; however, he did not control for whether it was the clergyperson's first or subsequent position. Since most clergywomen are in first positions, to compare their positions with men who have considerable experience may be misleading. Therefore, we will need to control for whether the respondents are in their first, second, third (or more) parishes.

Before considering variations by experience, it is instructive simply to compare men and women as to type of position as in Table 5.3. While 88 percent of the men are in sole and senior pastor positions, quite a different story is true for women. Overall, women are significantly more likely to be assistant or associate pastors than men and less likely to be sole or senior pastors of churches.

The pattern of positions for women varies by denomination. Presbyterian U.S., United Methodist, United Presbyterian, Lutheran Church in America, and UCC women are most likely to be sole pastor positions (ranging from 70 percent in the Presbyterian U.S. to 45 percent in the UCC). Over six of ten Episcopal women are employed as curates (assistant ministers). Likewise, four of ten Disciples women are assistants/associates. American Baptist and American Lutheran women are about equally divided among sole and assistant/associate positions. Almost three out of ten American Lutheran women serve as co-pastors and two of ten Baptists as Ministers of Christian Education. Thus there are denominational variations in the deployment of women. These variations reflect, in part, denominational practices in the deployment of starting ministers, since many of the women are in their first parishes.

Table 5.3   Type of Position in Ministry
(by Sex of Pastor)

Position	Women %	Men %
Sole pastor	47	66
Senior pastor	2	22
Co-pastor	14	2
Associate/assistant pastor	27	8
Minister of education	5	0
Interim pastor	4	1
Other	1	1
Total	100	100
(N)	(604)	(725)

In the Episcopal Church, for example, beginning clergy frequently serve as curates, while United Methodist and Presbyterian Church U.S. clergy often start as pastors of small parishes.

Twenty-five percent of the women and 5 percent of the men are part-time, most of whom work half or three-fourths time. As we shall see later, a large number of part-timers are married to another clergy-person. Part-time clergywomen are evenly distributed across denominations (ranging from 26 to 33 percent) with the exception of the Lutheran Church in America and United Methodists, who have 14 and 7 percent respectively. Until 1980, United Methodist polity prohibited a part-time appointment of an ordained minister. We will consider below the effect on salary of being part-time. Other than salary differentials, women working part-time are especially more likely to be married than those working full-time (81 percent to 46 percent). This probably also accounts for their greater unwillingness to relocate their residence to take a new position (true for both women and men part-timers). They are also significantly more likely to serve churches of less than 100 members (again true for both sexes).

Differences in types of positions between women and men reflected in Table 5.3 no doubt reflect the number of years of experience in ministry. Since the majority of women are relative newcomers to ordained ministry, it is more likely that they will be disproportionately in entry-level positions. In Table 5.4 we have controlled for whether the position represents the individual's first, second, third (or more) parish. Sole and senior pastor categories have been combined. All other categories have been combined with associate/assistant. In this table we have not further controlled for denomination.

Table 5.4 Position in Church and Pastoral Experience
(by Sex of Minister)

Present Position	First Church W	M	Second Church W	M	Third-plus Church W	M
	%		%		%	
Sole pastor/ senior pastor	42	68	49	85	60	92
Assistant/ associate pastor	58	32	51	15	40	8
Total	100	100	100	100	100	100
(N)	(233)	(74)	(169)	(120)	(187)	(518)

Tau Beta: −.14 (sig. .0002) for clergywomen
Tau Beta: −.19 (sig. .0000) for clergymen

The differences between men and women are striking at each point of comparison. Men are significantly more likely than women to be sole or senior pastors and less likely to be assistant or associate pastors. While the data are cross-sectional rather than longitudinal, it is tempting to interpret them longitudinally; that is, to suggest that women are more likely than men to enter the ministry in assistant or associate roles and remain there. Almost six out of ten women enter in assistant or associate positions; four out of ten women in third or more positions are at the same level. However, men progressively move to sole or senior pastor positions.

Are there also differences in the types of churches to which men and women are called or appointed? As we noted earlier, Lehman cited data from an American Baptist study that suggested that declining churches are more likely to call a woman pastor. We asked respondents to describe their churches on several measures. When we compare clergymen to women in first positions only, ignoring whether they are sole pastors or assistant/associate, there is only one statistically significant difference. Clergywomen are significantly less likely than men (48 to 63 percent) to describe the dominant theological position of their congregation as very or moderately conservative. Rather, their congregations are typically described as being either liberal theologically (31 percent) or mixed (21 percent), as compared to 25 and 12 percent, respectively, for men. Other than this difference, women and men are not significantly different in describing their churches as growing or declining when they first arrived. The size of the places in which the churches are located does not differ significantly; nor do church size, the age structure of the congregations, the congregations' social class composition, or the churches' financial positions differ significantly. Thus, considering all churches to which women are called, our data do not support Lehman's earlier findings. Rather, the major difference between first churches served by women and men is their theological position. Liberal churches are more likely to be open to women.

But, what happens to this picture of little or no difference when we compare the churches of men and women who are in their first positions as sole pastors? Table 5.5 presents these comparisons. It also includes comparisons of men and women in their second and third or more parishes. Because our sample contains too few male assistants or associates in second or third positions to allow for meaningful analysis, we consider only sole or senior pastors in the table.

Looking at first positions only, clergywomen and men are about equally likely to say that their churches were declining when they arrived (46 and 44 percent respectively); that they are located in a small city, small town or rural area (both 80 percent); that their churches are predominantly middle and upper class (54 and 56 percent respectively); and that the present financial health is excellent or good (40 and 46 percent). These differences are not statistically significant. However, there are significant differences between the first parishes of clergywomen and men at several points. Women are much more likely (by 26 percent) to be in churches of fewer than 200 members and (by 9 percent) to be in churches where two-thirds of the members are age 50 and older. Significant differences in the theological conservatism of the congregations remain, with men more likely (by 17 percent) to say their congregation members are mostly conservative. Thus, there are differences in first parishes served by women and men who are sole or senior pastors, but the hypothesis that women are more likely to be called or assigned to declining churches is not supported by our data.

Table 5.5 does, however, lend some support to a hypothesis that clergywomen do not fare as well as men in second, third and subsequent calls. There are strong and significant differences between women and men in their second and third or more parishes in several comparisons. The third or more parishes of women are more likely than those of men to be located in small cities, small towns, or rural areas, and to have older members; both second and third parishes of women are more likely than those served by men to be small (under 200 members), to have fewer middle and upper class members, and are *less* likely to be in good or excellent financial health. Thus, women who are in sole or senior pastorates do not apppear to keep pace with clergywomen in the kinds of positions to which they are called or appointed in their second or subsequent moves. It must be noted again that these

Table 5.5 Comparisons of First, Second, and Third-Plus Parishes of Clergywomen and Clergymen as Sole or Senior Pastors*

	Women %	Men %
1. Percent saying when first called church was generally declining:		
First parish	46	44
Second parish	52	45
Third-plus parish	52	46
Tau Beta:†	.03 ns	.003 ns
2. Percent saying the church is in a small city (less than 54,000), town, or rural area:		
First parish	80	80
Second parish	69	64
Third-plus parish	76	61
Tau Beta:	.08 (sig. .04)	.10 (sig. .002)
3. Percent saying the church size is under 200 members:		
First parish	72	46
Second parish	61	32
Third-plus parish	55	21
Tau Beta:	.09 (sig. .04)	.16 (sig. .0000)
4. Percent serving congregations where two-thirds of the parishioners are age 50 and older:		
First parish	33	24
Second parish	27	22
Third-plus parish	40	32
Tau Beta:	−.08 ns	−.09 (sig. .006)
5. Percent serving churches where two-thirds of the parishioners are middle and upper-middle class:		
First parish	54	56
Second parish	48	59
Third-plus parish	45	61
Tau Beta:	.06 ns	−.04 ns
6. Percent saying church's predominant theological position is conservative:		
First parish	54	71
Second parish	46	63
Third-plus parish	53	60
Tau Beta:	−.01 ns	.04 ns

Table 5.5—*CONTINUED*

	Women %	Men %
7. Percent saying present financial health of the church is excellent or good:		
First parish	40	46
Second parish	38	61
Third-plus parish	21	59
Tau Beta:	.05 ns	− .02 ns
8. Percent saying they are "quite willing" to relocate residence one hundred miles away from present residence in order to take a new position:		
First parish	60	61
Second parish	51	57
Third-plus parish	58	51
Tau Beta:	.002 ns	.04 ns

*Assistant/associate ministers are excluded.
†Tau Beta is used to test the significance of the difference for each sex between first, second, and third parishes, *not* between sexes.

data are cross-sectional, comparing three different groups of women at different stages of their careers. We cannot compare the same woman at differing career stages; nevertheless, the data support the hypothesis of differences in second and third-plus placements for men and women.

One other aspect of a minister's position for which comparisons are appropriate is salary. Overall, 39 percent of the clergywomen reported receiving a salary of less than $10,000, as compared with 10 percent of the clergymen. Since, however, there is a considerable difference in years of experience in the samples of men and women, the salary differential may simply reflect experience. Comparing women and men with five or less years of experience, the salary difference remains, although not as sharply. While 16 percent of the men with five or less years of experience earn less than $10,000, 40 percent of the women with comparable experience do so.

We also compared men and women in sole pastor positions, controlling as before on whether this was their first, second, or third-plus parish. Table 5.6 contains the breakdowns. The table reveals significant differences in the levels of cash salary between clergywomen and men in sole or senior pastorates within most categories. Only in two of the first parish comparisons are there insignificant differences. In the remainder, men consistently receive higher salaries than women.

Table 5.6 Cash Salary Paid to Women and Men Clergy in Sole or Senior Pastorates Comparing First, Second, and Third-Plus Parishes

Salary	Parish	Women %	Men %
$10,000 and under	First parish	39	23
	Second parish	36	11
	Third-plus parish	37	6
$11,000 – $15,000	First parish	53	55
	Second parish	52	42
	Third-plus parish	50	37
$16,000 – $20,000	First parish	5	15
	Second parish	7	31
	Third-plus parish	10	30
$21,000 and over	First parish	3	6
	Second parish	5	16
	Third-plus parish	3	27

Another likely factor contributing to the salary differences between men and women is the larger percentage of women working part-time. As might be expected, part-time employment is negatively correlated with the amount of salary earned, both for men and women. However, the correlation is stronger for women (tau beta: $-.37$) than for men (tau beta: $-.23$). Still, being part-time does not entirely reduce the differential between men and women. Twenty-seven percent of the women working full-time earn $10,000 or less. Only 7 percent of the men do so.

The difference between full-time men and women clergy increases when we compare clergy in first, second and third or more parishes. While men are 11 percentage points more likely than women to earn more than $10,000 in their first parish, they are 24 percent more likely to do so in their third parish.[12]

To assess the relative importance of various factors that might affect salary, we used multiple regression analysis separately for women and men. For women, being part-time has the most significant negative effect on salary. The number of years of experience in ministry plays a small but statistically significant positive role. For men, the reverse is true. Years of experience are most important positively in increasing salary, while being part-time is significant in its negative effect. For men, then, years of experience increase the chances for a higher salary, more so than is true for women. Marital status was not significant relative to salary, nor was support (or lack thereof) of judicatory officials.

No doubt other factors also contribute to salary difference. For example, Bonifield and Mills found the joint effects of church size and the position of the pastor (sole pastor or member of a staff) to be the most important factor affecting clergy salary.[13] This factor, however, should affect men and women alike. More to the issue of salary differences affecting women, Lehman found that having one or more special needs (e.g., family, education, spouse's job) affected the amount of salary earned by United Presbyterian women.[14] These needs set conditions that limit a woman's flexibility and thus her opportunities for better-paying positions. Probably most important, however, is the widespread tendency in many occupations for women to be paid less than men. Evidently the doctrine of equal pay for equal work is not any more observed by many churches than by other institutions.

Interestingly, in spite of the salary differences, women are more likely than men to say that they usually had sufficient money during the last year to live comfortably. Seventy-two percent of the women answered affirmatively, while 61 percent of the men did so. Is this because as one Episcopal clergywoman suggested, "Women priests are happy to have parish jobs that pay anything at all"? We used multiple regression analysis to assess the relative importance of various factors that might affect satisfaction for women and men. For both, having sufficient income to retire was the most important factor making one relatively satisfied, followed by total family income. Having a spouse employed was positively related to satisfaction with salary for women, but negatively so for men. For clergymen, having a working wife is often seen as a necessity to supplement an insufficient parish salary, as a number of men commented in interviews. Supplementing their husbands' incomes is less likely to be considered a necessity for married clergywomen. Finally, for men, but not for women, the number of years in ministry positively affects satisfaction with salary, no doubt reflecting salary differences between men and women at higher levels of experience.

In summarizing this section, the following inferences can be drawn: (1) while women and men seem to be able to secure first positions without undue difficulty, there are differences in the positions they secure, with women significantly more likely to be in assistant or associate positions; (2) there are more women than men functioning part-time, apparently related to restrictions that marriage and spouse's job place on mobility; (3) the career lines of women appear to be different from those of men, since women are more likely than men to be in assistant and associate positions or in small and financially precarious churches beyond their first parish positions; (4) women are no more likely than men to find placements in declining churches, although they are less likely to be in theologically conservative churches than men; (5) the cash salary paid to women is significantly lower than for men of comparable experience and for men in sole or senior pastorates, a finding that is only partially explained by the larger number of women clergy serving part-time; and (6) despite lower salaries, women are more likely than men to find their current salary sufficient.

These findings raise some important questions about careers in parish ministry for women and men that can only be fully answered by longitudinal rather than cross-sectional data. However, we believe it important to speculate on these issues as if our data were longitudinal. In particular we ask why the apparent differences in career lines and salaries paid to women and men, and why the relative satisfaction with salary that women express despite the differences?

One possible explanation is that women bring different values to careers than men, that they are less likely to demand upward mobility. Their goal, in contrast to that of clergymen, is not always to move upward to positions offering greater prestige and higher rewards. Women's socialization has been traditionally more service oriented, stressing nonmaterial satisfactions, and leading to a different set of motivations as clergy. This explanation is akin to the position, discussed in Chapter 1, that there are feminine characteristics or "special gifts" that women bring to the ministry that are different from men. Thus the different career lines, unequal in rewards though they may be, reflect different values that women bring to the ministry.

While we are unable from our data to confirm or disconfirm this hypothesis, we tend not to give it much weight. Joy Charlton's findings with reference to clergywomen's views of denominational structures seem more applicable here. Charlton found little evidence that women were dissatisfied with denominational organizations which tend to be pyramidal. "Their goal is to move *into* these organizations, not to challenge them."[15] We suspect that this observation also carries over to career mobility and rewards.

We note, however, that those who do explain the apparent differences in clergywomen's career mobility by the "different motivations" hypothesis are using what Cynthia Fuchs Epstein calls the "myth of the good woman;" that is, the myth that women possess, or should possess, higher moral standards than men and, in this case, therefore, are "too good" to get trapped in the upward mobility game. In her study of women lawyers, Epstein notes that however laudable this myth may be, it can be used "to legitimate the restriction of women to positions without power or prestige."[16]

If women do not choose assistant/associate positions or small churches on the basis of special feminine characteristics they probably choose these positions because there are desired rewards attached to them: for example, better salaries than are often available to women in sole pastorates, which are often small in size and relatively low in salary. Another benefit is that assistant or associate positions are often located in large towns or cities where there are more opportunities for support and interaction with congenial persons outside the parish. Let us add that we do not intend to depreciate either small churches or assistant/associate positions as being less important than larger parishes or sole pastor positions. The latter are simply viewed by prevailing standards as being higher on the career ladder.

Both of these explanations place the primary emphasis on personal choices made by women regarding their careers. The second explanation, however, suggests that women's choices are made within constraints or limits present in the job market. That is, the career line for women within the church system may be different, not simply because women personally choose to follow different career lines, but because the career lines open to them are to some extent different and carry with them different possibilities for movement and rewards. This is similar to a suggestion by Lehman that women may be "typecast"; that is they may enter a particular position initially and find themselves "locked into" similar kinds of positions for the future as well as for the present.[17] If such typecasting occurs, as we suspect that it does, it is probably neither blatantly nor maliciously done, nor even fully recognized. Rather it is probably much more subtly, even unconsciously done, reflecting the dilemmas and contradictions of status noted in Chapter 1. We would add, however, that its subtle and perhaps unconscious character does not make such typecasting any less unjust.

Despite the apparent injustice that clergywomen seem to be experiencing, why do they appear to be relatively satisfied with this situation, especially with their salaries? Based on the widely held belief in fairness or distributive justice, we would expect women not only to be dissatisfied, but quite angry about their situation. Why then are they not? We can only continue to speculate, but it may be that the women in our study are not using clergymen as their reference group or standard of comparison. Rather, they are viewing their situation in terms of the experiences of "pioneer" women parish clergy or of the stories they heard in seminary about how "grim" things are for women in parish ministry. With earlier women clergy as their reference group, the women in our study did not expect their rewards to be great, and therefore they express relative satisfaction with what they have found. Had they made clergymen their reference group (or *when* they make clergymen their reference group) their anger might have been (or *will be*) quite different.[18]

Clergy Couples

Before concluding this discussion of the job market for clergy, we look briefly at a relatively new phenomenon affecting clergy deployment, clergy couples. Increasing numbers of clergy are marrying other ordained persons, and both frequently seek placement in parish positions. It is not surprising that this is happening, with the large number of women and men together in seminaries; although, as one bemused Lutheran official said: "Clergy couples really took us by surprise. Somehow, we failed to anticipate that our men and women seminarians might marry each other!"

Clergy couples will be profiled in more detail in Chapter 8. Here, we deal only with deployment issues.

We did not draw our sample explicitly to include clergy couples; rather, we asked in the clergy interviews and questionnaires if their spouse is ordained. Of the 635 clergywomen interviewed, 195 or 31 percent are married to an ordained clergyman. Of the 739 clergymen, only nineteen, or 2.5 percent, have an ordained clergywoman as spouse. The large difference reflects the years in ministry of respondents. Women are relative newcomers and much more likely to have married during seminary. Most clergymen in our sample, as in the general population, have been in the ministry longer and finished seminary before the large influx of women seminarians. Indeed, in the total sample, of the 55 percent of the women who are married, almost two-thirds are married to an ordained minister. Of the 94 percent of the clergymen who are married, only 4 percent are married to an ordained minister. The very small number of men in the sample who are part of clergy couples in the sample makes it questionable to use their responses for more refined analysis; however, the profile of the women provides considerable insight into deployment issues for couples.

Because the issues of placement for ordained couples involve securing two jobs rather than one (or one shared job), and because two careers do not always run on the same track or at equal speed, an early decision that a couple faces is whose career goals will take priority. Such an issue is obviously not unique to clergy couples. All two-career families must face it. Approximately eight of ten respondents, men and women, indicated that both spouses' goals were given equal weight when considering a position. Of the remainder, the husband's goals took priority in the majority of cases. As one woman said, "We give his priority because of reality factors: he is more employable basically because he is male."

Clergy couples are little different from other clergy in reported ease of finding a first position; however, the options open to them and choices to be made may be somewhat different from others. For example, will they both seek employment in the same church, perhaps necessitating sharing a salary? If so, will one or both partners work part or full-time? Will they try to find separate church jobs, either a parish job for each, or a parish for one and some other church-related or secular job for the other? These options have obvious consequences for both work and marital relationships for the couple, and for the relationship of the couple to the church or churches they are serving. For example, one United Presbyterian woman whose husband serves a different church reported that her congregation was not happy that her spouse was relatively inactive in her church. They "have no opportunity to get to know him, and they occasionally use it as a way of expressing dissatisfaction with me." A United Methodist couple who serve parishes some distance apart are able to live together only for a part of each week. Said the wife: "When I first was appointed to the church and my husband would come to visit, my parishioners responded as if somehow we were 'living in sin.' Now they've gotten more accustomed to his visits."

The most popular option appears to be functioning in the same parish, either as co-pastors or in senior-assistant/associate relationships, with one or both clergy working part-time. Fifty-seven percent of the women and 72 percent of the men work in the same parish with their spouse. One-third of the women and one-fifth of the men work in different parishes from their spouses, with fewer than 10 percent indicating that their spouses are in non-parish work settings (typically in chaplaincy or judicatory positions).

If a choice must be made between full- or part-time work, clergy couple women are more likely to be part-time than men; although half of the women and two-thirds of the men report working full-time. As one clergy couple woman said:

> *Women may have family responsibilities. Never mind that the man does; it is not acceptable for him to go to work part-time. A woman can get away with being hired part-time and still find herself accepted very readily, whereas I think a man who takes on a part-time church position is thought to be somebody who can't make it.*

The part-time position for the wife in the clergy couple may also be relatively acceptable because laity often transfer to her traditional expectations for the pastor's wife. In many instances pastors' wives have functioned, or have been expected to function, as unpaid assistant ministers. For this reason, the part-time co-pastor wife may be more acceptable to some laity than a full-time, sole pastor woman.

When asked how satisfied they are with their present position, clergywomen who are part of couples differ little in their responses from the total number of clergywomen (41 and 42 percent respectively saying that they are very satisfied); however, the clergymen married to ordained women are significantly more likely (by 25 percentage points) to express some dissatisfaction. This may be due to the small sample of men in this category; however, it may also indicate that men perceive their hoped-for career mobility thwarted by the difficulty of neogtiating two clergy careers.

Neither men nor women who are part of a clergy couple are more likely than other clergy to anticipate a move "in the next couple of years." They are not significantly more likely to anticipate difficulty in making a move to a better parish than the one they now serve, nor are they more likely than other clergy to anticipate that judicatory staff will negatively affect their mobility. Men, but not women, who are part of clergy couples, however, are much more likely than other clergymen to express difficulty in planning a career strategy.

Do the churches clergy couples serve, either singly or as couples, differ from those served by other clergy? On the various measures of size of membership, size of community, financial health, growth or decline, and theological position, there are no major differences reported. In cash salary, however, women and men who are part of a clergy couple are somewhat more likely to report making less salary than other clergy. This is especially true for men at the upper salary level, where only 21 percent of men married to an ordained woman are making over $15,000 as compared to 51 percent of the total sample of men.

In summary, our data do not reveal striking differences between clergy couples and other clergy, especially in the types of churches they serve or their experiences in the job market. Perhaps most significant is the way they work out their careers. A majority serve in the same parish, and when a choice must be made for one partner to serve part-time, it is usually the woman who does so. How couples function in parishes and some of the concerns they have will be dealt with in Chapter 8.

Summary

The findings of this chapter are obviously mixed when it comes to the experiences of clergywomen in the job market. Neither women nor men have very much difficulty in securing a first parish position, and women are generally more optimistic than men about the situation for new entrants. Perceived ease of career mobility after the first position varies both by denomination and by characteristics of individual clergy, including age and experience of success or failure in previous or present parishes. Placement and career mobility are affected by the denomination's deployment methods. In those denominations using national deployment systems, use of the system is important for men and women at the early stages of job search, though regional judicatory executives and local congregation pastoral search committees become increasingly salient as the job search narrows. While the advocacy of judicatory executives is crucial to overcome lay resistance to a woman pastor, it does not always occur. Men and women find it relatively easy to find first positions, but the kinds of positions differ, with more women than men serving in assistant or associate pastor positions or as part-time pastors. Likewise, the career lines of women seem to be more "flat" than those of men. It appears that women continue to serve as pastors of smaller churches or in assistant or associate positions in second, third, and subsequent positions. Also, there are salary inequities between men and women, although women are more likely than men to report that their current salary is sufficient. Finally, as noted, clergy couples do not differ significantly from other clergy except in the ways that they work out their dual careers.

In general, while the findings regarding the job market for clergywomen contain much that is positive, inequities still exist. Only time will tell whether the inequities will continue, or if the greater numbers of women entering the job market and the consequent increased exposure of laity, clergymen and denominational officials to clergywomen will aid in overcoming them. The generally positive responses of laity to clergywomen are cause for hope. They reflect the importance of having first-hand experience of clergywomen. Until these inequities are overcome, use of formal denominational placement processes and the positive advocacy of judicatory officials, seminary faculty, administrators, and others able to influence congregational decision makers will be critical.

6

Clergy Effectiveness and Church Stability: A Different Equation for Men and Women?

In my opinion, for my pastor to do his or her job successfully, it takes cooperation from members of the congregation. When 95 percent of a congregation puts church and church work at the bottom of their list of priorities, the church will not grow as it should. . . . We have had and still have many inspiring and well written sermons delivered from our lady pastor and yet it doesn't sink in. . . . As for myself, I will serve, if able, no matter who the pastor is, but I will say a handsome, outgoing, friendly, energetic, magnetic-type man is what it takes to get the hard-to-get people to participate. Whether the pastor is a handsome, appealing man should not affect people's feelings. After all, it is wrong to worship the pastor. However, people do this.—PARISH LAY LEADER

Maintaining the Parish Organization: Implications for Hiring and Deployment

One of the major reasons women encounter difficulty in getting as good job placements as men after the first couple of parishes is opposition to having a woman pastor from laypersons in parishes, according to clergywomen, women seminary faculty, and denominational executives. Some of this resistance is a manifest and blatant expression of sexist attitudes; some more latent and subtle. Examples include: "Woman's place is in the home, not the pulpit"; "Women are temperamentally unsuited for ministry"; "I simply can't conceive of having a woman as a minister"; "I believe that religious leadership has been given by God to men and therefore would not favor a woman as a pastor of a church"; "Of course, women are subordinate to men and therefore cannot rule over men in the church." Whether manifest or latent, blatant or subtle, such statements often reflect unexamined, taken-for-granted definitions of the situation that become real in their consequences for women as they encounter the job market for clergy.

Lay leaders also may be reluctant to hire a woman simply because they believe that the majority of their congregation opposes women in the pulpit. In fact, Lehman postulates that a major block to parish hiring of women ministers is not lay leaders' personal sexism or opposition to women pastors, but rather their fear that hiring a woman might upset other parishioners, with ensuing, deleterious effects on the whole congregation.[1]

People who have a high degree of investment in the church, whether clergy or lay leaders, are likely to perceive this era as a precarious time, particularly if their loyalties and membership lie within the so-called mainline denominations. These denominations have experienced sharp declines in membership in recent years—so much so that some within them fear for their survival. Dean Kelley, a staff member of the National Council of Churches and generally sympathetic to the mainline churches, wrote *Why Conservative Churches Are Growing*. The book became a religious best-seller, in part because of mainline church leaders' anxiety over their own declines and their concern to discover the secret of conservative church growth. It is into this threatened organization that the great influx of women clergy has been pushing, and some of the reaction to them must be seen in this context.

There are a number of reasons why some women clergy may be perceived as an institutional threat. The primary one concerns the tension between tradition and change in which all organizations exist in modern society. This situation is exacerbated in the churches by the strong tie in the minds of most people between religion and tradition on the one hand, and on the other by continuing organizational precariousness of American churches as voluntary organizations. That is, they are dependent upon the loyalty and support of members; but these members receive little social disapproval in modern culture if they simply walk away from church conflict or problems. Given a strongly male-oriented clergy pattern in the Christian tradition, a woman in the pulpit may be expected to arouse concern among traditionalists and perhaps threaten an already shaky organization.

Another concern often only half-articulated comes from the observation that churches seem to have a large percentage of women as their regular clientele. While it thus seems particularly appropriate that these organizations should have female leadership, it also raises the issue of the public image of the church becoming that of a woman's organization. For all these reasons, lay leaders, despite their personal beliefs, may fear hiring a woman in the pulpit because, as Lehman postulates, it will hurt the stability of their church.[2] Similarly, some lay leaders may fear that having a woman minister will alter the kind of church that they now have, in its particular style of programs and types of parishioners, into "something else." They may not want their church to change—even should it become larger and more financially stable in the process.[3]

In this chapter, we will investigate to what extent Lehman's findings are replicated in this cross-denominational sample through questions such as: do clergy and laity differ by sex in how they perceive the clergypersons' effectiveness in various pastoral roles?; and do lay persons prefer that some activities be done pastorally by men or by women? We will also examine the extent to which clergy and laypersons' beliefs about hiring clergywomen and promoting women generally within the denomination and parish have a bearing on actual practices and other predispositions relevant to the future of women in ministry.

Another area we will examine in this chapter is the degree to which clergywomen and men feel they are effective in their ministry, not just to compare lay and clergy assessments of clergy competence, but as an issue in its own right. While clergy's assessments of their own competence partially reflect feedback from others they are presently working with or ministering to, self-assessments of competence are also based on standards the individual has internalized from his or her youth or other prior experiences.[4] A person's sense of competence in the core activities associated with a professional status (such as doctor, lawyer, social worker, teacher, or pastor) is the central ingredient of what has been termed "professional self-concept"—the extent to which one thinks of one's self as a full-fledged member of an occupation rather than a novice or layperson. The higher one's feelings of competence in the core activities of his or her professional work, the higher the individual's professional self-concept. The stronger the professional self-concept, the better able the individual will be to deal effectively with difficult aspects of the work, withstand strain, seek out new experiences, and maintain commitments to remaining in the profession.[5] This last consequence of a strong professional self-concept has been hypothesized by Jud, Mills, and Burch to be important to clergy in maintaining their commitment to the parish ministry in times of stress and frustration.[6] For these reasons, it is important to understand how clergy evaluate their own professional competence in a variety of ministerial activities, and how they assess their accomplishment in their ministry within the last year.

We will first look at the lay leaders' conceptions of how competent their pastor(s) are in a variety of ministerial activities, as it has been found that the way the professional's "clients" or audience react to the way he or she performs in the professional role is very important in the development of a professional self-concept, especially among beginning practitioners of medicine, law, music,[7] and probably parish ministers as well.

Stereotypes and Preferences of Lay Leaders

Not only may professionals have their own internalized ideas about competency in the professional task, but their clients and audiences may have their particularistic ideas as well of what competent professional behavior should be. Stereotypes people hold about the behavior and appearance of the ideal professional may affect the evaluations people give about the competency of a particular professional.

Three-fourths of these lay leaders questioned are in churches which have had a woman in a clergy position during the past ten years (70 percent of the men and 75 percent of the women lay leaders).[8] Therefore, it may well be that these laity are less inclined to stereotypical thinking about clergywomen than the majority of laity in parish leadership positions. It is also likely that because of their leadership positions they are better able than most parishioners to observe accurately their pastor's work and be cognizant of how he or she is perceived by other members of the congregation. However, the top lay leaders of any church may not be typical of the average member of that congregation in certain key aspects. Indeed, a number of lay leaders wrote comments on their questionnaires that their opinions would not be shared by all members of their churches. This possibility is further underscored in that 31 percent of the women and 42 percent of the men lay leaders indicated that they were "theologically more liberal" than the majority of their congregations, especially, it can be inferred, in their openness to ordained women in the pulpit.

Fortunately, the responses in this study can be compared to those in other studies. A number of items used in this study indicating lay attitudes toward women clergy were taken from Lehman's S.W.I.M. study of American Baptist clergy[9] and also appear in the United Presbyterian Church Panel in identical or similar form. These items appear in Table 6.1 for our study, with responses divided by denomination and sex of layperson.

Three-fourths of Lehman's American Baptist sample in 1977 perceived that, for most persons, there was a general incompatibility between the image of minister and that of woman. Our 1981 data, as can be seen, replicates this proportion generally, not only for American Baptists, but for all other denominations as well. If these lay leaders are correct about what most church members think, then it indeed seems

Table 6.1 Selected Attitudes of Lay Leaders Regarding Women Ministers*

	Denomination																	
	ABC		CC(D)		EC		LCA		ALC		PCUS		UPC		UMC		UCC	
	W %	M	W %	M	W %	M	W %	M	W %	M	W %	M	W %	M	W %	M	W %	M
1. There is a general incompatibility between the image of a "minister" and the image of a "woman" in the minds of church members	74	61	73	81	74	74	69	63	77	75	83	83	72	60	71	66	65	47
2. When a church has more than one minister on its staff, all things considered today, the senior minister should really be a man	45	48	41	62	37	48	35	32	50	36	52	58	27	43	31	49	18	35
3. Women who try to be both full-time ministers and wives and mothers are likely to have emotional problems due to all the demands placed on them by both jobs	35	59	41	47	29	36	31	38	32	36	41	67	38	24	39	50	31	49
(N)	(22)	(23)	(27)	(32)	(51)	(50)	(49)	(47)	(22)	(28)	(23)	(12)	(52)	(42)	(72)	(71)	(51)	(46)

*% = percent agreeing with statement.

that women ministers may have difficulty in their parish ministry—or at least that lay leaders fear that a clergywoman may be disruptive, even if they personally may have no objection to a woman minister.

There is no significant difference in the total sample between laywomen and laymen in their perceptions, with 72 percent of the women and 66 percent of the men believing that "clergywoman" is a difficult concept for church members to assimilate readily. In several instances across denominations, *men* were more inclined than women lay leaders to feel that church members would not have too difficult a time accepting the idea of a woman pastor. This is especially true of the United Church of Christ, where laywomen were 18 percent more likely than laymen to feel church members would have trouble accepting the idea of an ordained woman in their pulpit, and only slightly less true of the Baptist and the United Presbyterian laywomen and men. Overall, it could be said that the Presbyterian Church U.S. lay leaders anticipated the most negative reaction to having a woman pastor, particularly in the senior position, from the majority of churchgoers in their denomination, while the United Church of Christ laity anticipated the least.

The difference here seems to reflect directly the influence of local culture, since the PCUS is located almost entirely in the South, with many churches in rural or small-town settings, while the UCC is more dominant in northeastern, urban areas. Southern culture is still strongly male dominated, with a premodern understanding of "women's place" that puts a higher value on women in traditional roles than is true in most other sections of the country.

Overall, 45 percent of the laymen and 34 percent of the laywomen thought that the senior minister should be a man. Much of this attitude appears traceable to the desire for congregational stability or for a stronger public voice for the church. The proportion in this study is slightly less both overall and for the American Baptists specifically than that which Lehman found, probably because this present study uses lay *leaders* rather than churchgoers in general. Lack of personal bias against clergywomen was also indicated in Lehman's study by 71 percent of laity who thought that a "woman's temperament is just as suited for the pastoral ministry as a man's." Our study shows even more in agreement with the statement, with 88 percent of the men, and 92 percent of the women lay leaders giving this response. Those who disagreed tended to be among those who believed that it was at least probably correct that "women who try to be both full-time ministers and wives and mothers are likely to have emotional problems due to all the demands placed on them by both jobs" (44 percent of the men and 35 percent of the women lay leaders in the present study).

These figures, compared with the 1977 American Baptist study, where 57 percent of the laity agreed with the statement, and the 1980 Presbyterian 50 percent figure, conceivably reflect a change in social climate; however, it is much more likely that fewer laity in our 1981 sample perceive severe role conflict for a pastor who is also a wife and mother, because these laity are leaders in the congregation, and hence in a better position to observe how women clergy handle these roles. Some laity in our sample did, however, specifically comment on the difficulty they perceived their woman pastor to be having in juggling motherhood and ministry:

We had a female pastor for three years. Her husband was also a pastor. She was well accepted but with two children their home life suffered. They left and do not both serve as pastors.

While our congregation has been very pleased in having a woman minister, she has been under stress with three children and a husband still in seminary, so we are looking forward to an even better ministry when they both become our co-pastors within a few months.

The only question I have about younger women in the ministry is the extreme psychological and physical demand put upon them when they have children. The demands of their ministry and the demands upon them as new mothers seem to be almost irreconcilable. My heart aches when I see how exhausted our assistant looks after a sleepless night with a small baby.

Concerns about the image of the local church, whether within its membership or in the community at large, seem apparent in responses about particular positions lay leaders found acceptable for women clergy. While there was some slight preference, as we shall discuss in greater detail later, for some "balancing" of pastoral leadership by having a man *and* a woman minister, the majority of lay leaders expressed a preference to have a man in the senior position rather than as an associate or co-minister with a woman. The majority of these lay leaders, 85 to 86 percent, say they do not have a preference as to the sex of the assistant or associate minister, though very few (less than 8 percent) would *prefer* a woman. American Baptist laymen were most adamant across the denominations in saying they preferred a man even for the associate position (36 percent). It was only in two positions or tasks that preferences for women clergy in particular reached over 8 percent of the total sample (with again the vast majority saying that sex made no difference)—minister of education and minister of music. Since these are roles frequently held in past years by lay professional women, it seems evident that what is at stake here is not the ordination of women, per se, but the familiarity of the public functions they perform in the parish. This theme is repeated in a number of ways. For example, men clergy were preferred by the highest proportions of laity in those activities considered socially "masculine," especially "working with a contractor to renovate the church," where 50 percent of the men and 33 percent of the women lay leaders expressed preference for a man.

When it comes to more private clergy functions, the distinction blurs. Correspondence of clergy sex with that of the lay person seems the most important explanatory variable, since the greatest difference in preference among laymen and women was found in "advising about a personal problem." In the total sample 31 percent of the men preferred the man compared with only 9 percent of the women. Thirteen percent of the women to 2 percent of the men, however, preferred a woman minister to advise them about a personal problem, the remainder claiming that sex of the minister was not important (67 to 77 percent). Over 90 percent of both the men and the women did not feel that the sex of their minister was important in either leading a pastoral prayer or reading the Scripture lesson. Nearly 90 percent of both laymen and women also felt that it was irrelevant whether a clergyman or woman visited them in the hospital or developed programs for the church.

It was generally true across denominations that laywomen were less likely than laymen to express a preference for a male pastor in any parish slot or performing any pastoral activity or role. This is in direct contradiction to many statements that laywomen, particularly those in leadership roles in the church, are likely to perceive clergywomen as threats to their positions of influence, and so to prefer men in the clergy role. Differences between the sexes in laity-expressed preferences for a man or woman pastor were most pronounced among the Lutheran Church in America, and then the Episcopal, laity. The lack of difference between laywomen and laymen in these two denominations may seem surprising, due to the very short time women have been ordained to full ministerial status in their organizations. Perhaps it is the very novelty of having women ministers at all that predisposes laity in these denominations to have little or no preference as to sex of the minister fulfilling various church tasks, especially since laity in this study are relatively unique in having had women clergy as ministers. One may expect that persons in denominations with little experience of women in pastoral roles would be less ready than others to make the fine distinctions about functions within the larger role.

Some indication of the potential conflict accompanying the appointment of a woman pastor may be seen in the greater congruence of theological position perceived by male pastors concerning their own and their congregation's stance, as compared with women clergy. (The tau beta correlation of perceived positions was .20 for men, .12 for clergywomen.) A slight majority of both sexes, but more clergywomen than men, considered their own theological position to be more liberal than that of the majority of their congregations (69 percent of the clergywomen to 51 percent of the clergymen saying their own position was more liberal).

This finding suggests that greater acceptance of women clergy will be expedited by a strong orientation toward what we have termed "church feminism," or the openness to having women in leadership positions within the church and attention to using inclusive language.

The Feminist Issue in the Parish and Denomination

While clergywomen may be as competent and as temperamentally suited to the parish ministry as are men, there is not any very strong majority among clergy or laity who feel that women should be preferred to men as ministers or in a variety of pastoral roles. Neither do many respondents believe that affirmative action should be taken to ensure that women are placed in pastoral roles in their own congregations.

A majority of clergy and laity of both sexes agreed that "more women should be ordained to full ministerial status in my denomination" (81 percent of the clergywomen and 59 percent of the men; 71 percent of the laywomen and 62 percent of the men). Only a minority of either group, however, agreed that "if a ministerial vacancy should occur in my congregation (or finances permit an additional minister to be hired) the search committee should actively seek a woman candidate" (thirty-four percent women clergy to 40 percent of the men in their profession; 34 percent laywomen to 20 percent laymen).

Comments by clergy and lay respondents on the latter statement offer a variety of explanations. Primarily, all respondents express a distaste for using sex as a factor in choosing a minister, either negatively or positively. Rather they prefer to consider professional qualifications regardless of sex.

The following comments on this point were made by laity from a number of denominations:

I do not think women, minorities, etc., should be selected for a position simply because they fit a characteristic. Similarly they should not be prevented from equal chances. There are very few positions that are filled by men or women best.

I feel the time has come when people should be awarded positions by how well qualified they are for the job and stop worrying about their sex.

Women are people. Let them not be given positions because they are women!

A number of these lay leaders further commented that having a woman minister has changed opinions in their congregations as to whether a woman can be as qualified as a man for pastoral leadership. But as illustrated in the following quote, most lay leaders would still not approve of seeking a woman specifically:

We are so pleased with our woman minister, and the growth her efforts have brought our church, that this position in the future would be open equally to male and female candidates—choice based solely on competency.

A major catch, however, is that a number of lay leaders, though believing that sex should not be a criterion in selecting a minister, nevertheless want a man, especially as senior pastor. The following remarks indicate degrees of awareness or discomfort that lay leaders experience with their own ambivalence on this issue:

Our married co-pastors are doing an excellent job in shepherding our congregation, with their youthful exuberance and Christian devotion. They share equally in the work and are accepted equally. Still, personally, I would prefer a man if there was to be only one pastor, even though I know a woman would be as able.

While I have no strong feelings personally and my Pastor is one of the few successful female ministers, . . . experience leads me to admit men are superior local pastors. . . .

I believe sex or race should not be a factor in seeking a new minister; however, all other qualifications being equal, and having experienced both men and women's effectiveness as pastor, I would prefer the men.

Even though I am a modern, moderately liberal, extremely active grandmother, who feels women are capable of doing anything in the church as well as men, I prefer a male senior minister. I do not even know why!

An additional reason some laity and clergy advanced for not hiring a woman specifically to fill a position is their belief that it is beneficial to the church to have a balance of sexes, either in replacing the present minister or balancing the pastoral leadership between the sexes. Interestingly, clergywomen also tended to agree with this "principle of alternation," as one clergywomen put it. Only a third of the clergywomen agreed that a woman should replace them or, as more interpreted the question, join them in the pastoral leadership of their present parishes. The general feeling seems to be that it is important that a church not be typecast as one that only has women clergy, and that on multiple staffs, ministry is more effective if "there is a balance in the male/female emphasis." Since multiple staffs are relatively limited in number, considering the total number of churches, alternation between men and women pastors appear to be the best compromise, even for more liberal laypersons.

An equally equivocal response, but for somewhat different reasons, emerged as to whether respondents thought their "congregation should appoint or elect an equal number of laywomen to that of laymen on the parish governing board." Although most agreed, with clergywomen assenting 75 percent of the time, clergymen 59 percent, laywomen 64 percent, and laymen 61 percent, comments given indicated some confusion about the meaning of the question. What happens if the governing board is already predominantly women? Having an equal number of laymen would entail reducing the number of laywomen to make up the required ratio in a number of parishes. Here, too, the question of selecting on the basis of sex rather than competence emerges. Yet there is obviously more support for the concept of giving laywomen more power within the formal structure of the parish than there is for affirmative action in hiring women to fill the clergy slots.

Part of this may be the difference in the minds of the respondents between temporary and voluntary positions like those on church boards and the more permanent status of professional church leadership. Apart from permanency, the main reason is probably the theological or personal preference for men in the pulpit indicated by those lay leaders who feel that tasks carried out in the church by laity should be allocated regardless of sex. Furthermore, there are a number of Anglo-Catholic Episcopal parishes in the U.S.A. which would not tolerate a woman priest, but nevertheless have the vestry (parish governing board) scrupulously made up of equal numbers of laymen and women.

The importance of inclusive language varies greatly within the churches, with clergywomen most strongly advocating its usage and laymen least enthusiastic. Agreeing with the item, "inclusive language should be used in church publications and services," were 88 percent of the clergywomen, 53 percent of the clergymen, 44 percent of the laywomen, and 36 percent of the laymen. A number, especially laity, indicated "mixed feelings" here, because although they wanted inclusive language used in sermons and prayers, they were opposed to changing biblical language, as well as "going too far" in employing awkward constructions.

The following are some representative comments from laypersons on the "inclusive language" issue:

If inclusive means changing wording in texts to "humankind" from "mankind" and eliminating the word "chairman" even when referring to males, I disagree.

The "inclusive language" disturbs my continuity in worship service. I feel included in mankind and do not need a term for women or feel the necessity to change Father to Mother God. Too much emphasis is disturbing.

I feel compelled to say a word about the "inclusive language." Please leave the Bible as it is. These changes will only divide us more, and we have enough problems.

However, for the bulk of clergywomen coming out of seminary in the mid-seventies, the use of inclusive language in services is personally very important. Nonetheless, as a number indicated, they would take care as to how they introduced inclusive language into their worship services, and not force it on their congregations.

Clergywomen were also far more likely than clergymen or laity of either sex to agree that "there should be more women in executive staff positions in regional and national offices of my denomination." Eighty-five percent of the women clergy agreed with this statement, as compared with 53 percent of the clergymen, 58 percent of the laywomen, and 48 percent of the laymen. Some may have disagreed or had mixed feelings here because they did not feel that women had the competency, experience, or predisposition to do this effectively. Others, however, of both sexes among the clergy tended to interpret this question as "kicking the women upstairs," as has in fact been the case with many women who were ordained in earlier years. To quote one man in illustration:

This is not a simple question. Women tend to gravitate toward judicatory staff positions because they are blocked from moving up the pastoral ladder to the larger parishes. I would rather see more women in the parish to complement women in staff positions.

Some clergy, especially women, interpreted going into the judicatory staff positions as "copping out" in facing the difficulties and challenges in the parish. As one woman minister commented: *"No! They should be in the parish! They should be out there on the front lines."*

All in all, however, most of those who agreed with this item were concerned that some clergywomen, at least, should actively seek the judicatory and national power positions in their denominations, so that the cause of women clergy might better be advanced and women provided visible role models in the denominational hierarchy.

Although these general findings hold across denominations in most cases, there are denominational variations in espousal of various items and in the differences between clergy and lay, men and women. In most cases it is the clergywomen who stand out as being the most different from any of the other three categories of respondents.

Fewer differences among men and women were found in their perceptions of discrimination against women. Although clergy were overall more likely to agree than laity that "Women, whether lay or clergy, do not hold positions of influence in this area comparable to lay and clergymen of my denomination," the overall difference between the sexes in each group was not significant. (The percent agreeing with the statement is as follows: clergy—61 percent women, 53 percent men; laity—43 percent women, 41 percent men.)

The more lay leaders espoused the perspectives indicated by the index of Organizational Church Feminism (Chapter 4, p. 31), the more likely they were also to indicate that they at least did not care whether the minister was a man or woman, or whether various ministerial activities were carried out by a man or woman minister. Their response as feminists was not so much advocacy for women clergy as a kind of gender-blindness regarding the occupants of clergy roles.

In the majority of instances, women lay leaders' degree of espousal of feminist perspectives did not relate to how they actually evaluated their ministers' effectiveness in the variety of activities listed, with a few exceptions. However, men among these lay leaders who scored high on the feminism scale tended to be slightly more positive in their evaluation of the role performance of women clergy in various activities than men lay leaders who scored low on this scale of feminism.

Clergy's own degree of feminism was far less related to their self-evaluation of ministerial effectiveness. There was a slight tendency for men clergy to feel they did better work stimulating parishioners to minister to those outside the church if they were inclined to be feminist, whereas this relationship did not hold for women. This may obtain because those who scored feminist, on this scale, clergy or lay, male or female, tended to be more likely than their less feminist counterparts to stress values of the church relating to the community, advocating that the church become involved in the community in social justice issues, and the like. The correlations between a strong feminist orientation and advocacy of the church's involvement in the community and social issues was stronger for clergymen than for clergywomen, and higher for clergymen on all items to do with church and community. These findings reinforce the expectations that for men, feminism is logically part of a larger package of social justice issues, since it involves a concern for rights and recognition of persons other than themselves. For clergywomen, however, feminism of this type measured here may involve personal job security and advancement, with or without a wider social justice orientation. Clergymen of a feminist orientation hence are likely to pastor churches where they also stress that parishioners and the church become involved in social concerns. They are also probably more successful in achieving such an outcome than those male pastors who are less feminist and less advocates of church involvement in social issues. There is a slightly less significant correlation between feminism and advocacy for church involvement in community issues for clergywomen. It is also true that clergywomen are less likely than clergymen to be sole or senior pastors, and hence to be in a position to push the church and parishioners very effectively into becoming involved with the community.

Clergywomen were slightly less likely to rate themselves as very effective in recruiting new members to the church if they were feminist. This relationship, however, was slight, and there was no relationship between espousal of feminist values and self-evaluation of clergymen as effective in this activity. What interrelationship there is on this item is most likely due to the relationship of feminism to a liberal designation, where conservatism often is linked to a greater emphasis on evangelism.

It is clearly better for clergywomen if top lay leaders in churches espouse feminist values. The data indicate that, while they may not be preferred over men as ministers, neither will their sex be a deterrent to being hired and accepted by these lay leaders whose values are feminist. The one area of concern is that the lay leaders may very well not be typical of the majority in their churches. Indeed, the more feminist lay leaders of both sexes were also those most likely to report that their own theological position was more liberal than the majority in their churches. The question that must be asked concerns the extent of their leadership in the churches. Would these more feminist leaders be able or even want to influence the other members of their congregations to accept their openness to the appointment of a woman pastor?

Another question that becomes important at this juncture is, which comes first, the clergywomen or feminism among lay leaders?

The Impact of Having a Woman Pastor on Lay Attitudes

Though this study cannot compare lay attitudes before and after having a woman pastor for the first time, it can compare the responses of lay leaders who have experienced a woman pastor in the last ten years and those who have not. A recent study by Edward Lehman, however, indicates that individual parishioners do change their initial attitudes of resistance to women pastors to acceptance of an ordained woman in their pulpit after the actual experience of having a woman minister.[10] Dividing the laity in this study into those who have had a clergywoman in the past ten years and those who have not, it may be recalled that only about a fourth of the laity had never been members of a church pastored by a woman. Yet these latter lay leaders, correlations indicated, were significantly more likely to want their minister to be a man—in the sole, or assistant, position—but especially as the senior pastor. Further, no matter what the pastoral activity, they are far more likely to say they would prefer a man than lay leaders who have been or are in churches pastored by women. However, for lay leaders there was no relationship between whether they were in churches served by clergywomen and strong endorsement of having women in leadership positions within the church, or a high score on the scale of church feminism. So, to answer an earlier question, it would seem that the feminism of lay leaders comes before the clergywoman.

Although the evidence here is not direct, it seems that lay leaders are likely to oppose clergywomen as pastors of their church not just on the basis of their own prejudices, but on whether they feel their churches would be positively or adversely affected if the minister were a woman. As church leaders, their primary concern is the welfare of the congregations rather than the advancement of their privately held values. In short, though it undoubtedly helps if lay leaders are of a feminist orientation as they deal with hiring or facilitating the ministerial role of clergywomen, it will hardly be sufficient. Lay leaders are going to have to be convinced that clergywomen will not shatter the extant stability of their church organization.

Lay leaders at any rate seem more likely to view women as pastors positively after experiencing a woman in this status. It may also be that with a change to a pastor of a different gender, different individuals within a congregation become the top lay leaders. Since previous studies suggest that many lay leaders (as well as clergywomen and men) do not feel that a church should be typecast as one that just hires women ministers, what happens to the attitudes of lay leaders about women ministers if they are in a church where a man replaced a woman as sole pastor? While again, this study cannot look at real attitude *change* among lay leaders, Table 6.2, looking only at clergy in sole pastorate positions, is suggestive, although the numbers are small and the data are not over time.

Assuming the lay leaders remain the same in the change of pastors, the data suggest that a switch from a woman pastor to a man may exacerbate the differences in attitudes toward women in church leadership positions among men and women lay leaders. Both men and women lay leaders become more inclined toward a man in the pastoral role, with men lay leaders particularly so. From Table 6.2, it can also be seen that both women and men lay leaders are very strongly less

Table 6.2 Lay Leader Responses According to Whether They Are in a Church with a Sole Pastor Which . . .

A. was pastored by a woman (in the last ten years) but now has a man
B. has had a man continually in the last ten years
C. is now pastored by a woman

(*Sex of Lay Leaders*)	A		B		C	
	W	M	W	M	W	M
	%		%		%	
1. Percent saying would prefer a man as senior pastor	31	69	55	60	11	18
2. Percent saying "definitely correct" that women are as suited for ministry as men	68	23	69	33	71	58
3. Percent strong feminists (score 4 on scale of church feminism)	44	22	37	25	21	19
(N)	(16)	(13)	(55)	(62)	(135)	(19)

insistent on having a man as senior pastor. They are also more likely to feel that a woman's temperament is just as suited to the parish ministry as a man's in churches now pastored by a woman than in churches pastored by a man consistently. However, in churches that had a woman but did not have a man as the sole pastor, it seems that *men* lay leaders become most likely to want a man in the senior pastoral position and are more inclined toward stereotypical thinking about a woman's temperament and ministry. Laywomen do not show anywhere near the same percentage increase in desiring a man as pastor or in stereotyping.

In fact, as far as negative stereotypical thinking about clergywomen is concerned, it seems that men lay leaders are more likely to engage in this in churches that switched from a woman pastor to a man than in churches that had a man pastor all along. The fact that women do not show any significant change in stereotypical thinking from one kind of church to another suggests that it is not actual negative experience with a woman pastor than makes the men less open toward women clergy, but that the switch from a woman to a man pastor has exacerbated sex rivalries among the laity—men thinking a man is best, and women opting for the woman. This interpretation may also be adduced to explain the finding that the most strongly feminist (on the church feminism scale) of the lay women leaders are those in churches which had a woman but now have a man, and the least feminist are those women in churches which now have a woman. The feminist orientation of men lay leaders, however, does not seem affected by the type of church.

Having a woman minister presently appears to be a depressant on women lay leaders *strongly* endorsing women in leadership positions in the church and non-sexist language in services. But the fact of once having a woman minister who has now been replaced by a man may anger the women lay leaders. Hence, they become strong advocates of church feminism—significantly different from men lay leaders in such churches. At the very least, these findings suggest that the effect of women ministers on attitudes toward women in leadership positions within the church, women clergy in general, and use of inclusive language in church services, needs to be looked at over time to see how stable any attitude change here is, especially if the woman minister is replaced by a man, as she is likely to be.

Clergy's Perception of Their Effectiveness in Various Pastoral Activities

A strong professional self-concept is very important to clergy in performance of their pastoral duties and commitment to the ministry as a vocation. One of the major components of a strong professional self-concept, as discussed, is a feeling that one is competent in carrying out the core tasks of the professional status. On this indicator, it can be said that on the whole these clergy are in good shape. On a series of items asking clergy to assess their "effectiveness" in a number of ministerial tasks and roles, few evaluated themselves as even "somewhat ineffective" in any task, distinctions being made more between whether they were "very effective" or "quite effective."

It is evident from Table 6.3 that on the whole most clergy felt they were effective in the core and most visible aspects of their pastoral job; that is, preaching, planning, and leading worship. The only areas where a fourth or more thought they were "somewhat ineffective" were in "organizing and motivating paid staff and volunteers to do the work of the parish," "stimulating parishioners to engage in service to others outside the parish," and "recruiting new members for the church." In the first of these, both in self-perception and lay ratings, women scored consistently higher than men.

Women clergy, as can be seen from this table, felt that they were somewhat more effective than men did in the core and visible aspects of their pastoral position, such as preaching sermons and planning and leading worship. Clergywomen were less likely, however, than clergymen to feel they were particularly competent in managing the church budget, though they were more likely to feel they were effective in teaching children. Thus even in the strictly professional performance of clergy roles, standard sex role expectancies emerged. There were no other differences of any magnitude between clergymen and women's

Table 6.3 Ratings of Ministerial Effectiveness*

Task Area	Clergy Self-Ratings				Lay Leader Ratings			
	Sole/Senior Pastor		Assistant/Associate Pastor		Sole/Senior Pastor		Assistant/Associate Minister	
	Clergywomen %	Clergymen %	Clergywomen %	Clergymen %	Clergywomen %	Clergymen %	Clergywomen %	Clergymen %
Preaching sermons	55	48	54	45	48	45	27	31
Planning and leading worship	67	50	59	51	62	54	46	40
Managing the church budget	13	27	8	5	20	31	7	17
Teaching adults	39	35	41	49	41	41	36	43
Teaching children	34	17	40	27	48	28	45	53
Presiding over a meeting or a large group	34	42	30	34	51	49	26	36
Crisis ministry	48	42	40	38	50	53	41	42
Pastoral counseling	32	29	32	43	48	48	39	39
Parish/home/hospital visitation	43	39	41	43	50	50	48	45
Organizing/motivating staff/volunteers to do work of church	19	17	25	15	36	31	24	15
Stimulating parishioners to serve others outside church	9	8	13	10	18	19	17	19
Recruiting new members	17	14	11	16	21	23	23	20

*% = percent saying minister is "very effective" in task area.

self-rating of effectiveness, even controlling for whether they were in a sole-senior pastor position or an associate or assistant.

Laity generally agreed with the clergy's self-estimation in that the laity rated the clergywomen as slightly (but statistically insignificant) better than clergymen in preaching and leading worship, and were 10 percent more likely to rate clergymen more effective than clergywomen in managing the budget of the church. This factor, linked with the information in the previous chapter about the placement of clergywomen as senior pastors of churches that are financially struggling, continues to beg the question of whether their ability to manage financial affairs or the situations into which they have been called is the primary explanatory variable.

Though it is generally true that laywomen tend to give higher ratings to clergy than do laymen in all areas, the nearly equal distribution by sex of our lay leader sample should avoid any imbalance because of this factor. Overall, these findings accord with Lehman's prediction that lay leaders would not differ perceptibly in their ratings of clergywomen's ministerial effectiveness as compared to that of clergymen.

The generally high professional self-concept of clergy is evinced also in their responses to an item asking them in the last year whether they "usually," "sometimes," "never or almost never" felt they were "really accomplishing things" in their ministry. Less than 5 percent said "never or almost never," and fully 64 percent of the women and 53 percent of the men said they "usually" felt they were really accomplishing things in their ministry last year.

In this feeling of current accomplishment, however, the type of church the clergy are in did affect ratings. One of the working hypotheses of this study was that clergy from backgrounds which are discrepant from those of most of their parishioners would be less likely to feel a sense of accomplishment.[11] However, as can be seen in Table 6.4, the preponderance of lower–middle or working class parishioners in the church was more important than a match with the social class of pastor's family of origin in the pastor's feeling of accomplishment. Whatever the social class origin of the clergy, it appears that most feel they are somewhat more able to accomplish things in their ministry if they are *not* at churches where most of the parishioners are lower–middle and working class. In other words, it is more the social class orientation that clergy have achieved through their education than their parents' social class that affects the way they get along with laity in their congregations. But what may be most important to note here is that clergywomen equal or excel clergymen in feeling they have accomplished something in their ministry, whatever the social class characteristics of their parishioners.

Table 6.4 Social Class and Clergy Feelings of Accomplishment

Amount of Clergy Fathers' Education	Women			Men		
	Proportion of Parishioners Middle and Upper-Middle Class			Proportion of Parishioners Middle and Upper-Middle Class		
	Two-Thirds Plus	Divided as to class	One-Third or less	Two-Thirds Plus	Divided as to Class	One-Third or Less
High school, one year technical school, or less	69% (of 140)	61% (of 44)	53% (of 70)	51% (of 255)	45% (of 93)	45% (of 71)
Some college and college graduation	67% (of 111)	56% (of 18)	49% (of 39)	61% (of 89)	62% (of 34)	46% (of 24)
Graduate education	69% (of 102)	80% (of 25)	54% (of 41)	63% (of 92)	68% (of 34)	29% (of 14)

Summary

Clergy feel competent in their ministries and are indeed rated as quite competent by their lay leaders. Although women pastors are not evaluated by themselves or their lay leaders as highly in managing the budget of the church, in all other role activities they typically equal or excel clergymen in self and lay evaluations.

However, the fact that lay leaders perceive their own woman pastor as competent in these various ministerial tasks does not necessarily mean that they want their next minister, and particularly a senior minister, to be a woman. The best that can be said is that lay leaders claim they would not care if their next minister were a woman or a man. However, the typical feeling is that churches should not specifically try to hire a woman, or that it is best for the church if women and men clergy are alternated (even among those favorable to women clergy). This attitude does not bode well for a fast expansion in hiring of women to occur in the numbers of churches open to women pastors, though the data are suggestive that having a woman minister leads laity to change negative attitudes toward clergywomen into positive ones. (The stability of such change, if the woman is followed by a man again in the pastoral position, is open to question.)

Lay leaders, regardless of their own approval or disapproval of clergywomen, may fear that having a woman pastor will upset the stability of their churches. However, as more and more women serve effectively as pastors of churches, lay leaders may be increasingly open to considering women. But this rate of progress may be far slower than the rate at which women are completing seminary M. Div. programs. Also, actual competence in ministerial tasks and perception of clergy's competence by lay persons may not be as important as is how the clergywomen actually get along with various types of lay people. This area that will be examined in the following chapter dealing particularly with clergy's role relationships with types of laity as well as other ordained persons in their professional status as parish ministers.

7

Interpersonal Relationships
on the Job

One young fellow told me that he always felt they sent the bottom of the barrel to serve this church, and when he heard they were sending a woman, he felt this was the pits. He said he never thought he could communicate with a woman, but finds that he can communicate better with me than he has with anyone in the past. It is really great when they can tell you these things! ... I find in most of the churches that I have served, it hasn't been men whom I've had the most difficulty with, but other women, particularly older women who might have been doing what I was doing if they had been born twenty years later .... I think that even these women who tear you down don't realize what they are doing. I think that is why you can forgive them. It is an inadequacy within themselves, I think, or a feeling that "I really can be doing more than I am doing."—CLERGYWOMAN

In the one church that I am familiar with that had a female pastor, the men got along great with her, but the women didn't. (She was in her mid-forties, widowed with children.) With male pastors before and after her, both men and women worked well.—LAY LEADER

When I first came as an assistant, there were a lot of people who really had severe doubts about having a woman and were prepared to leave even though they had stuck it out in this parish through thick and thin. But my coming to the church was the last straw. (I didn't know the extent of the opposition, only that there had been "some.") These people were persuaded to wait until I got there, and they ended up not leaving. Some said things like: "I don't know if you know this, but your close friend now, my husband—or your close friend now, my wife—was dead set against you and was ready to leave." That is how I really found specifically who they were and the extent of the opposition. But up until they sort of made themselves known, I operated in a kind of naive innocence. That I think was probably my greatest protection because my energies were not siphoned off.— CLERGYWOMAN

Earlier we used the sociological concept of "status" in referring to the position that an individual occupies as an ordained minister. In the different roles one is called on to perform in the status of minister, he or she relates to various people who form what may be called the minister's "role set."[1] These include lay parishioners, a senior pastor if the minister happens to be in an associate or assistant relationship, clergy in other churches, and denominational officials. The quality of the interpersonal relationships that clergywomen and men develop with these various members of their role set are important ingredients in effective functioning and in satisfaction with the profession. We deal with various aspects of these relationships in this chapter; and, in the following chapter, we focus more on satisfaction.

Relationships with Laity

Positive relationships between a minister and the parishioners in his or her role set are critical for effective ministry. In the role of preacher and teacher, the ordained minister's capacity to persuade or inform is greatly enhanced when there are positive bonds of affection between her or himself and parishioners. In the pastoral role, clergy are permitted to share in parishioners' deepest personal experiences. As with preaching and teaching, effectiveness in this role is aided or hindered by the quality of interpersonal relationships between pastor and people. Clergy who are constantly in conflict with individuals or groups within their parishes, however justified these conflicts may be, are likely to have difficulty moving towards realization of their goals for ministry and find themselves frustrated and discouraged. Indeed, as our data show, the more difficulties clergy reported having encountered with lay leaders and parishioners during the past year, the more likely they were to have considered leaving their present parish. Moreover, they were also likely to have thought seriously of leaving the ordained ministry. Because clergy-parishioner relationships are so critical to effective ministry, we consider several aspects of these relationships in this section. What is the extent of conflict experienced by clergy in our sample? With whom are they in conflict? Do clergymen and women differ in the types of persons with whom they have difficulty? How do clergywomen and men handle conflict? To whom do they turn for support?

Slightly over half of the clergywomen and just under half of the clergymen said that at least sometime last year they were having trouble with one or more lay leaders. At the same time, 90 percent of both men and women clergy reported that in the last year they usually felt accepted, liked, and appreciated by most of their congregations. Few clergy (around 10 percent) described themselves as "usually" in conflict with one or more lay leaders in the year past. Overall, it seems that though men and women pastors do minister to harmonious congregations in which they are appreciated, most pastors also have had recent experience in dealing with individual parishioners who do not like them.

Sometimes clergy seem to have consistent difficulty with lay leaders of certain age, sex, and occupational types. We hypothesized that this was the case and asked respondents how well they typically got on with several different categories of lay persons. Ninety-five percent of both women and men pastors claimed they got on at least "satisfactorily" with all types of laity listed. But, in distinguishing between those types of laity with whom they got on just satisfactorily from those with whom they got on "very well," clergywomen reported most difficulty with businessmen and executives, middle-aged men, and middle-aged women. For example, 52 percent of the clergywomen said they got on very well with businessmen and executives compared to 67 percent of the clergymen; whereas 57 percent of the clergywomen said they got on very well with middle-aged women compared to 70 percent of the clergymen, who reported very good relations with middle-aged women.

The relationships of clergy, men and women, with businessmen and executives is especially interesting. Only about half of the women pastors report that they get on very well with businessmen and executives, regardless of denomination. It is interesting to speculate why this is so. Perhaps church members who are male business executives may have some difficulty in accepting a woman in a position of executive decision making, even or especially in the church. This putative resistance may not be conscious on the part of the executives in the congregations pastored by women. One faculty woman reported that in talking with clergywomen's groups or with individual women pastors who return to their seminary for a visit, she has discovered a common, but ironic, phenomenon: the executives who are now giving the woman pastors a hard time in their daily ministry are often the identical individuals who had been instrumental in extending her a call. Male business executives, the woman faculty member noted, are often very used to "equal opportunity" if not "affirmative action" hiring in their own corporations, and so have less difficulty with the idea of hiring a woman per se for a good position than would those who are infrequently involved in hiring staff. However, these same executives are not typically used to having a woman share decision making with them or have more power than they do in the organization of which they are both members. As the woman's pastoral ministry unfolds in a particular church, she may therefore find that the men who were her supporters in the hiring process are increasingly opposing her suggestions and undermining the policies or programs she most strongly supports. These executives, frequently middle-aged men, may very well not realize that the sex of their pastor has any relevance to why they are finding her style and decisions less and less to their liking.

When we examined denominational differences, clergywomen did not differ much in how they get on with businessmen and executives. However, differences between men and women pastors did emerge more strongly in some denominations than others because the men in such denominations reported themselves as especially high or low in ability to get along well with businessmen and executives. For example, differences between men and women pastors in the Lutheran denominations were either nonexistent (LCA) or slightly in favor of the women (ALC), because the male pastors in both denominations reported *less* ease in getting along with male business executives than did men in the other denominations. Conversely, differences between men and women pastors in the United Presbyterian Church and the United Church of Christ were greater than those in other denominations because United Presbyterian and UCC clergymen described themselves as having *more* ease as a group than men in other denominations in getting along with businessmen and executives. These denominational differences are probably in part due to how much respect and power the male pastors and businessmen and executives accord one another in church committee meetings, and congregational and community life.

Businessmen and executives probably like and expect to make decisions and exert influence in organizations of which they are members. Hence, they will probably get on better with the male minister who allows them some input into running the church. Indeed, it appears that clergymen of the denominations who get on best with the businessmen and executives, the United Presbyterians and UCC, are far more likely to describe themselves as being quite "democratic" in their typical leadership style than the clergymen who got on least well with businessmen and executives as a denomination, the Lutherans. For example, we utilized a ten-point scale, ranging from what is described as authoritarian behavior (but termed "directive" in order not to bias clergy against describing their behavior by a term they might deem pejorative) to what is described and termed as very "democratic." Forty-three percent of the United Presbyterian clergymen, compared to only 20 percent of the LCA clergymen, rated themselves between eight and ten on the "democratic" end of the continuum.

A directive style of pastoral leadership, often called the *Herr Pastor* style, is frequently associated with Lutheran Churches. Our data suggest that such pastors are not as likely to include businessmen and executives in the decision making of the churches as those with more democratic styles. This may be the major factor in straining the relationship between some male clergy and business executives. This hypothesis receives further support when it is noted that the American Lutheran Church, the one denomination in which clergywomen got along slightly better with businessmen and executives than the clergymen did, also was the denomination in which clergywomen were most likely to say they typically used a quite democratic leadership style. This has ramifications, of course, for clergywomen and men in all the other denominations. The most obvious one is that, if the pastor wishes to retain the good will and active support of businessmen and executives in the congregation, it would behoove her or him to allow these parishioners some voice in deciding congregational policies.

While we noted that both clergywomen and clergymen generally reported being able to get on very well with elderly men and women among their parishioners, 13 percent fewer clergywomen than men reported that they got on very well with middle-aged women in the congregations they had served as pastors. Clergywomen interviewed often volunteered that competitive feelings they engendered among some middle-aged women by their very presence as pastor apparently were the major cause of friction with this age-sex group. Some middle-aged women may be threatened by the woman pastor who has entered their primary arena of power outside the home—parish politics and church programs—and has achieved an official status in the church above theirs. Others may fear that their husbands may like the woman pastor —too much. For this reason, one woman pastor related that, while in seminary, her dean warned the women seminarians: "Avoid the middle-aged men and work instead with their wives in the church; and never ride in a car alone with a middle-aged married man!"

Though in seven of the denominations, clergywomen did not get on as well with middle-aged women as did the clergymen, in three denominations clergywomen got on so well with this age-sex group that there was no significant difference between the men and women pastors. These latter three denominations are the Presbyterian Church U.S., Disciples, and Episcopal (86, 69, and 63 percent of the clergywomen respectively saying they got on "very well" with middle-aged women). In contrast, the two Lutheran denominations stood out in having the lowest percentage of clergywomen saying they got on "very well" with their middle-aged women parishioners (31 percent of ALC and 36 percent of LCA).

Analysis indicates that a major cause of these denominational differences is probably the relative youth of the clergywomen in the Lutheran denominations as compared to the others. For example, while 43 percent of the ALC and 45 percent of the LCA clergywomen are age thirty and younger, only 29 percent of the Presbyterian U.S., 19 percent of the Disciples, and 5 percent of the Episcopal clergywomen are this young. In fact, as Table 7.1 reveals, the older the clergy of both sexes (the table does not include denominations), the better they get on with businessmen and executives and middle-aged men and women. Clergywomen thirty years of age and younger are far more likely to have difficulty with both middle-aged men and women than young clergymen.

The middle-aged parishioner groups, particularly those of business-executive families, may be problematic to clergywomen, because they are apt to be the present or rising lay leaders in the churches, those who would have the power to give the clergywomen difficulty if they so chose. (Slightly under half of both the men and women lay leaders in this study were between the ages of 40 and 60). As noted, middle-aged men in business positions with supervisory responsibility might resent any clergyperson's attempting to exercise power in churches where they are lay leaders, but this is particularly likely for clergywomen, and especially a young clergywoman. Middle-aged women may also be particularly resentful of a younger woman who is both attractive and engaged in pastoral activities in the church that they themselves might like to have been doing. Also, younger clergywomen may not be as adept as older clergywomen in knowing how to navigate around such hostilities and jealousies. The data suggest, however, that, in time, clergywomen do learn these interpersonal skills.

Over the years, it is the rare pastor who will experience no conflict

Table 7.1 Getting Along with Types of Laity*
(by Clergy Age and Sex)

| | *51 +* | | *40 − 50* | | *35 − 40* | | *31 − 34* | | *30 −* | |
	W %	M %	W %	M %	W %	M %	W %	M %	W %	M %
Business executives	58	70	57	65	50	68	48	56	47	58
Middle-aged men	70	77	60	66	48	68	45	44	42	73
Middle-aged women	60	77	66	69	53	65	55	54	44	72
(N)	(89)	(300)	(99)	(208)	(127)	(103)	(142)	(77)	(113)	(33)

*% = percent saying they got along "very well" with this type of person.

with parishioners. In describing the kinds of issues that have caused conflict in their ministries, clergy most frequently pointed to theological or value differences between themselves and the laity involved. Fifty-three percent of the clergywomen and 40 percent of the clergymen cite this area as important in conflicts. Often these theological or value differences merge into power issues, for example, how much power the clergyperson should exercise in the parish, in what areas, and in what manner, as compared to the laity in the congregation. Also important is whose side the pastor takes in conflict over power between lay groups in the parish.

A slight majority (62 percent) of the clergywomen indicated that probably the fact that they are women played some role in conflicts and difficulties which occurred with individual laypersons over the years, but only 27 percent of the women believed their sex was an important factor in any such conflicts. Certainly, a woman pastor's age, experience, theological perspective, political and social values, leadership style, and personality, in comparison or contrast to similar attributes of laity in the congregation, may be a more important source of conflict than her gender. However, as several clergywomen noted, how much the fact that they are women enters into their occasional difficulties with laypersons is often hard to ascertain. Laity who object to a clergywoman because of her gender are unlikely to voice this complaint directly to the clergywoman or to those in the church who have hired her; instead, they often couch their objections in more acceptable terms having to do with her competence, personality, or style.

How does having a feminist perspective relate to conflict? Our hypothesis was that feminists would be more likely to engender conflict. Clergywomen, who by the Index of Church Feminism (see Chapter 4) are more feminist in their orientation, are indeed more likely than less feminist clergywomen to say that they sometimes have difficulties with laypersons *because* they are women. Whether this occurs because a strong feminist perspective exacerbates difficulties with laity, or because feminist clergywomen are more likely to recognize lay prejudice against women pastors is not clear.

Rejection by one's parishioners, for whatever reason, is painful. This includes rejection because of one's gender; however, being able to attribute an experience of rejection to the fact of being female may give women ministers some psychological advantage, as one clergywoman explains half-humorously:

> *There is one advantage for women ministers in the prejudice against women and the difficulties of breaking through that. This is that ordained women right now have a tremendous advantage over their male col-*

leagues. When they get the door slammed in their faces, or somebody gets into a snit at them, they can sit back and say, "Well, it is just because I am a woman." If you think about it, this is a tremendous advantage, because it immediately depersonalizes the whole thing.

Now, people's ministries are rejected for all kinds of reasons: Your hair is not the right color; your voice is not the right kind. There are thousands of reasons why people's ministries are rejected; and if you are temporarily in a position where you can tell yourself categorically that rejection has nothing to do with your intrinsic being, that it is just a matter of being female, that gives you a tremendous amount of freedom, and keeps you from getting terribly depressed and upset. But when three people in one morning say something mean to their minister who is a man, he has to take it personally!

The almost inevitable conflicts and misunderstandings that arise between pastor and parishioners raise the question regarding the degree that parish ministers should have confidants and close personal friends among their parishioners. Opinion is divided here generally, as well as among the clergy in this study.[2] Seminary and denominational staff frequently exhort clergy to develop their own support groups wherever they go, including developing support and feedback groups within the parish. Nevertheless, they caution clergy against being seen as "playing favorites" among parishioners. About half the clergy, but more men than women, said that in handling conflicts among or with parishioners, they would "quite likely" go to one or more parishioners for assistance or advice on how to handle the conflict (47 percent of the women and 59 percent of the men). Far fewer would go to anyone outside the congregation (with the exception of a family member) to get support or assistance in a personal conflict with parishioners or a church fight. If the clergy is not fortunate enough to have other professional staff in the church to whom he or she can turn, then parish leaders or friends in the congregation are sometimes not only the best option, but the only option. Having special individuals in the congregation who can provide a sounding board and support sometimes works out well for both parties, but sometimes it does not. The following three clergywomen's experiences of having close friends in their parishes to whom they went for advice and support are illustrative:

There was one couple about the second year into my ministry there who realized I was under some strain. We had an intentional covenant with one another, no matter what time of day or night that I felt the need to talk. . . . We talked about what it would mean for them to be that kind of support for me, that it might mean they would come under fire. You know the old stereotype: "Don't make friends with anybody in the congrega-tion." But we talked about that, and we talked about the good things that could happen and the bad things that could happen, and we made the covenant with one another. . . . But when I left, when this whole conflict thing came up (with the senior minister), they were very supportive of me, and it was difficult for them to stay in the church. He was the Vice Chairman of the Board and she was in charge of all the programming of the church, and they were both ready to drop out of the church. We had to talk this through, but they stayed.—YOUNG SINGLE CLERGYWOMAN

There is one woman in the church that I kind of feel that I can go and tell her anything I want to and know it would go no further. I know she would be sympathetic and listen and probably have something to say that I would need to hear. I have dumped on her, and she does the same thing to me. There are other people in the church that I can tell certain things to, but not everything. I do have outlets in the church, but I guess I am really struggling with that, whether that is a good thing to do or not.—YOUNG SINGLE CLERGYWOMAN

I have done what I suspect a lot of male ministers have done, and that is discover that you really can't share intimately with members of your con-gregation. When I first went to the church, I was needing a lot of support, a lot of nurturing. One of the women in the church and I became very good friends, and she wanted me to be her "best friend." She used those words. We got along well, probably too well; and I was too dependent on her, and she gloried in it. Finally, I realized it couldn't go on. Partly because, while I never told her anything I was to keep in confidence, we did talk about other things having to do with the church; and she spoke when she ought not to have. So I had to break that off, and that was kind of painful. . . . I think we have both done very well, because she still respects me. But we aren't nearly as close.—MIDDLE-AGED SINGLE CLER-GYWOMAN

Finding a source of support and friendship is particularly problemat-ic for single clergywomen, and especially for those in rural communities or small towns that do not provide other clergy or professional groups. We will come back to the subject of support for clergy. But at the moment, it is important to note that probably for all clergy, but partic-ularly for single women pastors of churches outside of metropolitan areas, more attention and discussion needs to be given to how and to what extent clergy can and should develop friendships and support groups within their congregations.

Despite some problems of occasional conflict with lay leaders, dif-ficulties with certain types of laypersons, and the dilemmas of establishing friendships with parishioners, overall both clergywomen and clergymen report generally harmonious relations with parishioners. Difficulties which do sometimes occur between pastors and parishioners befall women clergy only slightly more frequently than men. Considering that these women have far less experience in parish ministry than the men in this study, these results should be interpreted as evidence of successful relations on the whole between women pastors and parishioners. These findings confirm those of recent denominational studies of women ministers that indicate that, once in the churches for a while, clergywomen are well accepted by their parishioners.[3]

Ministerial Style, Dress, and Address

In their study of a small town in upstate New York, Arthur Vidich and Joseph Bensman commented on the high social visibility of the minister in such towns: "People take an interest in his public behavior and his private life and judge him on the basis of his personality and how he 'fits' into the life of the community."[4] While urban anonymity may reduce the community visibility of the ordained minister, there is still considerable interest within congregations about the minister's style and behavior. Learning to relate one's ministerial style and behavior to the expectations of parishioners, without at the same time compromising one's integrity, is certainly an important ingredient in a harmonious pastor-parishioner relationship. Based on the generally positive relationships reported in the preceding section, it would seem that most clergy in our sample have learned to adapt style and behavior reasonably well. In this section we look at three aspects of style and behavior that contribute to or detract from clergy-parishioner harmony: leadership style, dress, and mode of address or preferred title.

Before turning to the data, further reflection on why style, dress, and mode of address are important aspects of the clergy-parishioner relationship may be helpful. As leaders within a congregation, clergy exercise authority, or legitimate power, in their various roles. Jackson Carroll has called attention to several aspects of clergy authority that are important in pastor-parishioner relationships.[5] He distinguishes between the authority an ordained minister has that is derived from the formal clergy office or status and that which is derived from his or her personal attributes. He further distinguishes between clergy-lay authority relationships which are symmetrical and those which are asymmetrical. The more symmetrical the relationships, the more clergy and laity share power in church affairs. In asymmetrical relationships, either clergy or laity, but typically clergy, have more power than the other. If there has been a trend in recent years, it seems to be towards more symmetrical relationships in the church and in American society more generally. Finally, Carroll notes that the amount and kind of authority that the ordained minister exercises is to some extent relative to the particular congregation in which she or he exercises it. That is, a pastor's authority is dependent, not only on his or her attitudes and actions in the congregation, but also on what parishioners in that congregation believe is the appropriate exercise of authority for their minister.

This subtle "relational" aspect of authority often gets expressed by the way clergy and laity agree or disgree over the issues such as leadership style, appropriate dress for a clergyperson, and the way he or she is addressed. How clergy and laity view these issues may be taken as indicators of a preference for either authority based on the formal clergy office (more formal dress and mode of address) or a more personal basis of authority (less formal dress and mode of address).[6] Likewise, asymmetrical authority relations imply a leadership style that is both more autocratic and formal (in dress and address) than the more democratic and informal style implied in symmetrical relationships. Symmetrical relationships, however, risk becoming ambiguous and conflict-prone if the areas in which clergy and laity each exercise authority are not clearly defined or at least tacitly agreed on, or if the pastor has certain atypical personal characteristics, such as a woman's body.

In the preceding section, pastoral leadership style was discussed as we considered the way clergymen and women get on with male business executives. How clergy usually go about making decisions in their congregations (on their own or by seeking the opinion of others in the church) is one way they exercise their authority. In her study of women seminarians, Joy Charlton points out that women may seek to reduce the status discrepancy of being a female in an authority position, which has been "sacredly" and traditionally male, by advocating for themselves a more participatory or symmetrical view of how they will exercise authority within the congregation. Charlton describes how women, in preferring the image of "facilitator" as opposed to "Herr Pastor," are in effect "ideologically reconceptualizing the ministry" as a means of dealing with the status dilemma:

> *If just being a woman in the position is challenging, they can reduce the problem by in effect saying "I don't really intend to take over the male authority position." They understate the authority, and in addition express it in a way consonant with more traditionally female styles of leadership. . . . [In this way] they are broadening and redefining the occupational status so that it includes the traditional expectations associated with sex status.[7]*

Although there was a range in the way clergy in our study depicted themselves on a ten-point scale going from one, "directive" (making decisions on own), to ten, "democratic" (seeking the opinion of others), democratic or symmetrical authority ideals dominate. For example, less than 20 percent of both women and men thought of themselves as usually somewhat "directive" in leadership style (scores one to four); and only slightly more clergywomen than men described their style as quite "democratic" (scores eight to ten)—43 percent of the women to 36 percent of the men.

Several clergy noted that their parishioners might evaluate their leadership style quite differently than they themselves did, for two reasons. First, their predecessor in the pastorate might have been either very autocratic or exceedingly laissez-faire in leadership style, making their present pastor appear far less directive or democratic by comparison. Second, laypersons may unconsciously expect different leadership styles of men and women and evaluate the same type of leadership style differently if the pastor is a woman rather than a man. This differential may be especially strong in churches and traditions where even laywomen are seldom or never seen in top leadership roles. For example, a black woman pastor of a black parish said that, while she would place herself on the democratic end of the leadership style continuum, her parishioners would probably describe her as rather authoritarian, or near the directive end. She said she believed this perception reflects unconscious sexism. That is, if a woman makes *any* input into a decision it may be regarded as unduly autocratic, whereas the same behavior would go unnoticed in a man. She described an incident in which she made a decision that nearly precipitated a major church crisis of authority when she climbed up on the parish roof along with the male trustees to see how much repair was needed, so that they could make some decisions about the maintenance budget. The trustees were infuriated at what they considered her autocratic manner, remarking that she "should have let *us* make the decision." If she were a man, she would have been expected to act precisely as she did. Her behavior would probably have been noted as rather democratic, since the trustees were included in the assessment and decision making.

In our sample, lay leaders tend to agree with the clergy's self-reports of leadership style, seeing their clergy as rather democratic on the whole in decision making. The data suggest that men as well as women are adopting a more democratic leadership style in the parish, perhaps to accord with more general cultural norms in favor of this style of leadership. From our vantage point, this can be seen as advantageous to women clergy, in that the more democratic leadership style, as Charlton's analysis suggests, is more consonant with appropriate feminine behavior and hence may make the exercise of women's pastoral leadership more palatable to traditionalists in their congregations. From another perspective, the locus of pastoral authority is certainly clearer in the autocratic leadership style than the democratic one, and women may find themselves challenged in their leadership roles when using a democratic style more so than men. Nevertheless, no pastor is immune to challenge to authority. Research has shown that these challenges have increased in recent years for clergymen as well as women.[8] This suggests that differences in how men and women pastors exercise power in their congregations may not be overt, if indeed they exist at all. Both men and women pastors—and their laity as well—may at times experience some confusion as to how they should exercise their pastoral authority, and what such authority means, in this era of flexibility, informality and nonhierarchical relationships.

This informality is also apparent in clergy dress. Seventy-three percent of both men and women pastors report that they never or almost never wear a clerical collar outside of Sunday morning worship or other religious services. However, it should be noted that non-clerical garb cannot always be equated with a democratic leadership style. In judicatories of certain denominations, typically East Coast Lutheran and Episcopal, it may be the strong expectation that clergy wear collars at all public functions and while visiting parishioners, symbolizing authority of office, regardless of whether they are democratic or relaxed in other ways.[9] Indeed, the data on wearing the collar outside of Sunday and other services show strong denominational differences. Women and men pastors in the Episcopal Church and the Lutheran Church in America differ from clergy in the remaining seven denominations. While at least three-fourths, and typically over 85 percent, of the clergy in these latter denominations say they never wear a collar outside of church services, this is true for less than 40 percent of the LCA clergy (39 percent of the women and 30 percent of the men) and seldom true for clergy in the Episcopal Church (20 percent of the women and 6 percent of the men).

Whether or not clergy wear clerical collars, the style of clergy clothing is often of concern to denominational staff and to clergy themselves. At least one denominational study has put stress on appropriate dress for women pastors,[10] and a "dress for success" article for men pastors was recently published, urging clergymen to dress in conservative two-piece suits on all but the most informal occasions, as a means of appearing credible and trustworthy to those within and without their parishes.[11] Furthermore, clergy in our study were sensitive to what effect their clothing had on people. About 60 percent of the women and 50 percent of the men indicate that at least sometimes they consciously alter their clothing in order to facilitate their ministries on different kinds of occasions and with different types of people. Denominational differences here were less dramatic, with the Episcopal and LCA clergymen and women not significantly different from clergy in other denominations. Disciples clergywomen were most likely to alter the dress to facilitate their ministry, and UCC clergywomen second most clothes-conscious among the women. American Lutheran and United Methodist clergymen were least likely to change their style of clothing (yet 42 percent of the ALC and 44 percent of UMC clergymen at least occasionally did so).

A good number of these clergy explained why they did or did not alter their style of clothing to fit the people or the occasion. For example, two clergywomen commented, "Appearance is the first thing people notice," and "How we present ourselves affects our ministries." Another woman explained: "If I dress not to be criticized, I can deal with more important things." Clergymen also made similar kinds of comments on why they were conscious of dress. For example, "I don't want clothes to be a barrier to what I am trying to communicate." Clergywomen were 13 percent more likely than men to be very conscious of their clothing. This is illustrated in the following woman pastor's comment that "I strategize every time I change clothes!"

Even comments from those clergy who never, or almost never, alter their clothing for events or people indicate an awareness of the potential importance of how they dress. A few indicate that they did not change their style of dress on principle. For example, a clergyman commented, "I stopped dressing for people a long time ago." Likewise, a clergywoman said, "I dress the way I like, and if the parishioners don't like it, too bad!" However, most who never or almost never dressed for particular groups or occasions said either they couldn't afford to do so ("My income doesn't give me the luxury of changing styles of dress"), or that the parish or community dressed so informally all the time that changing clothing styles was not necessary. Said one clergywoman, "My congregation dresses informally, and I dress as they do. To do otherwise would be stuffy." And a clergyman explained, "This is a very casual community. If I wear a coat and tie, someone will ask, 'Who died?' "

The majority of clergy are similarly flexible in how they prefer their parishioners to address them. Only 8 percent of the women and 13 percent of the men prefer that members of their congregations use their clerical titles alone or in conjunction with their first or last names. Clergywomen are more likely than men to prefer parishioners to address them by their first names (68 percent of the women to 48 percent of the men). Clergymen typically said they do not care one way or another how parishioners address them. However, a number of women in associate/assistant pastor positions or co-pastorates pointed out that they do not care how parishioners address them *as long as* they are addressed in the same way as the senior pastor or any other minister in the church. As one clergywoman expressed it: " 'Pastor Karen' is fine if the congregation also addresses the senior minister as 'Pastor John.' " Consistency in the use of titles appears particularly problematic to Episcopal clergywomen in those dioceses where the clergyman is commonly addressed as "Father." The parallel use of "Mother" is not always popular with laity or with the women priests themselves. Hence, Episcopal clergywomen would typically prefer parishioners use their first names. Still they do not like the distinction being made between how parishioners address them and how they address any male priests that may also be in their parishes. Address can be as important symbolically as collars and clothing in daily interactions between pastors and parishioners.

We can make a generalization at this point. Although the majority of both women and men pastors opt for a relaxed, more "symmetrical" style of relating to parishioners and others, there is also an underlying strong concern of these clergy that they retain the dignity of their clerical status in such exchanges if only in order to have sufficient legitimacy and credibility to minister effectively to those they hope to serve. Clergywomen, whose credibility and legitimacy may be more in question generally, seem to feel more need to be conscious of how they and others use the symbols of their clerical status than do clergymen. However, even a clergyman who endeavors to introduce a very democratic style of leadership in a congregation unaccustomed to highly symmetrical relations between pastor and parishioners, may run into difficulty. This may especially be the case if, at the same time he is trying to change the mode of pastoral decision making, he is also presenting an appearance (through dress or mode of address) to the congregation which they do not deem appropriate for a pastor. Keeping some degree of consistency in the components of the "front" of clergy in their occupational role of pastor[12]—that is, being a pastor who acts and dresses in the manner expected by parishioners—is often a necessary presentation of self to ensure maximum credibility and legitimacy among many parishioners. One clergywoman, for example, recounted how she brought a church back "from death's door" (which sad state had resulted from her male predecessor's combination of informal manner and sloppy appearance) partly by her own strict adherence to her parishioners' preference for their pastor to appear in clerical attire at most functions and to "run a tight ship" as far as her involvement in church decision making was concerned.

This example again raises an issue of how far clergywomen can *in fact* deviate from parishioners' expectations of how pastors should appear and behave, especially since such women are already deviant from the normative appearance of a pastor as a man. It may also explain why there is actually very little difference between clergymen and clergywomen in self-reported pastoral leadership style, or in the way that laity view their styles. Women may find a democratic style more in keeping with a traditionally feminine style; however, where that style is not the expected one, they appear to be willing to adapt in the interest of harmony.

Getting Along with Other Clergy

(1) The Senior Minister

I think that sometimes in the first call for a woman particularly, paternalism really rises up. . . . The senior minister worked diligently at protecting me and trying to show me everything to do. With some things you have to take the risk of failing, you have to be allowed to take that risk.—
CLERGYWOMAN

There were some conflicts that evolved between the senior minister and myself which were very difficult for me to define as to whether in each case it was a woman's issue, because he wanted to be so accepting, that he was accepting in a paternalistic, protecting type of way. For at least a year there were people coming to him telling him things about me that he should have told me, or he should have told them to tell me, that he was protecting me from. . . . I have talked to some other women who have been in the associate's position and also experienced this. Yet when we talk about it, we have to ask ourselves, "Is it simply a woman's issue or is it any associate minister's issue?" The senior minister's concept was that I was beginning to learn everything, and he had to show me the ropes . . . trying to help me along like he would have liked to have been helped, I guess. He maybe had a lower estimate of what I could do than I had. . . . I got some support at the time from one man who was an associate minister in another church and was having problems with his senior minister."—
CLERGYWOMAN .

For many men and women clergy in our study, an important person in their role set with whom they had to relate soon after they began their parish job was their senior minister. Although women are far more likely to be presently working as assistant/associate ministers, nearly three-fifths of both clergymen and women have worked under senior ministers at some time in their professional lives.

Most clergy report relatively positive experiences with the senior pastors. At least half the clergy of both sexes reported that "they and their senior ministers spent an hour or so discussing the ministry of the parish" on a regular and frequent basis. Most of the remainder said such a discussion occurred "sometimes." Although over three-fourths of both clergywomen and clergymen said it was rarely or never the case that the senior minister was "overly critical" of their work, clergywomen were slightly more likely than clergymen to believe their senior minister was overly protective of them, not giving them sufficient critical feedback. Thirty-seven percent of the women reported this happened "often" or "sometimes" as compared with 27 percent of the men. On a broader level, it seems the major complaint against the senior minister was that he was too laissez-faire in his supervision of the junior minister and/or would not or could not teach the junior much of value. Less than a fifth of the clergymen and women said that it was often the case that the senior minister made good suggestions on how they might improve their preaching, teaching, or counseling. Almost 50 percent indicated that they "rarely" or "never" received constructive suggestions from the senior minister.

Part of this relative absence of crediting their senior ministers with much positive impact on their own ministerial skills may be that the senior minister's method of relating was perceived as unhelpful. As one clergywoman put it, "The senior minister and I had regular meetings, but you couldn't call them 'discussions,' because he did most of the talking!" Another alternative is that the senior ministers were not perceived as good mentors to their junior clergy because they were not considered as competent in various ministerial tasks as the juniors believed themselves to be. Also, it may be that the senior ministers were reluctant to instruct their assistant/associate ministers too well, less these junior pastors surpass them in pastoral skills and popularity with the congregation.

"Threatened" senior ministers appear to be a relatively common phenomenon, according to these present and erstwhile assistant and associate ministers. About half the clergywomen (51 percent) and 40 percent of the clergymen say that at least "sometimes" their senior minister felt threatened by them. A number of former or present assistants or associates commented on the perceived threat felt by the senior minister. For example, one woman said, "I was twenty-eight; the senior minister had been in the church twenty-eight years." Said another, "The senior minister ignored me for the most part. He did not want an associate, he wanted to run it alone." Similar comments in this vein were also made by clergymen. For example: "He was on the verge of retiring. I was the young whippersnapper"; and, "The church of one thousand members forced him to take an associate. He was always afraid I wanted his job."

Others attributed the threat they perceived they posed to the senior minister as part of the senior's general personality difficulties. For example: "He had mentally retired and didn't like people much," or, "He was extremely threatened by everything and everyone." Some clergywomen and clergymen felt that their senior minister was justified in feeling threatened by them, since they indeed were more competent. To illustrate, two clergymen remarked: "I was a stronger preacher than he"; and, "He feels very threatened by my popularity." Two clergywomen similarly commented: "My senior minister felt threatened because he was incompetent"; and, "We got along O.K. I did most of the work, he was kind of lazy . . . but when he found that I had mustered more support in the congregation than he was comfortable with, he would become very 'picky.' " "I know more theology than he would know if he lived to 100 years old. He was not too swift."

For the women clergy, the fact that they *are* women was credited by half as playing some role in difficulties which developed between them and the senior minister, but only about a fourth of the clergywomen felt the fact of their gender was really important. Even then it was not as important as other differences between themselves and their senior ministers. Comments volunteered by some clergywomen indicate that it was more often the senior pastor's wife who objected to the fact that the assistant was a woman. For example: "His wife was a major problem. She was manipulative and hated me. We had nothing in common."

Since the senior minister typically has a major if not deciding voice in who the assistant or associate will be, one would not expect the fact that the junior minister is a woman to be a major negative factor in itself in any conflicts which develop. Nonetheless, the senior minister, though agreeing to have a woman as assistant or associate, may unconsciously carry stereotypes of traditionally feminine behavior, which, when not forthcoming, provokes difficulties in the relationship. For example, when asked for reasons for any trouble that occurred between themselves and their senior ministers, women were more likely than men to volunteer explanations having to do with their "assertiveness" which irritated the senior. For example: "He needed to please. He was a fence sitter. I am an activitist"; and, "He felt insecure, not a democratic person. He did not like assertive persons." It is interesting to note that difficulties with the senior minister (as was the case with difficulties with laity) were significantly more likely to be reported by clergywomen with a strong feminist orientation to women's leadership in the church (by the Church Feminism Scale) than those clergywomen with a weaker or non-feminist perspective. The more feminist clergywomen were particularly more apt to say that the fact they were women played a role in the conflicts or difficulties which developed between themselves and the senior minister. A strong feminist orientation either enabled clergywomen to perceive difficulties with the senior minister more clearly, or, in some instances, actually increased conflict between these women and the senior pastors.

According to both clergywomen and men, the most important factor in conflict with the senior minister was "personality, value, or style differences." Only a fourth of both sexes report that this factor was unimportant. This observation points to the importance of matching the junior with the senior on these factors whenever possible.

Another important reason for difficulties in the junior-senior relationship cannot be readily corrected by such matching—that of simply being in the associate or assistant position. Approximately two-thirds of both the men and women clergy indicate that difficulties inherent the associate or assistant role played some role in conflicts which developed; however, women were somewhat more likely than men to say this was important in problems they had with the senior minister. Such inherent difficulties for the associate or assistant include not having final say on pastoral matters, or being perceived by the laity as a lesser minister—as one clergyman expressed it, "the frustration in being second cucumber on the vine." A young clergywoman described her "associate pastor problem" in ministry to laity as follows: "People do not know what to do with associate pastors. The associate pastor can make a call, and they still feel they have not been called on by *the* minister, because the senior pastor has not called."

Age differences, our analysis indicates, may be very important in junior-senior clergy relations, especially for clergywomen. The *older* the clergywomen were when they entered seminary (and hence when they first encountered a senior minister as an assistant), the more likely they are to spend time with the senior minister discussing the ministry of the parish, the more likely to credit the senior minister with making good suggestions to them, and the less likely to say they threatened the senior minister. They are also less likely to say that the fact they are women entered into any conflicts which may occasionally have developed between them. This finding parallels that reported previously that older clergywomen have less difficulty in working with middle-aged laity. Being older seems generally to enhance clergywomen's ability to work effectively with others in carrying out the tasks of a parish minister. It also seems to reduce their threat to others who also wish to exercise leadership roles in the parish (that is, senior pastors and lay leaders). Perhaps an older, "mother figure" in the pastoral role is less threatening to lay leaders and senior pastors than a younger "professional woman" is, since the leadership of elderly matriarchs (especially in religious matters) is not uncommon in traditional systems and families, while similar leadership attempts from young women would probably have a far greater risk of rebuff. In terms of equity theory or "distributive justice," the investment that greater age implies in terms of experience and wisdom may partially compensate for the pastor being of lesser status because of her sex in the minds of some traditionalists. Hence, she is more deserving of their esteem than would be the case with a younger, less experienced woman.[13]

(2) *Other Clergy in the Area or Judicatory*

An important group within the role set of the individual minister is other clergy, either within one's own denomination or in other denominations. Clergy not only relate to each other as colleagues (and sometimes as competitors), but they also occupy the same status and thereby share common problems and concerns. Therefore, the possibility for supportive relationships with other clergy, or even joining forces to meet common problems, is an important issue. A study of ex-pastors who left the parish ministry found evidence of considerable isolation from professional peers on the part of men who left the pastorate as a contributing factor to their leaving. They reported having significantly fewer friends among other pastors than did those who had not left the pastorate.[14]

We asked several questions regarding relationships with other clergy, both in one's denomination and in other denominations, and (for clergywomen) relationships with other ministers' wives. They were asked how well they got along with these others. Additionally, as a rough indicator of the degree of integration a clergyperson has with other clergy colleagues, we asked about how many other clergy they talk with fairly regularly (at least once a month). Finally, we also asked about involvement in colleague-support groups with other clergy.

Very few clergy of either sex said they did not have good relationships with other clergy. Two-thirds of both the men and women said they got on very well with other ministers in their own denomination; and slightly over half (53 percent of the women and 56 percent of the men) said they got on very well with clergy in other denominations.[15] There were some differences between men and women pastors within certain denominations on how they got on with other clergy. This discrepancy is greatest in the Episcopal Church, where Episcopal women are over 20 percent more likely than Episcopal men to say they get on better with other ministers both in their denomination and in other denominations. In fact, there are only two denominations in which clergy women report getting along better than the men with clergy in other denominations, Episcopal and American Lutheran. The reasons for this seems mainly to lie in the fact that Episcopal and American Lutheran clergywomen are not only more likely to report that they talk with over ten or more other clergy on a regular basis than clergymen in these denominations, but are also more likely to do so than are the women pastors in the remaining seven denominations. Since it is unlikely that clergy of other denominations would be more discriminated against by other clergy than are Episcopal and ALC women, the message here seems to be that getting on well with other clergy requires taking an active role in keeping open lines of communication.

In general, both clergywomen and men are more likely to get on better with other clergy in their own denominations than in other denominations. From one perspective, this seems understandable. Both men and women pastors probably have more structured opportunities to interact with clergy of their own denomination than with those of other denominations. From another vantage point, however, the possibility of competition for parish openings between men and women of the same denomination, given the difficult job market in some denominations,[16] suggests that women might get on worse with clergy in their own denomination than in other denominations. As yet, however, women probably do not pose a threat to the mobility aspirations of clergymen. Their numbers are too small to cause any reduction of interaction or collegiality with men on the grounds of job competition.

In fact, the women in this study were quite apprehensive about antagonistic reactions from male clergy in their denomination if a woman should get a "plum" parish more so than were clergymen. We asked what would likely be the reaction of male pastors if a woman were called or appointed to "the most prestigious parish in your judicatory as senior pastor?" Overall, 43 percent of the women and 24 percent of the men said that if this event occurred, the majority of male pastors of their denomination would be resentful, suspicious, or both. The only denomination in which women anticipated less hostility than did men was the Episcopal Church (35 percent of the women to 46 percent of the men anticipating resentment or suspicion). The finding can probably be accounted for mainly by the fact that Episcopal women priests are clustered in dioceses friendly to women, whereas more men priests in this study are drawn from dioceses which have few or no women, and do not want any! The denomination in which the highest percentage of clergywomen foresaw an antagonistic reaction from ordained men in the denomination—a projection partly affirmed by these men— was the United Methodist Church (59 percent of the women to 33 percent of the men). In terms of United Methodist deployment practices, this fear is understandable. Several Methodist clergy of both sexes indicated that other things being equal, "plum" parish jobs go to the person with the most seniority in the region. Clergywomen are simply too new to ministry to have acquired the requisite experience. An appointment of a woman to such a position would be viewed as a violation of the reward system and an injustice. In denominations where competence is not equated so closely with seniority, or where seniority is not given precedence over competence, a clergywoman presumably will have a greater chance of obtaining a "plum" parish position without undue hostility and suspicion from her male colleagues in the denomination.

However, while competition for parish openings can be expected to increase competition among clergy in the area or judicatory, it may not create more competition between the sexes than it does among clergy of the same sex. Clergymen may be more able to reduce pangs of jealousy in seeing a woman given the top parish position in their area by rationalizing that she got it through "affirmative action," than if a man obtained this position. Both clergymen and women may use their own sex as a comparative reference group in determining whether they are better or worse off.[17] In fact, other data discussed from this study suggests that same-sex comparisons with other clergy are probably more typical than cross-sex comparisons. Women are probably still too marginal to the profession of ministry to be used by clergymen as reference individuals in judging their own career progress; and women may be as likely to compare themselves to those who are in "the same boat," that is, to other women. Given the previously discussed inequity in salary between women and men pastors with similar experience, and the greater anticipated difficulties women will have in moving from entry level positions than men, there is a far greater likelihood that clergywomen will feel "relatively deprived" in comparing themselves to clergymen than vice versa. However, the woman who too easily (or too quickly) obtains a top pastoral position may find herself the butt of resentful feelings from both men and women clergy of her denomination. For example, a black clergywoman described what happened when she was made pastor of the largest black church of her denomination in the region soon after she had been ordained. She found herself the target of hostility, not only from black clergymen in her denomination, but also from white clergywomen, who were typically in smaller churches and/or poorer paying positions.

While competition and jealousies no doubt exist between clergywomen and men within and between denominations, overall the situation seems to be one of good professional and collegial relations between the two groups. Nevertheless, it may well be that these positive relations between men and women occur mostly in professional capacities, denominational meetings, and perhaps, clergy support/study groups, rather than on a more purely social or informal basis. That this is the case is suggested by the fact that over half the clergywomen said they got on at best satisfactorily with other ministers' wives.[18] For most of the respondents, "satisfactorily" was checked only because the clergywomen seldom came in contact with clergy wives. Several of the clergywomen who said they got on very well with ministers' wives indicated that this was because they took special efforts to do so. A number of clergywomen also mentioned that their good relations with the clergy wives occurred because they were once non-ordained ministers' wives themselves, and hence better understood how to interact with these women. A couple of women pastors married to nonclergy spouses commented that clergy wives may have as much or more difficulty with "what to do with the male spouse of ordained persons" (as one put it) at clergy social functions.

Slightly over half of the women are members of colleague, professional, or interest groups composed predominantly or only of women. Three-fifths (61 percent) of the clergywomen believe that women pastors should join or establish such groups, mostly for personal support and sharing of professional concerns related to being a woman in the ordained ministry. Women who are opposed to or ambivalent about joining such groups primarily indicated either that this was because they feel that excluding men is "isolating" and wrong, or simply that they find support and sharing in mixed sex groups more valuable. Others indicated that the mechanics of trying to get clergywomen to meet together or with other professional women could be more effort than it was worth, or even than was possible, where travel, time, and money are considerable factors in coming together.

Clergywomen in the Disciples of Christ are most likely to be presently members of an all-woman professional support or interest group (77 percent). Those in the Presbyterian Church U.S. and the American Lutheran Church are least likely to be members of such groups (21 percent and 32 percent respectively). Location and the accompanying ease or difficulty of assembling clergy and other professional women is probably a major explanatory factor: clergywomen in the Disciples are least likely among the several denominations to be serving churches in rural areas (only 18 percent), while PCUS and ALC women are most likely to be in such areas (57 percent and 44 percent respectively).

A dilemma is indicated in these differences. While it may be more difficult to bring together women in rural churches—so difficult that it is rarely done—it is precisely these women (especially if they are young and single) who are in most need of the support of other women clergy. In fact, a number of clergywomen who were only lukewarm about the value of such women's groups indicated that they had sufficient nearby women friends in the parish ministry and other social-service-related occupations with whom they could interact informally. Nevertheless, they realized that such groups would probably be very important for women in rural pastorates, for women who are strangers to a particular region, and especially for women who are new to the parish ministry altogether.

Quite a few clergywomen expressed the conviction that experienced women pastors should make an effort to reach out to provide support, assistance, and advice to women who are in their first pastorates. Such help is neither always forthcoming nor is it always accepted. Some clergywomen no doubt are "queen bees" who do not relish the thought of other younger clergywomen moving into "their" territory. Also, there are reports that efforts of experienced women pastors to offer friendship and assistance to newly ordained women have been rebuffed in some instances, apparently because of the latter's own insecurities and competitive feelings concerning her more experienced sister. Overall, however, there is far more sense of responsibility among these women ministers for the support of other clergywomen (particularly those new to the ministry) than there is hostility or irritation at having any such demand being placed on them. (It should also be pointed out that most of the clergymen who were respondents in this study reported that personally they would try to be supportive to a woman pastor in their area. Fully four-fifths of these men would be willing to be a clergy supervisor to a woman seminarian or intern in their church.)

Possibly as a combination of competition with other clergy and/or lack of clergy colleagues with whom they could speak frankly, a good number of both men and women clergy, but especially women, said they were able to obtain support from therapists, counselors, seminary professors, former seminary classmates, or other clergy friends who lived at a distance. It seems that the telephone can become an important instrument in providing support and reducing isolation for many clergywomen, providing of course they have some supportive colleagues to whom they can turn.

(3) Clergy Integration into the Professional Network and Formal Organization of the Judicatory

Despite the fact that women clergy tend to have been in their present judicatories a shorter time than clergymen (75 percent of the women to 40 percent of the men have been in their present judicatories seven years or less), they are at least as well integrated into the social and professional network of the clergy in their judicatories as the ordained

men are. Whether this situation is because women are inclined to be
more social than men, whether it is because they have graduated more
recently than most of the men from seminaries where the value of
establishing peer relationship has been more heavily stressed than a
generation ago, or whether it is because judicatory executives and clergymen are taking special care to incorporate new women pastors into
the life of the judicatory—or some combination of such possibilities—
these women pastors generally talk to slightly more other clergy regularly per month than men pastors; 56 percent of the women compared
with 43 percent of the men report talking to over ten other clergy
regularly (with Episcopal and ALC clergywomen being the most social
in this regard as indicated previously.) Also, although two-thirds of
both the men and women clergy belong to clergy support/study groups,
the women were 9 percent more likely to be a member of such groups
than the men. Furthermore, clergywomen are about equal to clergymen in being incorporated into the formal power structure of the
judicatory; only around 10 percent of these clergy have never been a
member of a judicatory commission or committee, and 76 percent of
the women and 73 percent of the men are currently members of such a
commission or committee.

Though women may anticipate a bit more negative impact from
judicatory executives on their careers than clergymen, they are generally as happy with their *present* judicatory executives as men are, and
seem to receive equal time and attention from these executives. On the
average, they talk with the executive of their judicatory (that is, bishop,
conference minister, executive presbyter, area minister) as often as do
men; for example, 47 percent of both men and women pastors had
talked with their judicatory executives three or more times in the two-
month period preceding this study. Likewise, there is no difference
between women and men clergy in how well they know their executive,
or how supportive or helpful this executive has been to them in professional or ministerial career concerns, problems with their churches, or
personal matters. Fifty-seven percent of the women and 63 percent of
the men said they knew their judicatory executive at least "quite well"
(about a third of these men and women said they knew the executive
"very well"). Lutheran clergy, both men and women, reported knowing their bishop least well of all the denominations, probably because
Lutheran bishops are in charge of much larger geographical areas typically than is true of executives in most other denominations. (This last
finding would have perhaps also obtained for Methodist clergy if they
had been restricted to answering how well they knew their bishop
rather than the bishop *or* the district superintendent.) Presbyterian
U.S. clergy (especially clergywomen) were the most likely of all

denominations to say they knew their executive very well personally. The PCUS "cousin system" described earlier obviously extends to integrating clergy not only well with one another in a presbytery but also with their executives.

Clergy were most likely to credit their executive in helping them with professional or ministerial career concerns. (The executive was "quite helpful" for 58 percent of the women and 42 percent of the men.) In contrast, 31 percent of the women and 30 percent of the men said their executive was "quite helpful" on problems with their churches, and only 21 percent of the women and 23 percent of the men said their executive had been "quite helpful" to them in personal matters. It is seldom the case that the executive was reported not to be helpful, but more that the executive was not asked for help in these latter two areas as much as in the first. While in large part due to the clergy's feeling that they have no problems in their church or in their personal lives which would be benefitted by consultation, it is also difficult to take personal or church problems to the person who is also to some extent their judge, and who can reward or punish them through giving or withholding support for their professional careers.[19]

Clergy were asked how likely they would be to turn to their denominational judiciary executive for advice or assistance in resolving a church fight or a conflict between themselves and parishioners. While two-thirds could envision at least "some possibility" of calling in the executive, only a third indicated they would be "quite likely" to discuss the situation with their executive should it arise. The remaining one-third of both the men and women said they were "unlikely" to bring matters of church conflict to the attention of the judiciary executive. Some further commented that they would only tell the executive if the conflict was very serious. As for less than crisis-proportion difficulties and conflicts within the congregation, to quote one clergywoman: "Never let the bishop know if you are having a problem!"

Whatever assistance the judiciary executive was or was not able (or allowed) to provide in resolving congregational and personal problems of clergy, clergywomen were 16 percent more likely than clergymen to report that their executive had been "quite helpful" in their professional career concerns. Across denominations, this difference favoring clergywomen (or not differing significantly from men) was most pronounced in the Episcopal and American Lutheran Church, where Episcopal clergywomen were 16 percent more likely, and ALC clergywomen 19 percent more likely, to report their executive as "quite helpful" than the clergymen in these denominations. Although these Episcopal and ALC clergywomen did not speak more frequently to the executive than the other clergywomen or men, they tend to know more clergy to talk with on a regular basis. Conceivably, they are adept at using the power/influence structure in their denominations more effectively than their counterparts; or their outgoing manner makes them more appealing to the executives; or these women's judicatory executives themselves have taken more trouble to help the women professionally than is the case for men, and they are concerned that the women have good support networks with other clergy.

Of course, there is always the possibility that, no matter how hard judicatory executives may try, given the poor job market or particular job requirements of clergy, they simply may not be able to provide much help in clergy career concerns. However, our data certainly indicate that clergywomen are typically as well integrated into their judicatories as are clergymen. Despite some frustrations with getting the amount and kind of advice and support from professional colleagues they may need and want, clergywomen are in large measure supported and feel supported by other clergy and laity.

Summary

We have examined a variety of relationships the clergy have with members of their role set. Although both women and men pastors get on well generally with their parishioners, a fact of parish life is that conflicts and disagreements are endemic. Clergy will not be able to avoid having at least some problems with laity. Like the men, the majority of clergywomen got on at least satisfactorily with all types of laity. However, the types that gave them the most trouble were businessmen and executives and middle-aged men and women. A democratic leadership style appears to be useful for both clergymen and clergywomen in maintaining harmonious relations with businessmen and executives, who probably expect to have some decision making power in any organization to which they belong. Increased years of living appears also to be especially beneficial to clergywomen in getting along with laity who fall into these three categories.

Laypersons can be a good and important source of personal support to clergy in their parishes and in ministry generally. There are always some potential difficulties in using parishioners as best friends and confidantes, but creating a group of supportive individuals in the parish can be an effective means of ministering to a congregation and to oneself. Other clergy in the community, both of one's own denomination and others, are also potential sources of personal and professional support. Clergywomen seem as able to obtain such colleague support as clergymen, even though the former have typically been in their judicatories and in the parish ministry a far shorter time. Judicatory executives also appear to be supportive to those clergywomen, sometimes even slightly more helpful to the women than to the men in their charge. Clergywomen may encounter resentment from clergy wives, and also from other male and female clergy, but especially if they are seen as obtaining positions or other rewards for which the others believe they are not qualified (or not as justified in receiving as these others would be).

All in all, however, relations with professional colleagues are good for clergywomen. Even complaints about present or former senior ministers are not unduly skewed by the sex of the current or erstwhile assistant or associate minister. Clergywomen acknowledge that the fact they are women probably enters to some degree in misunderstandings and conflicts with laity and with senior pastors. They do not, however, perceive their gender to be as important as other differences between themselves and their role-partners among laity and clergy, such as value, style, theological, and personality differences. Also, the assistant or associate ministerial status, regardless of the sex of the person filling it, can create problems both in ministering to laypersons and to one's own sense of autonomy and competency.

On the whole, these men and women clergy seem to be opting for symmetrical relations between themselves and their parishioners. They tend to avoid clerical garb outside of church services, do not mind if their parishioners call them by their first names, and see their style as somewhat democratic in the way they try to make decisions in the church. However, this rather relaxed style of ministry and reciprocal role relations with parishioners do not connote necessarily a laissez-faire style of operating. On the contrary, both clergy men and women are very intentional about their ministerial style, and many change their dress and, perhaps, demeanor to produce a good impression on people in ways which will facilitate, rather than block, their ministry. Women, to some extent, appear to take more care in how they present themselves as clergy because of their atypical gender as a cleric. Both men and women clergy are always to some degree constrained in their appearance and behavior by the expectations of laity, but women clergy may find that they have to be somewhat more conforming in behavior and appearance than men clergy in order to expedite their ministry with laypersons in their congregations.

8

Personal Life and Pastoral Commitment

*When I first came here, I thought, "This is my first church, and I am not going to say 'no' to anything"—a big mistake! There were times when people called me to do all sorts of things, join all kinds of groups; I immediately accepted. I let them govern my life. I began to feel put upon. But I blame myself for that because I allowed it to happen. Now I am starting to say to myself "Wait!" before I agree to do something, and I am starting to claim some time for myself. But it has taken me five years to do this! . . . I also discovered that if I make plans to do something on my day off with other people, I am more likely to actually take the day off, than if I just say to myself, "Well, why don't I go off into the woods today?"—*SINGLE CLERGYWOMAN

Women intending to be pastors have got to be more aware of the real difficulties in handling family and parish demands. I think a lot of women pastors who are trying to handle both family and ministry are fooling themselves and their parishes on how much is possible—like having a baby in the parish and assuming they are going to be able to carry on full-time right away. Such an assumption is especially unrealistic when it is the first church and baby! . . . I think the church is afraid to face up to some of the hard problems of family and profession for ordained women because they are afraid they are going to look anti-feminist.— SEMINARY FACULTY WOMAN

We are in separate churches. Although mine is a part-time position (since there are only forty adults in the congregation), it is some distance away from his church and where we live; and I am "it" at this church—so it can take up a good deal of my time. With two young children, we are kind of running a relay race. Scheduling is always a problem. "I've got a meeting this night, when is yours? . . . I wonder if we can get a babysitter? What are we going to do? . . . I'll be home at 12:15. If you can hang on and not leave 'till 12:30. . . ." Life gets terribly, terribly cluttered, particularly when one of you has to commute in addition. It might be easier if our parishes were side by side. For us, one of the really major drawbacks to being in different parishes is that we are not together on Sunday morning. We find that fragmenting. . . . We are very well acquainted now with the problems of having separate churches and are hoping we can be together in the same church as ministers eventually. But we are not naive enough to think there will be no problems from being in the same church.—CLERGYWOMAN (Part of a Clergy Couple)

In the last chapter we described relations clergy have with different types of people with whom they interact in their status or position as ordained ministers. These people make up their "role set" with reference to ministry. But clergy are also other's close friends, spouses, children, parents, or other relatives, as well as being their "own" person. These other statuses that clergy occupy also have their role sets or others with whom the clergyperson interacts as father or mother, relative, or friend. Not only may people in the role set attached to their status of minister make onerous or sometimes conflicting demands on them, but also their demands may conflict with those of the people who are part of the role set attached to their other statuses as family member or tennis partner, for example.[1] Clergy may experience feelings of anxiety, stress, or frustration if obligations put on them by members of one role set, or from different role sets, are overdemanding in terms of their available time. Consider this scenario, for example. It is a pastor's day off. She or he has planned a game of golf with a friend. The phone rings. A parishioner has entered the hospital for emergency surgery. And to cap it off, the school calls to say that the pastor's child is ill and needs to come home. The spouse has already left home for the day. How will the pastor cope? Such "role strain" potentially can be reduced for individuals if they can manage to arrange their personal and professional lives so that demands on them and on their time will not be too onerous or conflicting in content or scheduling.[2] Issues to be considered in this chapter are the ways clergy attempt to reduce role strain, their success in actually minimizing overwork and conflicting demands on their time, and the effects that their efforts at reducing strain have on clergy's satisfaction with their present position and their commitment to parish ministry.

Balancing Parish and Private Life

A problem in varying degrees for most clergy is maintaining some degree of separation between their ministerial duties and their private lives; however, this problem seems generally more acute for clergywomen. For example, only 47 percent of the women pastors in our study said they were "usually" able to maintain a separation between their ministerial duties and their private lives; and 10 percent more women than men said they could "*never*" accomplish this feat. Although some of the older single clergywomen said they did not even try to make this separation—that the parish was their life—most of the women wished that they could better manage their time in order to have more of a life of their own. The reason that many clergywomen report greater difficulty than men in juggling their schedules to create some time for themselves may be that women have had less experience in parish ministry than most of the men in our sample. As one of the clergywomen quoted at the beginning of this chapter remarked, it had taken her five years to learn to say "no" to overdemanding parishioners.

There is some debate about whether it is "easier" to be a parish minister if one is single or married—at least if the parish minister is a woman. There seems to be little doubt in Protestant circles that an ordained man who wishes to be a pastor is better off if he is married. The fact that 94 percent of the men compared to only 55 percent of the women pastors in this study are presently married may be taken as support for the near necessity in the eyes of pastoral search committees for a clergyman to be married. Although clergywomen in this study are far more likely to be younger than the men (46 percent of the women are under 35 years of age compared to only 16 percent of the men), their relative youth does not seem a very valid explanation for the greater likelihood of the women to be unmarried. It is probably true most of the men were likely to have married during or prior to attending seminary. Bock, using 1960 census data, discovered that "age for age," clergywomen are less likely to be married than clergymen. He accounts for the discrepancy as resulting from the greater conflict women experience in combining clergy and marriage roles.[3] Another explanation for the greater propensity that still exists for women pastors to be single *may* be that, unlike women who have never worked, or who have worked in relatively low-paying or low-prestige jobs, clergywomen have higher expectations of the kind of equitable marriage relationship they wish to enter. Data for women in a range of occupations suggests that clergywomen are far from unique in this regard. A study by Elizabeth Havens, also using 1960 census data, disclosed that among the working female population, the higher a woman's income, the more likely she was to be single. Havens attributes this result to the lesser willingness of the higher income women to enter into or maintain marital relationships they find confining or unhappy.[4]

There is, at any rate, no relationship in our data between the marital status of clergywomen and how easy or difficult they find balancing their personal and private lives. Neither is there a relationship between marital status and other general factors indicating satisfaction with life and ministry, such as feelings of boredom and frustration by the limits of the particular parish situation, or whether the clergyperson was considering leaving the parish ministry. While the total amount of difficulty or anxiety clergywomen may experience is not strictly dependent on whether they are married or to whom, nevertheless married clergywomen may encounter different kinds of problems than do single clergywomen. In the 1980s, perhaps the most striking phenomenon about clergywomen's marital status is that they tend to be married to other clergy. As reported in an earlier chapter, of the married clergy, 60 percent of the clergywomen in our sample, as compared with only 4 percent of the clergymen, have a spouse who is also ordained. When this situation is compared to other women professionals, clergywomen do not seem to be unique. Cynthia Fuchs Epstein reports that nearly one-half of women lawyers are married to other lawyers. She adds:

> The favored marriage pattern for women attorneys, like other women in male-dominated professions, seems to be what sociologists call homogamy —"like marrying like"—in this case, along professional lines. A similar pattern is seen among women in other male-dominated professions such as medicine, science, and engineering.[5]

Again, our data show no difference between women pastors who are single, married to clergy spouses, or married to those in other occupations in ability to manage time effectively or in satisfaction with life and ministry. Clergywomen in these various types of marital statuses may have equal difficulty in balancing parish and private time effectively, but their difficulty results from somewhat different causes.

Single clergywomen, for example, do not have the "legitimate" excuse of a husband or children to use in keeping overdemanding parishioners at bay. One single woman pastor reported having developed a clever escape by taking her day off at her vacation home, for which the church does not have the telephone number! Apart from such measures as this to protect one's private time, single clergywomen may need to take special precautions to have a private social life, since with *whom* they spend their free time may be a topic of intense interest to some of their parishioners. The single clergywomen in rural areas or small towns, on the other hand, may have difficulty finding any congenial individuals to socialize with on an intimate basis in their free time.

Married clergywomen are likely to have problems in juggling ministerial duties and their private lives. Married clergywomen, almost by

definition, are more likely to be in "dual-career" families than are clergymen, who are more likely to have wives who do not work outside the
home or who work only part-time. The married clergywomen, who, as
previously indicated, are younger than the clergymen, are also more
likely currently to have children under ten years of age than their male
counterparts. While we speculate that clergywomen may well be in
more equitable marriages in terms of allocation of household duties
between spouses than the clergymen in our sample, just the sheer difficulties of scheduling time in two-career families creates problems.
This is especially true when there are young children as well, and little
money for household help. Such a situation is bound to create problems
in time-management for the clergywoman, as illustrated by the quote
from one young married woman pastor cited at the beginning of this
chapter. Among those who had children under ten when they were also
engaging full-time in ministry, clergywomen in each of the nine
denominations were more likely than men to say they had a very difficult time when their children were this young. Overall, 29 percent of
the clergywomen reported that it was "relatively easy" to do this compared to 64 percent of the clergymen.

In balancing church and home demands when there are young children, the difference for clergywomen seems not to be in whether or not
they are married to an ordained man. Rather, the location of the husband's job seems to be the more important factor. Clergywomen whose
clergy husbands are in the *same* church are more likely to say they
had/have a "relatively easy" time carrying on a full-time ministry when
their children are ten and under than clergywomen whose husbands are
pastor of a different church (35 percent to 19 percent respectively).
That more equitable child-rearing practices are expected in clergy couple marriages may partly be indicated in this study by the fact that
clergy*men* with ordained wives (though they constitute only 4 percent
of the married male clergy) are more likely than those whose wives are
not ordained (and also typically not working full-time) to report difficulty in carrying on a full-time ministry when their children are under
ten. To be sure, some young clergymen may look forward to the
responsibility of caring for their children, no matter how difficult this
may be in combination with full-time ministry. However, some clergy
couples are in the situation of attempting to resolve both the strain of
full-time ministry and child-rearing by sharing a single salary as co-
pastors of a church. They do so partly in order for both to participate
equally and fully in combining ministry and parenthood, and probably
partly as well so they can be together in the same parish.

How well clergy are able to cope in carrying on a full-time ministry
with young children not surprisingly has some consequences for the

marital relationship. Both men and women pastors who said it was relatively easy to carry on a full-time ministry while their children were young were also most likely to say that their spouse was "never or rarely resentful" of the time and energy they invested in their ministerial work.

As far as this last indicator of marital harmony is concerned, it appears generally to be the case that clergywomen are more likely to have spouses who are understanding and supportive of their careers than are the clergymen. About two-thirds (68 percent) of the married clergywomen say that their spouses are "never or rarely resentful" compared to only about a half (48 percent) of the clergymen. A good part of the reason clergywomen have more understanding spouses is that they are far more likely to be part of a clergy couple than clergymen. And, as can be observed in Table 8.1, women married to ordained men are 18 percent more likely than women married to non-ordained men to report that they have very understanding husbands who were "never or rarely resentful of the time and energy" they put into ministerial work. Whether or not clergymen have an ordained wife apparently has no effect on whether they perceive their wives as resentful of the time they devote to their ministry; however, the numbers of men with clergy wives in the sample are really too few to make statistically reliable judgments. Among the clergy married to a nonordained spouse, women are only slightly more likely than clergymen to believe their spouses are almost never resentful of the time they devote to ministerial work. It is clear that marital homogamy, choosing a spouse with the same profession, is benefical to clergywomen in terms of allieviating some role strain and conflict. This is not, however, to infer that clergy couple marriages are without conflict or scheduling difficulties.

Dual-career families, whether clergy couples or not, have economic, scheduling, and other problems having to do with balancing career and

Table 8.1 Spouse Resentment of Ministry

"Overall, how resentful is your spouse of the time and energy you invest in your ministerial work?"	Spouse Not Ordained		Spouse Ordained (Clergy Couple)	
	Women %	Men %	Women %	Men %
Never or rarely resentful	57	49	75	48
Sometimes resentful	39	47	22	47
Frequently resentful	4	4	3	5
Total	100	100	100	100
(N)	(134)	(488)	(199)	(19)

family life that do not exist to the same degree and kind in the more traditional marriages where the wife remains in the home. Role strain from sheer overload of time commitments, and from conflicts in obligations arising from career, family, or both has been reported as endemic in many dual career families involved in secular occupations.[6] At the same time, dual-career marriages may be as happy and stable as more traditional marriages. Since clergy couples are such a recent phenomenon in any significant numbers, there is insufficient history as yet to say whether generally, or in particular denominations, these marriages are more or less stable than when one of the partners is not working or working in a secular occupation. This study provides no evidence that clergy couple marriages are less happy and stable than other clergy marriages. Only 14 percent of the total sample had been divorced, 91 clergywomen and 80 clergymen. A number of women volunteered that they had been divorced before they began seminary, and this may well be the case for most of the divorced clergywomen. For example, of those divorced, 73 percent of the clergywomen and 51 percent of the clergymen said their divorce was not at all related to their work as ministers, either to the time that it requires or the nature of the job. Whatever the cause of the divorce, the consequences of divorce are felt by about a third of the divorced clergy to have been detrimental, especially in their ability to get another parish call or appointment. Divorced clergy who have custody of young children may find parishes particularly resistant to hiring them. As an indication that this is not solely a problem for women, one divorced clergyman, who had custody of his eight-year-old son, complained that his "refusal to put in 100 hours a week, so I could be home with my kid, led twelve families to leave the church!"

In addition to clergy's satisfaction with their own ways of working out marriage, family, and career relationships, we were interested in how parishioners viewed these relationships (as perceived by the clergy). Among clergy with working spouses, clergywomen are more likely to have spouses who are top professionals and business executives than is true for clergymen, whose spouses are more likely to be lower status professionals and clerical workers. Also, clergywomen, as we have noted, are far more likely to have spouses who are ordained than are clergymen. It is perhaps for these reasons that clergywomen are more likely than the men to believe that their parishioners respect them more because of their spouse's occupation (57 percent of the women to 37 percent of the men). Clergymen, on the other hand, are more likely to say their spouse's occupation does not affect their parishioner's opinion of them (60 percent of the men to 33 percent of the women). The spouses of clergywomen tend to be less active in their churches than the spouses of clergymen; for example, 27 percent of the women's spouses are "rather inactive" in their churches compared to only 4 percent of the spouses of the men. However, overall, clergywomen were only slightly less likely to report that parishioners are satisfied with the degree of their spouse's participation in their church than were clergymen.

From comments made by the clergy, it seems that generally clergy see parishioners as expecting more from the spouse who is a wife than one who is a husband. Also, about a third of the clergywomen's husbands were pastors of a different church from their wife, which no doubt makes their non-attendance at their wives' Sunday services understandable. One of the women quoted at the beginning of this chapter commented on the fact that she and her husband did not like their inability to be together on Sunday mornings and at other church affairs because they were serving different congregations. This sentiment was echoed by other clergy couples included in this study. Clergywomen whose husbands had responsibilities in another church frequently also volunteered that, not only did they tend to be more active in their husbands' churches than their husbands were in theirs, but their participation in their husbands' churches was more expected of them by the parishioners there than vice versa. The following comments of two clergywomen reflect this:

> My husband is a minister in another church, and although he is relatively inactive in my church, my parishioners do not seem to mind. They relate to me as a single person overall, but are glad to see him when he comes to non-Sunday activities. He has more negative reponse from his church about my not being involved there!

> Before we got this church together, he was a minister of one church and I another. He was inactive in my church; they seldom saw him. I was more active in his church, and I resented that. My parishioners didn't think about it—they did not seem to care. It was more of an issue for me.

Some of the problems for clergy couples of being together in the same church are often financial, especially if they are sharing one or one and a half positions. Also there is at least the potential difficulty that one of the "team," namely the woman pastor, will be seen as the lesser minister, as illustrated in the following clergywoman's comment:

> Part of the danger of clergy couples answering one call as we did, is that people will think of the woman as the "pastor's wife." I am pregnant, and I know that a question in some of the people's minds is "How can she be a mother and a pastor?" Most respect and approve of my husband, but some question his judgment for allowing me to be co-pastor.

Difficulties of this nature, plus potential conflict over whose ideas should prevail in particular aspects of parish planning, and also the possibility of too much "togetherness" sometimes arise for clergy couples who function as co-pastors of the same parish. However, they seem to handle these problems without undue stress. A clergywoman suggests that she is better able now to handle these particular problems of a co-pastorate than she was when she and her spouse were new to the ordained ministry:

> *There was a time when . . . I would have gotten very brusque and very upset with people calling the house wanting to "talk to Father, please." That really would make me angry. But I think that over the past few years, I have learned a lot about how people respond to their clergy. Different people respond in different ways, different people have different needs, and that is one of the strengths of having more than one ordained person on the staff of a church anyway. . . . We enjoy different aspects of parish life, we have different approaches, different ways of thinking about things . . . instead of putting a lot of effort and energy into what we don't like to do, we can divide it. . . . We don't agree about everything either, so there will be times when we will be fighting with each other . . . but we can also share. . . .*
>
> *People project a whole lot of stuff on you just because you happen to be ordained. Most of us walk around with a little cloud of stuff that doesn't belong to us at all. . . . What is essential is that you hold on to your own identity. . . . But if you are somebody who has a hard time dealing with other people's images and projections, one of the things that would make it easier, I would expect, would be to make sure never to work in the same parish with your spouse, because if you start to believe what other people perceive you to be or your spouse to be, then you get in terrible difficulties.*

As one woman seminary professor put it, the important thing for clergy couples is that they not "go off idealistically into the sunset of team ministry, not understanding or ready for possible conflicts, resistances, and low income." Whether married or single, clergywomen need to beware that they not fall victim to a "superwoman complex" which, as a United Methodist study of clergywomen described it "is an insidious, creeping kind of phenomenon that often invades personalities without one being aware of it."[7]

It seems to be especially important for clergywomen to be able to maintain a separation between their ministerial duties and their private lives, even if, on the whole, they experience more difficulty in doing this than clergymen. For clergywomen, but not for men, there is a significant correlation between difficulty in making this separation and feelings of loneliness and isolation. Furthermore, for clergywomen, this relationship holds regardless of whether they are single, married to a man who has a secular job, or part of a clergy couple. It holds also whether the clergywomen live in a rural area, town, small city, large metropolitan suburb, or a large city. Women clergy, being so relatively new and unique to the congregational scene, are probably observed more closely than their male counterparts, and they are aware of being in the "fishbowl." Erving Goffman describes people in a variety of occupations as being performers. They manipulate their "appearance" and "manner" consistent with how they believe ideally they are expected to behave, especially when they are being observed by their clients or other publics.[8] Being always "on stage" can be tiring and very isolating. The woman pastor who has difficulty making a separation between her ministerial duties and personal life may well feel as if she is always "on stage," that she must constantly behave as a pastor is expected to, and cannot really be herself.

There are other correlates and causes of feelings of isolation and loneliness expressed by clergywomen. To these we now turn.

The Problems of Loneliness

Feelings of loneliness and isolation are at least an occasional problem for slightly over half of all clergy in the study. Sixty-one percent of the women and 55 percent of the men indicate that they were at least "sometimes" lonely and felt isolated during the last year. While this was a regular state of affairs for only 14 percent of the clergywomen and 6 percent of the men, this leaves a slight majority who are sometimes lonely. Such an experience may have negative consequences for their ministry. As we note below, feelings of loneliness—especially if accompanied by depression about the particular congregation being served—can lead the clergyman or woman to think seriously not only of leaving his or her present parish, but also the parish ministry altogether.

Unfortunately, the structural panacea most frequently used to deal with clergy isolation—the formation of clergy study-support groups and interactions with other clergy on an informal basis—appears to have little effect on whether or not these pastors felt lonely and isolated. Of course, the number of clergy one interacts with regularly each month, or whether one belongs to a regularly meeting clergy group, says nothing about the quality of the support provided through these relationships. There may be certain kinds of clergy colleague groups or study groups that indeed assist in reducing isolation and loneliness for their members; however, our broad measures of these groups did not show them to be very effective. Similarly, neither the total number of women clergy of one's denomination in the regional judicatory, nor the number of women clergy talked with each month, nor whether the clergywomen were members of an ongoing group composed predominantly of women, had any significant effect in reducing women pastors' sense of isolation. These are areas needing further study in greater depth than we have been able to provide.

Clergywomen, who are still more rare in pastorates than clergymen, will have greater visibility than the men and feel greater pressure (from themselves or from others) to "perform" well as parish ministers. The rarity of clergywomen gives them a "token" status in many judicatories. As Rosabeth Moss Kanter argues for "token" women in general, this status may lead other clergy to set them apart by exaggerating the differences between clergywomen and clergymen, applying all manner of stereotypes, which Kanter theorizes leads to isolation of the "token" woman.[9] Of course, the number of other clergywomen of the particular denomination in any judictory never approaches the roughly 40 percent of women necessary to be a "tilted" group in Kanter's theory, in which the negative effects of tokenism are reduced. However, there may also be a flaw in Kanter's hypothesis that the negative effects of tokenism can be reduced by an increase in numbers of those in the "token status." Cynthia Fuchs Epstein suggests that increasing numbers of women in male-dominated professions may simply lead to greater toleration of women by the male establishment, but not true acceptance of them, especially not acceptance into the power positions within the particular profession.[10] This interpretation helps to explain why the numbers of clergywomen in the judicatory had no relationship to other effects of "tokenism" that we suspected might be the case, including: how easy or difficult it was for the clergywomen to maintain a separation between their ministerial duties and private life; whether or not women were satisfied with their present position; whether or not they felt they were really accomplishing things in their ministry; or whether or not they felt lonely and isolated. The number of women in the judicatory made no real difference in relieving any of these concerns.

Clergy loneliness and feelings of isolation were dependent in part on three very concrete factors: where clergy lived, whether or not they were married, and their age (or how recently they had been ordained). Both older male and female pastors were significantly less likely to feel lonely and isolated than the younger pastors of either gender, regardless of marital status. Part of this is probably the greater experience of older clergy in finding supportive friends and effectively managing their professional and personal lives. Single clergy who have never been married are the loneliest clergy of all, lonelier even than the widowed and the divorced. They tend to be the youngest clergy, as well. Younger age and singleness reinforce each other in producing loneliness. Marriage per se is not as important in reducing loneliness as the amount of spouse support. For both men and women, the loneliest among the married clergy were those whose spouses tended to resent the amount of time they devoted to their pastoral work. Whether or not their spouse was ordained had no effect on how lonely clergywomen were.

Marriage is, however, a more important buffer in itself against clergy feelings of isolation in different types of locations. Clergy in rural areas were lonelier than in any other place, and least lonely if their churches were located in a large city. However, further analysis showed that there was almost no difference between married clergy in rural churches and those in city churches in loneliness and feelings of isolation. For both, marriage reduced the isolation. Church location was of primary importance for the never-married clergy, especially the younger ones. These young, unmarried women and men were considerably (25 to 28 percent) more likely to feel lonely and isolated if their congregations were located in rural rather than urban areas. This situation was especially true for the young unmarried clergywomen in this study. One can infer from the data that it is better to send older widows or young married clergywomen (particularly those who are part of clergy couples) to the rural pastorate, than to send young single women. Not only is the young woman likely to find it difficult to escape close scrutiny in all aspects of her professional and private life, but her social life will be restricted because of a greater difficulty of finding close, supportive friends with whom she can be herself.

It is still possible for clergy to be lonely and isolated in their parishes, regardless of marital status, age, or location, depending in great part on how satisfied they are with their ministry in the particular parish. Using multiple regression analysis, we examined the relative effects of a number of factors associated with feelings of isolation among clergy. The analysis reveals that those factors discussed above are of some importance in either fostering or reducing isolation, particularly for clergywomen; however, of greatest importance is the degree of boredom and frustration with the limits of one's particular parish job. Young, single clergywomen who are bored and dissatisfied with the present parish are especially likely to feel lonely and isolated if they also anticipate that their judicatory executive will not help them to find another position.

Whether loneliness comes before, after, or develops in conjunction with frustration and dissatisfaction with present pastoral position cannot be clearly determined from our data. However, an additional regression analysis shows that loneliness, feelings of non-accomplishment in ministry, boredom and frustration with the limits of one's particular parish, and difficulty in getting one's ideas supported by the church's governing board, are among the most important factors contributing to clergy dissatisfaction with their present ministerial position. There is no difference for men and women. Ease of maintaining a separation between their ministerial duties and private lives is not significantly related to satisfaction with the particular parish. It is only when an inability to make this separation results in, or is associated with, loneliness that clergy—especially women—are dissatisfied with their present parish. Any one or combination of these reasons that leads clergy to be dissatisfied also leads them to want to leave the present parish for another, or to leave the parish ministry altogether.[11]

Satisfaction with Ministry in the Particular Congregation and Commitment to the Parish Ministry

Given the rather limited possibilities for mobility that clergy presently experience in several Protestant denominations, it is perhaps fortunate that a majority of clergy are generally satisfied with their present positions. Overall a few more men than women expressed relative satisfaction (67 percent of the men and 59 percent of the women). However, clergywomen were more likely than the men to say that last year they "usually" felt they were accomplishing things in their ministry (64 percent of the women to 53 percent of the men). At the same time, they were less likely than men to say it was "definitely" true that their present position offered them maximum opportunities for expression of their talents for ministry (40 percent of the women to 50 percent of the men). As we indicated in Chapter 5, clergywomen do not tend to be in as prestigious churches or positions as are clergymen of comparable experience. Therefore, their lower evaluation of the opportunities provided by their present parish is understandable. Further, 64 percent of the women and 70 percent of the men said they never really thought seriously in the last year about leaving the parish ministry for some other kind of work. There are no significant differences among denominations or between men and women pastors in each of the nine denominations in commitment to the parish ministry.

Younger clergy are more likely to consider seriously the possibility of leaving the parish ministry than older clergy. For example, among those clergy born before 1941, only 25 percent of the women and 28 percent of the men had, during the previous year, thought seriously about leaving the parish ministry; however, 41 percent of the women and 38 percent of the men born in 1941 and later had considered leaving. As indicated, clergy who seldom or never feel lonely and isolated, who believe they have maximum opportunity to use their talents for ministry in their present situation, and who find a sense of accomplishment in their ministry, are unlikely to have thought seriously in the preceding year about leaving the parish ministry. For clergymen, but not for women, there is a significant relationship between believing that they will have a relatively easy time getting another parish and their commitment to the parish ministry.

These findings from this study generally parallel those obtained by Hoge, Dyble, and Polk in a 1978 study of clergy from seven Protestant denominations in the Chicago metropolitan area. In that study, too, it was seen that ministers were committed to their own pastorates, but even more strongly committed to the pastoral ministry as a career. Also, the authors concluded that, "Among younger ministers especially, career development is a concern, and when it is impaired, vocational commitment will weaken." They suggest that if denominational officials cannot improve the opportunities for changing to (better) positions, they should try to help young ministers enhance their present positions to make them more "challenging and absorbing."[12]

While our data suggest that clergywomen presently are less likely than men to have their commitment to parish ministry affected by their perceptions of ease of finding a better parish position, this by no means indicates they are not concerned with career development. It is probably more the case that clergywomen, despite their shorter experience as parish ministers, feel sufficiently personally competent, satisfied, and challenged by their success in being pastors and meeting difficulties well, and that their commitment to the parish ministry is strengthened in the process.

Summary

Demands made on clergy time and energies are great, both in professional and personal relationships. Many pastors experience some role strain and stress in balancing these often competing demands. Women pastors seem to have slightly more difficulty than men in negotiating these role demands on their time and activity, partly because they have had less experience in the pastoral ministry than the vast majority of men, and no doubt also because the expectations of how women ministers should balance their professional and private lives are less clear than for men in pastoral ministry.

The sheer amount of difficulty clergywomen experience in juggling such role demands is not related to their marital status; however, it seems that single clergywomen, women married to nonordained spouses, and those who are part of clergy couples have different kinds of problems in accomplishing this balancing act effectively. Single women pastors may have more difficulty in convincing parishioners they have the right to a private life outside of their pastoral duties than married clergywomen do. Married clergywomen, who almost by definition are in dual-career families, have more difficulty in scheduling their home and parish responsibilities so that neither suffers unduly and they have some time left for themselves. This scheduling may be easier in many cases if the clergywoman has opted for marital homogany in terms of marrying a clergyman. Certainly, a major reason why clergywomen report less resentment from their spouses than do clergymen with reference to their ministerial work is because over half the married clergywomen (compared to a tiny proportion of clergymen) are part of a clergy couple. This is not to say that clergy couple marriages do not have problems of scheduling, competition, and other strains, particularly when there are young children and little money for household help. It seems a little easier in terms of time management if the clergy couple serve the same church. However, there is no evidence in this study that clergy couple marriages are less stable than marriages where only one spouse is ordained.

Clergywomen are still relatively unique to the congregational scene, and this token status in parish ministry makes their actions very visible. Constantly being observed in their pastoral role makes it more difficult for clergywomen to relax, be themselves, and perhaps find close friends. This type of experience is isolating, and, for many clergywomen, a feeling of loneliness ensues.

Clergymen also experience loneliness. For both women and men, feelings of isolation and loneliness were exacerbated if they were young, unmarried, and in rural pastorates. Young single women are clearly better able to avoid feelings of loneliness if they work in metropolitan churches. Loneliness and isolation were also accompanied or intensified by the feeling of being ineffective ministers in their parishes, or being bored and frustrated in attempts to do something worthwhile. If such feelings become too prolonged or intense, our analysis suggests that the man or woman is likely to think seriously of dropping out of parish ministry altogether.

Fortunately, the clear majority of both women and men pastors are satisfied with their parishes, feel competent and challenged in their ministerial work, and are highly committed to remaining in the parish ministry. Women's commitment to the parish ministry is less tied to their perceptions of ease of career mobility than are those of young clergymen. Instead, their commitment to the parish ministry seems more closely related to feeling challenged and effective in their parish work and not overly bored or isolated. Thus, in coordinating the conflicting demands made on them, women pastors seem to be managing their professional and private lives, perhaps with some difficulty, but nonetheless relatively well; and their commitment to their parishes and to parish ministry is strong and solid.

Some Concluding Reflections: Milk, Honey, and Giants

The Lord said to Moses, "Send men to spy out the land of Canaan, which I give to the people of Israel; from each tribe of their fathers shall you send a man. . . . Moses sent them to spy out the land of Canaan, and said to them, " . . . see what the land is, and whether the people who dwell in it are strong or weak, whether they are few or many, and whether the land that they dwell in is good or bad, and whether the cities that they dwell in are camps or strongholds. . . .

At the end of forty days they returned from spying out the land. . . . And they told [Moses], "We came to the land to which you sent us; it flows with milk and honey, and this is its fruit. Yet the people who dwell in the land are strong, and the cities are fruitful and very large; and besides, we saw the descendants of Anak there.—Numbers 13:1-2, 17-20, 25-28 (RSV)

. . . It will not make our task easier if people conclude that there are "no problems" as we seek advocacy for women's full participation in the life and ministry of the Church."—CLERGYWOMAN, Denominational Official

The report of the spies to Moses surely has to be one of the earliest "good news–bad news" stories on record; and that, in effect, has also been the message of this book. On the whole, the findings from our study have brought good news about the acceptance and functioning of women as parish clergy. While "milk and honey" may be too exaggerated a metaphor to describe what these women clergy have found in occupying traditionally male territory, most of them seem to have found it a "good land." But our study has also uncovered some bad news. Along with the "milk and honey," there are still "giants" to be met. Thus, while women now contemplating entering parish ministry—or laity considering calling a clergywoman—can find satisfaction in the good news, we would not want to understate the obstacles that still remain "to full participation in the life and ministry of the Church." In these final pages, we wish to reflect further on both the good news and bad news that we have observed and to consider some of the implications of these findings. We will not attempt a full summary but rather will call attention to some of the more important conclusions that indicate both "good" and "bad" news.

The "Milk and Honey"

There is much of a very positive nature that has been reported in these pages. Aspiring clergywomen, laity in congregations, and denominational and seminary officials can take much encouragement from them.

To begin, the women who have entered parish ministry are generally dedicated and competent individuals who have a strong sense of calling to serve God as ordained ministers. In the past, many of these women would have had to be content to serve as highly committed laity, frustrated perhaps, but resigned to their exclusion from the ranks of ordained ministry. Indeed many of the current clergywomen and women seminarians have served in this lay ministry capacity before the doors —either personal or institutional—opened to allow them to pursue ordained ministry. That this situation was the case for many women in our study is attested to by their relatively older age on entering seminary. This "graying" of the ordained ministry is an important social fact to which we will return below.

As women entered seminary in the years when they were still pioneers—roughly prior to the early 1970s—they typically experienced the seminary as a male enclave in which they were curiosities at best, and unwelcome intruders at worst. Our study reveals that this situation has changed considerably. While it would be a mistake to assume that all seminary obstacles to full acceptance of women have been removed, the majority of the women in our sample, especially more recent graduates, found the seminary to be a comfortable environment and their experience in seminary to be positive.

The news from the job market for clergywomen is mixed, but there are a number of positive aspects that deserve highlighting. Recalling once more that our survey includes only those already in parish ministry positions, thus perhaps excluding women (and men) who have been unable to secure a position, we nevertheless note that women did not, on balance, experience unusual difficulties being ordained. Neither has securing a first parish position been unduly difficult. Also, contrary to some reports, the women in our study were not more likely than men to be sent to declining churches or churches in trouble. In securing calls or appointments, many, but not all, clergywomen find the denominational deployment systems useful and are appreciative of the advocacy of regional denominational officials on their behalf in the appointment or call process. Similar findings were true for clergy couples. Thus, there is some very good news about the job market for women, and we predict that it will likely continue to improve as local churches and denominations have wider and longer exposure to clergywomen. All of this good news is not to gloss over the problems that persist for clergywomen as they try to maneuver in the job market; nevertheless, the positive findings reported here are significant and cannot be gainsaid.

As they enter parish positions, clergywomen are functioning competently as pastors. Positive self-assessment of clergywomen regarding various areas of ministerial functioning equal or excel those of the clergymen in our sample. Furthermore, their positive assessments are confirmed by lay leaders who have experienced clergywomen in positions of pastoral leadership. Additionally, clergywomen are no less likely than men to maintain harmonious relationships with parishioners; although several types of laity seem more problematic to women clergy than to men. In general, therefore, fears that having a clergywoman would bring on decline in the parish are not supported. Having a woman pastor is not an institutional threat to a congregation's future.

The generally favorable experiences that lay leaders have had when their congregations have been served by women pastors appear to have had an important positive effect on their attitudes towards clergywomen. While there is no groundswell among laity for affirmative hiring of clergywomen, and while there are only limited numbers of lay leaders who would actually prefer a woman pastor over a man, those with direct experience of a clergywoman are much more likely to say that the pastor's gender makes no difference. As the generally positive experiences of these laity with clergywomen become commonly known throughout the church system, the apprehensions of other laity about having a woman pastor should be reduced.

Not only are clergywomen relating well to most parishioners, but they report generally positive relationships with other clergy and judicatory officials. This fact is important, since the clergy profession in the denominations studied is tied to the larger organizational system of the denomination. Not only does this broader system play an important role in facilitating parish clergy pursuing their careers through serving in a succession of local congregations, but clergy find social and professional fulfillment and support in various relationships, roles, and responsibilities in this broader system. Not all clergywomen are as yet well integrated into this larger system. Nevertheless, the majority seem to be, and their experiences bode well for clergywomen in the future.

Finally, to return to the matter of the relative maturity of many clergywomen—the "graying" of the ministry referred to above—there is "good news" here as well. While their maturity is a consequence of the clergywomen's relative age and experience rather than their gender, nevertheless, we noted a number of instances in which maturity and previous experience as lay leaders in congregations proved salutory for effective ministerial functioning and positive interpersonal relationships. There are those who have argued that maturity and experience ought to be the norm for ministerial leadership in the church, and that it is a fundamental mistake to "inflict" on churches young seminary graduates with little or no experience of leadership in the parish. They cite the early church's selection of "elders"—persons of maturity and experience—to lead congregations.[1] From this perspective, the delayed entry into the ordained ministry, which is the case for many women and an increasing number of men, is a positive phenomenon. They come into parish leadership, not as "wet-behind-the-ears" novices, but as mature individuals with a number of years of leadership experience in parishes. We are not arguing here for restricting entry into ordained ministry only to older clergy, but simply noting that the "graying" of the ministry may have positive benefits for clergy leadership in parishes. In this instance, the large number of mature clergywomen are leading the way.

The "Giants" Still to Be Met

Not all, however, is flowing with "milk and honey." As is clear from the findings, clergywomen still face obstacles to their full participation in the ordained ministry of the church. In almost every instance of "good news" reported above, there was a corresponding negative note.

In contemplating a career in parish ministry, women are less likely than men to be encouraged by either their parents or pastors. Cultural stereotypes about appropriate roles for women apparently continue to operate and deprive women of needed support at an important time of personal decision making. And once they have made the decision—at least to enter seminary—they will still find faculties with a heavy male majority, especially at the senior professor levels. While this may be more a fruit of tenure systems and low faculty turnover than overt sexism, it remains as a negative factor to be encountered by women seminarians (and women faculty) along with other aspects of lingering sexism.

It is in the clergy job market that a number of "giants" remain to be met. The resistance of some judicatory officials to women clergy, ranging from polite neutrality to refusal to allow women clergy in the judicatory, is a major obstacle to women seeking calls or appointments to parishes. Moreover both the inequities of salary between clergymen and women with comparable experience and the apparently more "flat" career lines of women—the "typecasting" hypothesis—point to serious institutional issues that need to be confronted in the churches. To be sure, charges of gross injustice must be tempered by the fact that some women choose to remain in lower paying or less "prestigious" parish ministry positions, often because of what were referred to in Chapter 5 as "special needs" that restrict their willingness to move to other positions. Nevertheless, we do not believe that "special needs" account for all of the differences uncovered between salaries and career lines of male and female parish clergy. Rather some of it seems to reflect a residual sexism that "rewards" women with lower salaries and positions with less status than their male colleagues in the ordained ministry, as is also the case in many secular occupations.[2] But unlike many secular institutions, churches are legally unaffected by equal employment regulations that seek to rectify inequities. Regrettably, an institution committed to justice and love among humankind perpetuates injustice among a significant number of its professional leaders.

There are also obstacles to the full acceptance of women pastors by lay members, as our data have revealed. The image of a minister is still, for a large number of laity, a masculine image. And even when exposure to a clergywoman reduces significantly the expressed preference for a male minister, there is no overwhelming preference for a female. Nor are laity much inclined to act affirmatively to employ clergywomen; and some types of laity—businessmen and executives and middle-aged men and women—offer special challenges to clergywomen, especially younger women.

While many clergywomen have experienced little difficulty with being accepted and integrated into judicatory structures and clergy support networks, our data show that there are significant problems for single clergywomen in rural areas and small communities. The same is true to a lesser extent for single clergymen. There, the lack of the support of a spouse or of nearby clergy with whom one can join in a support group, along with the "fish bowl" existence that rural and small town clergy experience, often lead to loneliness and serious questioning of one's vocation. Additionally, there are the obstacles of balancing one's career with marriage and family responsibilities that clergywomen, especially, seem to face. Even in more "modern" marriages, where couples have worked to overcome traditional, sex-role distinctions, combining full-time ministry and motherhood poses a problem for a large number of clergywomen.

Relative Success and Persisting Inequities

There are then both "milk and honey" and "giants" yet to be met for women in parish ministry. To acknowledge the positive aspects of the situation which our "scouting" report has revealed is quite important; on balance, we believe that the positive aspects substantially outweigh the negative, and that women clergy have made important gains in overcoming the dilemmas and contradictions of status which we discussed in Chapter 1. This was confirmed when, in the course of this study, we shared preliminary findings with several experienced clergywomen. When, for example, we lamented that *fully* 55 percent of the lay leaders in our survey expressed negativity regarding having a clergywoman as senior minister, one of the clergywomen present replied, "But don't ignore the fact that *fully* 45 percent of the laity expressed a positive attitude!" She continued, "That is a very encouraging statistic. It would not have been likely to occur as little as a decade ago." It is highly important, therefore, to see the *relatively positive* findings of the study for what they are—a considerable improvement over what they would have been only a few years previously.

At the same time, we would be remiss if we did not also emphasize the distance that remains to be travelled before persisting inequities between clergymen and women are fully overcome. It is important that current clergywomen, women contemplating a call to the ordained ministry, and all those responsible for making the church system work, do not ignore the obstacles that remain. Overcoming naivete with realism —especially among women entering the ordained ministry—is crucial.

Why do these inequities and obstacles remain? It is important to identify some of the major causes, even though a full discussion of them is beyond the scope of this book.

The most obvious and insidious cause of the inequities is the persistence of sexism in the churches as well as in the culture. Sexism can be defined as any attitude or action by individuals, groups, institutions, or cultures that treats individuals unjustly because of their gender and rationalizes that treatment on the basis of biological, psychological, social, or cultural characteristics.[3] This definition calls attention to both individual and institutional aspects of sexism. At the individual level, as we noted in Chapter 6, sexist attitudes and actions can be manifest and blatant, or they can be more latent and subtle. While we encountered, in the course of our study, a few individuals who were blatantly intentional about their negative attitudes towards women, we were struck more often by the prevalence of latent sexism, sexist attitudes that seemed to us unintended and unrecognized. Because of their subtlety and generally unrecognized character, such attitudes are sometimes more difficult to deal with and alter than more blatant ones.

As this chapter was being written, we received a publication for seminary students in which an author discussed pressures facing parish ministers today. His article used the male pronoun frequently and exclusively to refer to ministers, ignoring the gender of almost half of the audience for whom he was writing; the article also contained a list of successful persons, including clergy, as examples of the kinds of individuals with whom parish ministers are often compared and encouraged (pressured) to emulate. Not one example given was a woman! While the author would likely maintain that no sexism was intended (and this is probably true), sexism nevertheless is present and no less negative in its consequences for being unintentional. The image of the minister the article conveys and perpetuates is distinctly a male one.

But attitudinal sexism is only a part of the problem. Sexism, like racism, is often institutionalized in the customs, laws, and structures of society, including those of the churches. Institutional sexism can perpetuate inequities even when individuals in the institutions do not have sexist intentions. The restriction by church law of ordination to men, which none of the denominations in our study now practice, is an obvious example of institutional sexism, as is also the practice, noted in Chapter 5, of paying clergywomen less than men, even when their years of experience are similar. Typecasting of women into particular kinds of clergy positions, which was at least suggested by our findings, also reflects institutional sexism. The use of masculine forms of religious language is also reflective of not only of individual sexism, but institutional, as well. Language is also one of our most powerful cultural institutions, and it is a shaper of consciousness and behavior. When religious language uses predominantly male images, whether in reference to God or as a designation for clergy, consciousness is shaped in the direction of excluding women. Thus sexism, whether individual or institutional, whether intentional or unintentional, is a major obstacle to the full participation of women in the ordained ministry.

There are at least two other factors that play lesser but contributing roles in hindering women's full participation in ordained ministry. One, already alluded to in previous chapters, is the current situation of mainline Protestantism as an "imperiled" institution. As is well known, many mainline Protestant denominations have experienced serious institutional problems since the mid to late 1960s. These have included: unprecedented declines in church memberships that have only recently begun to slow and perhaps "bottom out"; the combined impact of inflation and membership declines on church finances, with a growing number of congregations experiencing severe financial exigencies; and, in some denominations, an oversupply of ordained clergy.[4] None of these trends has a necessary connection with resistance to clergywomen; however, as we noted, they create a climate of anxiety among laity and clergy about the future of the church. This anxiety no doubt fosters a resistance to any innovation which might be suspected of further endangering the already fragile institution—women clergy being such an innovation. Under these conditions latent sexism can rise to the surface but be rationalized in terms of anxiety over the institution. We hope that the positive findings of our study will help to show this fear to be groundless; nevertheless, we strongly suspect it has been an obstacle to the full acceptance of clergywomen.

Another factor contributing to resistance to clergywomen rests in characteristics of the clergy profession itself. For one thing, at its very center is the profession's focus in religion. The profession is the guardian of the religious heritage. While one function of religion is to nurture visions of the future on the basis of which social change can occur, religion also has a conservative function. It is a promoter of stability, a preserver of tradition, lifting up to sacred status aspects of the social order considered vital. The aura of sanctity given to the tradition of an all-male clergy is a case in point. The "sacredly masculine" image of the clergy, as we have seen, is a hard one to shake.

Other attributes of this profession also make resistance to women clergy more likely than in some occupations, or make it possible for sexist attitudes to come into play in more subtle, less obvious ways.[5] Unlike some professions, parish clergy do not have clients or patients. Rather, they relate to parishioners who are considered colleagues in ministry. While ordination recognizes the special training of clergy and sets them apart for special functions in the church—preaching, teaching, celebrating the sacraments, administering the affairs of the congregation—the doctrine of the "priesthood of all believers" emphasizes that ministry belongs equally to all Christians. Ordained clergy are *primus inter pares*, first among equals. Clergy perform their special functions of ministry to enable laity to perform their ministry. Such an emphasis, while salutory from our perspective, nevertheless can lead to a blurring of lines of authority when it is not clear what the clergy's primary tasks are, how their role differs from that of laity, and who, in the last analysis, is in charge. This can make it difficult for any clergyperson to exercise authority;[6] and it may be especially difficult for clergywomen, as we noted in Chapter 7. This ambiguity of the clergy role is compounded by the additional ambiguity that some have of accepting a woman in the status.

Added to these problems is the fact that there are rarely clearly defined standards for evaluating the performance of clergy. It is relatively easy to evaluate the performance of an engineer—man or woman— where one can assess the adequacy of the efficiency of a new product that he or she has designed. It is much less easy to evaluate the adequa-

cy of a theological idea which the minister has communicated in a ser-
mon or lecture. Or should the laity's evaluation be placed rather on the
minister's effectiveness in leading a person to salvation? Or on her or
his ability to build up the institutional life of the church? Such diverse
and ill defined criteria for evaluating clergy performance make it easy
for evaluators to let latent or manifest sexist attitudes color their evaluation. Those who resist the idea of a woman minister can usually find
some aspect of performance to criticize, blowing it out of proportion,
while ignoring other more positive aspects of her performance. The
absence of clear and agreed on criteria makes this likely.

Let us add that the clergy profession is not alone in sharing many of
these characteristics. It is important, nevertheless, to acknowledge
some of the important reasons that the various inequities and obstacles
to women's full participation in ordained ministry exist. By understanding these issues, it is possible to develop strategies that may alter
the situation into a more favorable one for clergywomen, and beyond
that to address core issues of ministry and mission related to entry of
women into ordained ministry.

Overcoming the Giants

The theologian Paul Tillich once observed that there are three ways
in which the church has exercised leadership in social change: (1)
through the exercise of direct political power, as in a theocratic state;
(2) through offering prophetic criticism, holding up before the society
and its leaders the contrast between valued forms and those actually
practiced; and (3) the way of silent interpenetration in which change is
subtly wrought by behavior and example.[7] We are not concerned here
so much with the change of society per se, but more directly with
change in the church; yet, each of these broad methods of change is
indicative of particular strategies which our research has shown to be
necessary.

One of the major "messages" of our research findings has been that
time and increasing exposure to women pastors have had a generally
salutory effect on the acceptance of women as ordained ministers. This
reflects the third of Tillich's change strategies: the way of silent interpenetration, through which change comes subtly by behavior and example. Women clergy are now approaching becoming a critical mass
within the churches and these numbers will be bolstered considerably
by women presently in seminary. Their silent (or not so silent) interpenetration of the church's ordained ministry should reduce the
present inequities and overcome some of the obstacles to full acceptance of women clergy. The fact that many current women seminarians, according to the women faculty we interviewed, are not strongly

feminist in orientation, makes it likely that silent interpenetration will be a major change strategy.

Yet, silent interpenetration is a slow means of bringing about change. Another generation may grow up in the church before we are able to assess fully the kinds of subtle influences that may result in the full acceptance of women as ordained ministers. Other, more immediately effective strategies may speed up the process of acceptance.

One strategy that continues to be needed is Tillich's second method of change: prophetic criticism. Active, vocal advocates—women and men—for full acceptance of women as ordained ministers are crucial if the process of change is not to be interminably slow. These include judicatory officials who will press pastoral search committees or pastor-parish relations committees to accept women clergy, especially as senior pastors in the larger churches, and who will work to overcome salary inequities between men and women pastors. Advocates are needed to ensure the representation of women in positions of leadership within the denominations. In addition, continuing, if sometimes irritating, advocacy is needed to rid church practices, language, and cultural images of sexism. The goal is to create an environment which filters out inappropriate uses of gender that hinder women's full participation in the church's ministry and undermine the church's broader witness to justice and liberation.

It is unlikely, given the more professional orientation of many women seminarians and clergy, that large numbers of clergywomen (or men) will be strong vocal prophetic critics of sexism; nevertheless, however unwelcome it may be, such advocacy is essential if the change process is to be pushed forward. A lesson from the black experience is important. Blacks have gained considerable acceptance in recent years through the "silent interpenetration" of black men and women and children into schools, business and the professions, civic leadership and government. But this silent interpenetration could not have been possible without the strong and often costly prophetic criticism and advocacy of the black civil rights movement. And, as the political situation at the time of this writing makes clear, continued strong prophetic criticism and advocacy by blacks are needed if blacks are to continue to consolidate gains and overcome injustice and oppression.

Finally, the present situation of clergywomen can be considerably helped if clergywomen are better prepared for the situations that face them as ordained pastors. Naivite needs to be overcome with realism and wisdom. A major objective of this book has been to provide the kind of information that will help women to understand the "land" they are trying to occupy. Clergywomen—and almost all that we say is equally applicable to clergymen—need to have a realistic picture of what the current situation of ordained ministry is like. This information needs to include an understanding of what the job situation for clergy is in their denomination, what salaries are reasonable to expect, how the denominational deployment system works, and how to use it. There is a need for better understanding of power and the political process within congregations and denominations, so that Tillich's first change strategy may be used. What are appropriate leadership styles in dealing with situations for which there are few cultural models for women? Finally, there is need for greater realism about balancing the demands of marriage, family, and career. The "superwomen" myth is not a helpful one for effective ministry or healthy personal and family life. Realism and wisdom regarding these and other issues of parish ministry will not, in themselves, reduce the obstacles and inequities that women pastors face, but they will reduce the likelihood of being caught off guard by them. Both realism and wisdom are necessary first steps, not only of successful coping, but for effective change.

Women and the Promised Land

Much that we have dealt with in this book has focused on career and organizational concerns. What kinds of careers are women able to carve out in the church? How are they accepted? What institutional obstacles remain? Some may believe that these questions are penultimate or secondary, that what really matters in the last analysis is what difference does it make for the larger ministry and mission of the church that women are full participants in ordained ministry. We agree that this is a primary issue, and that we have concentrated heavily on what are really secondary concerns—important but nonetheless secondary. While we concede this, we believe that these issues of blocked access to full participation in ministry by women and other marginal groups are too compelling, too dominant, to allow the broader discussion without first addressing these issues.

Yet, it may also be that in addressing what some may believe to be secondary issues of careers and organizations, we are also indirectly raising primary issues of ministry and mission. It may be that, as churches have addressed the issues of whether women should be ordained, they have been led to a deeper understanding of what ministry and calling mean for all Christians. In raising concerns about salary inequities between clergymen and women, perhaps broader issues of justice will be focused. Perhaps, too, the abysmally low salaries paid to a majority of clergy, both male and female, will also be addressed. It may also be that, in the growing exposure of laity and male clergy to clergywomen, a new cultural image of the ordained ministry will emerge, one that is androgynous, neither male nor female, but incorporating the strengths and gifts of both. If these things occur, then women will not only have reached the "promised land" of full acceptance into ordained ministry. They will have contributed to the quality of life in that "land" for all who occupy it.

Appendix:
Overall Individual Responses to
Clergy Interview/Questionnaire

Number in Total Sample (the number responding to each question is not reported except where only a part of the sample responded)	*W* 635	*M* 739

Part I: Family Background and Preseminary Life

	Percentage	
	W	*M*
1. *Was your decision to enter ordained ministry:*		
gradual?	65	58
at a specific time in your life that you remember well?	24	40
both: gradual and specific?	11	2
	100	100
If "both" or "specific," at what age was this?		
18 or younger	23	46
19–22 years	20	31
23–26 years	18	11
27–36 years	22	10
37 plus years	17	2
	100	100
(N)	(211)	(305)
2. *By whom were you raised?*		
(Categories not mutually exclusive.)		
both parents	92	91
mother only	5	6
father only	1	1
grandparents	2	3
other	2	3
3. *In what year were you born?*		
1900–1930	16	41
1931–1940	17	29

	Percentage	
	W	*M*
1941–1946	21	15
1947–1950	26	11
1951–later	20 ·	4
	100	100

4. *How active were your parents (or guardians) in a church when you were growing up?*

unchurched	7	8
nominally church related	14	13
average church relationship	12	15
active church relationship	12	17
very active in church	55	47
	100	100

5. *In what denomination were you raised?*

Baptist	12	10
Disciples/Christian Church	7	7
Episcopal	8	10
Lutheran	16	14
Presbyterian	13	16
Methodist	19	19
Congregational/United Church of Christ	11	9
Roman Catholic	2	1
mixed/nothing	10	8
other	2	6
	100	100

Denominational stability or change?

in same denomination	69	72
have switched denomination	22	19
no previous denomination	9	9
	100	100

6. *What was the highest level of education of your father (or male guardian)?*

less than high school graduation	16	33
high school graduation	22	21
technical training, secretarial school, vocation education	5	5
some college	12	12
four-year college degree	16	9
some graduate or professional graduate-level education	5	6
master's degree	14	9
doctorate	10	5
	100	100

	Percentage	
	W	M

What was the highest level of education of your
mother (or female guardian)?

	W	M
less than high school graduation	12	26
high school graduation	28	28
technical training, secretarial school, vocational education	9	11
some college	22	16
four-year college degree	19	11
some graduate or professional graduate-level education	4	3
master's degree	5	4
doctorate	1	1
	100	100

7. What was your father's major occupation while you
were in junior and senior high school?

	W	M
minister	12	13
top professional, diplomat, senator	11	4
business executive, banker, large-business owner	7	3
school teacher, social worker, social service worker, pilot, engineer, librarian, newspaper editor, military officer, musician, artist	11	8
small-business owner, administrative personnel, insurance agent, semiprofessional, paraprofessional, reporter, sheriff, actor, mortician, computer programmer, lab technician, photographer, travel agent	22	21
clerical worker, sales worker, owner of little business (self-employed), postal worker, policeman, salesman, military personnel (nonofficer)	9	11
farmer (owner)	9	10
skilled manual laborer, fireman, machinist, hair stylist, carpenter	18	28
not in labor force, homemaker, retired, unemployed	1	2
	100	100

What was your mother's major occupation while
you were in junior and senior high school?

	W	M
minister	1	1
top professional, diplomat, senator	1	>1
business executive, banker, large-business owner	>1	>1
school teacher, social worker, social service		

	Percentage	
	W	M
worker, pilot, engineer, librarian, newspaper editor, military officer, musician, artist	14	8
small-business owner, administrative personnel, insurance agent, semiprofessional, paraprofessional, reporter, sheriff, actor, mortician, computer programmer, lab technician, photographer, travel agent	8	4
clerical worker, sales worker, owner of little business (self-employed), postal worker, police officer, salesperson, military personnel (nonofficer),	16	11
farmer (owner)	1	>1
skilled manual laborer, fireman, machinist, hair stylist, carpenter	4	6
not in labor force, homemaker, retired, unemployed	56	70
	100	100

8. *What post–high school education and degrees have you obtained?*

post–high school technical training	4	8
four-year college degree	97	96

What was your major in college?

English, journalism	16	15
languages	3	2
speech, arts, music	13	5
history, political science, economics	9	20
library, nursing, agriculture, business	4	3
education	10	4
religion, philosophy	27	25
anthropology, sociology, psychology	12	17
hard science, earth sciences, mathematics	6	9
	100	100

Was the college you attended:

public?	39	28
private, nonreligious?	16	15
private, religious?	45	57
	100	100

Do you have graduate education in secular fields of universities, professional schools? — 22 — 18

In what areas of study?

English, journalism	14	7
languages	1	3

		Percentage	
		W	*M*
speech, arts, music		9	5
history, political science, economics		6	16
library, nursing, agriculture, business		11	3
education		23	16
religion, philosophy		8	11
anthropology, sociology, psychology		24	30
hard science, earth science, mathematics		4	9
		100	100
	(N)	(138)	(129)

Number of years studied?

1		43	40
2		40	31
3		5	19
4		2	5
5 or more		10	5
		100	100
	(N)	(96)	(117)

Graduate degrees received?

none		25	29
certificate		9	6
master's degree		62	54
doctorate		4	11
		100	100
	(N)	(96)	(103)

Seminary Education: Seventy three seminaries were listed by respondents as the schools from which they graduated. Seminaries with the largest number of women graduates included Union Theological Seminary (36%), Princeton Theological Seminary (29%), Yale Divinity School (29%), Andover Newton Theological School (21%), and Garrett-Evangelical Theological Seminary (21%).

Date began first degree program?

Before 1960		10	53
1961–1965		8	17
1966–1970		14	15
1971–1973		27	8
1974–1976		38	7
1977–after		3	0
		100	100

Date completed first degree program?

Before 1960		8	41
1961–1965		6	17

	Percentage	
	W	M
1966–1970	9	16
1971–1973	7	9
1974–1976	24	7
1977–after	46	10
	100	100

Degrees received? (Categories not mutually exclusive.)

B.D., M.Div	45	87
M.A. or S.T.M.	9	9
M.R.E.	6	1
Ph.D. or Th.D.	2	3
D.Min.	5	9
Other	6	8

9. *How active were you in the church as a young adult (18 to 22 years of age)?*

unchurched	8	5
nominally church related	16	11
average church relationship	13	12
active church relationship	18	27
very active in church	45	45
	100	100

10. *Did you decide definitely to enter seminary (or study for ordination):*

before college?	10	35
during college?	41	44
or after college?	49	21
	100	100

Part II: Seminary and Ordination Experiences

1. *How old were you on first entering seminary?*

under 21 years	12	20
22 years	27	31
23–24 years	19	19
25–28 years	17	17
29–35 years	12	9
36 plus years	13	4
	100	100

2. *What was the response of your family, best friends, and pastors, or pastors you knew at this time, to your entering a seminary program? Were they supportive, neutral, antagonistic, or sharply divided (some supportive, some antagonistic?)*

| | *Percentage* | |
	W	*M*
Family		
supportive	63	80
neutral	13	9
antagonistic	9	4
divided	15	7
	100	100
Best friends		
supportive	69	71
neutral	16	20
antagonistic	5	1
divided	10	8
	100	100
Pastor(s)		
supportive	77	93
neutral	10	4
antagonistic	5	1
divided	8	2
	100	100

3. *What was the most important reason for your selecting the seminary you did?* (% = % of total sample; categories not mutually exclusive.) Most frequently given reasons included:

	W	M
near me, near my family	22	18
recommended by my pastor, denominational executive, or other clergy; my pastor attended	15	21
my family or friends went there; it was associated with my undergraduate college	11	11
area of the country (liked urban setting, loved California, wanted to go East, etc.)	20	16
liked the focus or curriculum or theological intent of the program	18	15
had some women; was open and friendly toward women; good women in ministry program	7	1
it was denominational	11	19
had a good academic reputation; excellent faculty; famous names; academically sound	10	13

4. *When you first got to seminary, approximately how many women were there:*
Among the student body?

	W	M
1–5	18	45
6–10	18	21

		Percentage	
		W	M
11–20		26	17
21–40		23	11
41 plus		15	6
		100	100
	(N)	(506)	(590)

In your entering class?

0–1	10	37
2–4	25	27
5–10	31	24
11–20	21	8
21 plus	13	4
	100	100

	(N)	(561)	(566)

On the faculty?

0	41	47
1	31	28
2	15	13
3	7	5
4	3	3
5 or more	3	4
	100	100

5. *On first entering seminary, how important were each of the following for you?*

Personal spiritual growth, faith development:

primary reason	60	40
secondary reason	30	47
not a reason	10	13
	100	100

Discovering in which ways to best serve Christ in the church or world:

primary reason	64	51
secondary reason	26	38
not a reason	10	11
	100	100

Preparing to be a parish minister:

primary reason	35	73
secondary reason	26	19
not a reason	39	8
	100	100

6. *How were you treated by the seminary faculty generally?*

impartially; like any other student	22	59
friendly, but didn't take me seriously	10	5

	Percentage	
	W	*M*
gave me preferential treatment	11	8
were cold, indifferent, or hostile toward me	4	1
friendly, warm	44	24
other	9	3
	100	100

7. *Did any seminary faculty clearly encourage you to enter parish ministry?*

yes	53	51
no	40	49
	100	100

8. *Did any faculty at seminary ever discourage you from entering parish ministry?*

yes	16	8
no	84	92
	100	100

9. *How valuable have you found your seminary education for your work in parish ministry?*

quite valuable	64	70
somewhat valuable	32	28
of little value	4	2
	100	100

10. *How important were each of the following in your decision to definitely seek ordination as a full minister in your denomination?*

Members of your family:

quite important	28	35
somewhat important	21	29
not important	41	28
not relevant, don't know	10	8
	100	100

Minister(s) of church(es) you attended:

quite important	40	50
somewhat important	27	29
not important	26	16
not relevant, don't know	7	5
	100	100

Regional or national denominational executive(s):

quite important	21	15
somewhat important	17	17
not important	44	44
not relevant, don't know	18	24
	100	100

	Percentage	
	W	M
Clergy field work or intern supervisor(s):		
quite important	34	19
somewhat important	23	25
not important	28	34
not relevant, don't know	15	22
	100	100
Friends:		
quite important	48	24
somewhat important	29	38
not important	18	28
not relevant, don't know	5	10
	100	100
Clergywomen or women pastors (this question not asked of clergymen):		
quite important	29	
somewhat important	17	
not important	20	
not relevant, don't know	34	
	100	
Seminary faculty or other personnel:		
quite important	37	25
somewhat important	32	35
not important	24	29
not relevant, don't know	7	11
	100	100

How important were the following experiences in your seeking ordination?

	W	M
Courses in Bible, theology, or church history:		
quite important	44	50
somewhat important	31	32
not important	21	14
not relevant, don't know	4	4
	100	100
Courses in preaching, worship, or counseling:		
quite important	51	47
somewhat important	24	34
not important	19	14
not relevant, don't know	6	5
	100	100
Your work in a parish as a seminarian, intern, paid assistant, or volunteer:		
quite important	70	57
somewhat important	14	27

| | Percentage | |
	W	*M*
not important	10	11
not relevant, don't know	6	5
	100	100

How important were the following possible motivations in seeking ordination?

Greater acceptance of your ministry by having official church legitimation as an ordained minister:

quite important	58	47
somewhat important	24	23
not important	14	23
not relevant, don't know	4	7
	100	100

Desire to administer the sacraments, and perform other priestly acts:

quite important	56	35
somewhat important	22	34
not important	18	26
not relevant, don't know	4	5
	100	100

Desire to change the sexist nature of the church (this question not asked of clergymen):

quite important	27	
somewhat important	29	
not important	36	
not relevant, don't know	8	
	100	

Conviction God wished you to be ordained:

quite important	77	67
somewhat important	13	21
not important	7	8
not relevant, don't know	3	4
	100	100

11. *After completing your studies, how easy was it for you to get ordained to full ministerial status?*

quite easy	54	78
somewhat easy	18	15
somewhat difficult	16	5
quite difficult	12	2
	100	100

12. *In what year were you ordained?*

before 1956	3	33
1957–1969	7	39
1970–1975	21	16

| | Percentage | |
	W	M
1976–1978	39	7
1979–1981	30	5
	100	100

13. *From the time you were ordained, about how long did it take for you to obtain a parish position?*

	W	M
less than 6 months	85	95
6 months–1 year	6	2
1–2 years	4	2
2–3 years	2	1
3–4 years	1	0
4 years or more	2	0
	100	100

14. *Do you think that seminary graduates in your denomination will have an easier or more difficult time than you had in getting ordained in 1981?*

	W	M
easier	44	7
about the same	39	45
more difficult	17	48
	100	100

Do you think that seminary graduates in your denomination will have an easier or more difficult time than you had in finding a first parish position in 1981?

	W	M
easier	31	5
about the same	34	37
more difficult	35	58
	100	100

15. *Have you ever had full-time secular employment?*

	W	M
yes	69	62
no	31	38
	100	100

Was this employment:

	W	M
prior to ordination?	90	85
after ordination?	7	10
both?	3	5
	100	100
	(431)	(453)

What was the nature of this work?

	W	M
church-related work, as a layperson	>1	1
top professional	2	2
business executive, banker, large-business owner	2	2
school teacher, social worker, engineer, pilot,		

	Percentage	
	W	*M*
librarian, newspaper editor, musician, artist (professional), military officer	45	17
small-business owner, administrative personnel, insurance agent, semiprofessional, paraprofessional, reporter, sheriff, actor, mortician, computer programmer, lab technician, photographer, travel agent, artist (nonprofessional)	25	30
clerical worker, sales worker, owner of little business, postal worker, police officer, salesperson, military (nonofficer)	21	23
farmer (owner)	0	2
skilled manual laborer, fireman, machinist, hairdresser, carpenter	4	23
unemployed, housewife, retired	0	>1
	100	100
(N)	(424)	(423)

How many years did you do this work?

	W	*M*
less than one year	20	23
1–2 years	21	20
3–4 years	22	21
5–9 years	21	20
more than 10 years	16	16
	100	100
(N)	(430)	(410)

16. *Do you presently have part-time secular work?*

	W	*M*
yes	6	6
no	94	93
full-time work	0	1
	100	100

If yes, what is the nature of this work?

	W	*M*
church-related work, as layperson	4	2
top professional	29	32
business executive, banker, large business owner	0	2
school teacher, social worker, engineer, pilot, librarian, newspaper editor, musician, artist (professional), military officer	27	29
small-business owner, administrative, insurance agent, semi-professional and paraprofessional, reporter, sheriff, actor, mortician, computer programmer, lab technician, photographer, travel agent, artist (nonprofessional)	23	22

	Percentage	
	W	M
clerical, sales worker, owner of little business, postal worker, police officer, salesperon, military (nonofficer)	10	4
farmer (owner)	5	0
skilled manual labor, fireman, machinists, hairdresser, carpenter	2	9
unemployed, housewife, retired		
	100	100
(N)	(48)	(59)

Approximately how many hours do you spend on this work per week?

	W	M
1–2 hours	12	10
3–4 hours	10	12
5–9 hours	25	14
10–20 hours	29	33
21 plus hours	24	31
	100	100
(N)	(41)	(51)

17. *In how many different congregations have you worked since ordination?*

	W	M
1	39	10
2	29	17
3	14	23
4–9	16	46
10 plus	2	4
	100	100

18. *How many years have you worked as a parish minister altogether?*

	W	M
1	10	1
2	16	2
3	16	3
4	16	3
5–6	18	6
7–14	18	26
15 plus	6	59
	100	100

19. *Have you ever been in a nonparish church-related position?*

	W	M
	34	21
What was this position?		
denominational staff	1	6
chaplaincy (hospital or prison)	34	28

	Percentage	
	W	*M*
social services, administration	11	16
seminary faculty, administration, or teaching		
religion in a college	5	10
specialized ministry to particular groups	16	17
missionary	8	8
campus ministry, college chaplain	13	12
CPE, clinical pastor center, pastoral counselor		
in private practice	4	2
DRE, or music or church consultant	7	2
Have you ever been on a regional or national		
denominational staff?	*10*	8
Have you ever been an instructor or professor		
in a seminary?	10	7
part-time (total sample N = 85)	89	83
full-time (total sample N = 14)	11	17
	54	36

Part III: Present Parish Position and Mobility Prospects

No Present Parish position

	9	3
(N)	(57)	(23)
Present occupation (secular):		
top professional	11	0
school teacher, social worker, engineer, pilot, librarian, newspaper editor, musician, artist (professional), military officer	22	57
small-business owner, administrative, insurance agent, semiprofessional and paraprofessional, reporter, sheriff, actor, mortician, computer programmer, lab technician, photograph, travel agent, artist (nonprofessional)	11	29
clerical, sale worker, owner of small business, postal worker, police officer, salesperson, military (nonofficer)	45	14
student	11	0
	100	100
(N)	(9)	(7)
Present occupation (church, other than parish):		
denomination staff	23	54
chaplaincy (hospital or prison)	30	15

	Percentage	
	W	*M*
social services, administration	7	23
seminary faculty, administration, or teaching religion in a college	6	0
specialized ministry to particular groups	0	8
missionary	3	0
campus ministry, college chaplain	17	0
CPE, clinical pastoral center, pastoral counselor in private practice	7	0
	100	100
(N)	(30)	(13)

Not employed		
retired	18	80
unemployed	47	20
not looking for work	29	0
returned to school	6	0
	100	100
(N)	(17)	(5)

PARISH EMPLOYMENT   91   97

1. *For this parish, do you work:*

full-time?	75	95
¾-time?	7	1
½-time?	14	3
less than ½-time?	4	1
	100	100

What is your present position in the parish?

sole pastor	47	66
senior pastor	2	22
co-pastor	14	2
associate/assistant	27	8
minister CE	5	0
supply/interim (2 months plus)	4	1
other	1	1

2. *How many other ordained clergy besides yourself are there in this church?*

1	72	54
2	17	26
3	6	12
4	3	5
5 or more	2	3
	100	100

	Percentage	
	W	M
Are any of these women?		
yes	4	22
no	96	78
	100	100

3. *How many years have you been in this parish?*

less than 1 year	17	12
1 year	16	5
2 years	25	12
3 years	17	12
4–5 years	16	19
6–9 years	7	22
more than 10 years	2	18
	100	100

4. *Please describe this church as it was when you were first called/appointed as minister:*
   Overall was it:

growing and developing?	18	14
holding its own?	43	42
generally declining?	38	43
new church?	1	1
	100	100

In regard to the members' view of their church and its possibilities, when you were first called, were they:

mostly indifferent, apathetic?	10	15
in conflict among themselves, angry and distrustful of one another?	22	26
mostly optimistic and enthusiastic?	49	43
other?	19	16
	100	100

5. *In approximately what size community is this church located?*

under 2,500 (rural, open country)	26	15
2,500–10,000 (town)	19	21
10,000–50,000 (small city)	19	25
50,000/over (metropolitan suburb)	13	15
50,000–250,000 (metropolitan inner city)	12	11
250,000–1,000,000	5	8
large city or megatropolis of over 1,000,000	6	5
	100	100

6. *How many members does this church have?*

fewer than 100	18	8

	Percentage	
	W	*M*
101–199	20	15
200–399	25	29
400–699	17	25
700 plus	20	23
	100	100

7. Please characterize the majority of parishioners
   in your church as follows:
   What proportion are age fifty and over?

	W	M
two-thirds or more	31	29
divided as to age	32	41
one-third or less	37	30
	100	100

   What proportion are middle and upper middle class?

	W	M
two-third or more	60	62
divided as to class	15	23
one-third or less	25	15
	100	100

   What proportion of the members are Sunday-morn-
   ing only's?

	W	M
two-thirds or more	29	32
divided as to church participation	33	40
one-third or less (most participate in other church activities as well)	38	28
	100	100

   What is the predominant theological position of the
   majority of this church?

	W	M
very conservative	5	4
moderately conservative	42	56
moderately liberal	26	26
very liberal	4	2
mixed, neither	23	12
	100	100

   How would you compare your own theological posi-
   tion to the majority in this church?

	W	M
more conservative	5	6
equally conservative	8	20
equally liberal	11	15
more liberal	69	51
mixed, neither	7	8
	100	100

   Presently, would you say the financial health of this
   church is:

	W	M
excellent?	15	29

| | *Percentage* | |
	W	M
good?	29	31
tight but adequate?	35	28
in some difficulty?	17	10
in serious difficulty?	4	2
	100	100

8. *How much difficulty have you had in the last year in getting your ideas for the church supported by the governing board of the church?*

	W	M
little or no difficulty	74	74
some difficulty	21	21
quite a bit of difficulty	5	5
	100	100

9. *How satisfied are you with your present ministerial position in this church?*

	W	M
very satisfied	42	40
satisfied	17	27
mixed, both satisfied and frustrated	33	29
dissatisfied	4	1
very dissatisfied and frustrated	4	3
	100	100

10. *Does this position offer you maximum opportunity for expression of your talents for ministry?*

	W	M
yes, definitely	40	50
yes, to some degree	31	35
no, not really	29	15
	100	100

11. *How likely is it that you will move from this church in the next couple of years?*

	W	M
very likely	39	27
somewhat likely	20	23
somewhat unlikely	15	25
very unlikely	26	25
	100	100

12. *Regardless of your plans, suppose you did leave this church for another position. Further, suppose the search/pulpit/pastor-relations committee had narrowed the choice of a new pastor down to a woman and a man. Assuming all other characteristics besides sex of the two candidates were equal, which would this committee probably prefer?*
If both candidates are:
single persons in their middle twenties, committee would:

	Percentage	
	W	M
prefer the man	43	71
prefer the woman	9	2
it would make no difference	43	24
neither	5	3
	100	100
about sixty years old and widowed, committee would:		
prefer the man	40	69
prefer the woman	11	4
it would make no difference	41	24
neither	8	3
	100	100
divorced, committee would:		
prefer the man	38	65
prefer the woman	8	2
it would make no difference	41	29
neither	13	4
	100	100
widowed with children under ten years of age, committee would:		
prefer the man	46	70
prefer the woman	11	7
it would make no difference	39	22
neither	4	1
	100	100
obese, committee would:		
prefer the man	47	67
prefer the woman	4	1
it would make no difference	42	29
neither	7	3
	100	100
physically a very attractive person, committee would:		
prefer the man	47	65
prefer the woman	6	5
it would make no difference	47	30
neither	0	0
	100	100

13. *In the last five years, about how many inquiries have you received (if any) from other churches about the possibility of being their minister?*

	W	M
1	19	9
2	22	18

	Percentage	
	W	M
3	19	18
4–5	15	22
6–9	12	16
10 plus	13	17
	100	100
(N)	(306)	(458)

United Methodists: In the last five years has your bishop or district superintendent asked you to consider a change of pastoral appointments?

yes	39	60
no	61	40
	100	100
(N)	(140)	(109)

14. *Of all inquiries, how good were these church positions (in terms of salary, working conditions, location, growth potential) in comparison to the position you held at the time?* (United Methodists: If you answered yes on question 13, was the move or change offered better or worse than your pastoral charge at the time?)

worse on the whole	20	9
about the same	15	21
some better, some worse	29	38
better on the whole	36	32
	100	100
(N)	(342)	(490)

15. *What would you prefer your next call, position (United Methodist: appointment) to be?* (Categories not mutually exclusive.)

another parish position	70	69
nonparish ministerial or denominational position	26	14
in secular work	4	4
retired	4	11
other	16	1

16. *Do you feel that you have adequate information about all church or church-related vacancies in which you might be interested?*

yes	60	62
no	40	38
	100	100

17. *Are you presently using the placement services of your national denominational office handling clergy*

	Percentage	
	W	*M*

*deployment; e.g., is your updated profile in this of-
fice?* (United Methodists skip this question.)

yes	57	66
no	43	34
	100	100
(N)	(465)	(556)

*If yes, how helpful have you found the national of-
fice deployment services in getting you interviews at
churches or an actual position?*

very helpful	21	20
somewhat helpful	24	31
not very helpful	24	21
of no help at all	13	11
not sure	15	11
not used	3	6
	100	100
(N)	(266)	(416)

If no, why not?

too much trouble	3	5
waste of time	4	6
prefer to get jobs without the help of national office	3	6

If some other reason, what?

don't trust national office and/or process or like categories used	6	8
profiles still have to go through judicatory executive or parish calling comittee who may not use them "right," or at all	1	3
churches find profiles too complicated to use, don't understand them	0	4
not presently looking	60	49
prefer to go through regional office	9	8
regional and personal ties are also necessary	17	12
national service inefficient, incomplete, too slow, out of date as to parish openings	2	8
computer service is too mechanical or unresponsive	2	5
didn't know we had a national office for deployment	3	3
	100	100
	(235)	(146)

18. *Should you want another parish position, slightly
better than the one you now have, how easy do you
anticipate that it would be to get?*

	Percentage	
	W	*M*
very easy	12	9
somewhat easy	28	35
somewhat difficult	38	41
very difficult	22	15
	100	100

19. *How willing would you be to relocate your residence one hundred miles away from your present residence in order to take a new position?*

quite willing	55	52
willing if necessary	18	27
rather stay here if possible	11	13
definitely do not wish to move that far	16	8
	100	100

20. *How easy or difficult do you find it to plan a career strategy (e.g., decide on what kinds of ministerial positions you will try to obtain in five, ten, fifteen, etc., years from now)?*

very easy	11	14
somewhat easy	19	29
somewhat difficult	33	36
very difficult	30	15
don't try to plan	5	3
plan to retire	2	3
	100	100

21. *In a number of denominations, judicatory executives (e.g., bishops, presbyters, area ministers, etc.) often have informal, if not formal, power over which clergy can transfer into their area to accept a parish or other church-related position. To what extent do you anticipate such "executive discretion" negatively affecting your occupational mobility?*

a great deal	7	5
quite a bit	10	6
some	28	18
little	23	29
not at all	32	42
	100	100

22. *Suppose the most prestigious church of your denomination in your region called/appointed a woman as senior pastor. How would the majority of clergymen in your denomination in the region feel?*

| resentful | 39 | 21 |
| puzzled | 27 | 33 |

	Percentage	
	W	M
pleased	21	35
other	13	11
	100	100

Part IV: Your Ministry in the Parish

1. *How effective, on the whole, do you think you are with your present congregation in doing each of the following?*

	W	M
Preaching sermons:		
very effective	55	48
quite effective	42	49
somewhat ineffective	2	3
do not do this	1	0
	100	100
Planning and leading worship:		
very effective	63	51
quite effective	34	46
somewhat ineffective	1	2
do not do this	2	1
	100	100
Managing the church budget:		
very effective	10	24
quite effective	34	43
somewhat ineffective	20	12
do not do this	36	21
	100	100
Teaching adults:		
very effective	40	37
quite effective	48	50
somewhat ineffective	5	7
do not do this	7	6
	100	100
Teaching children:		
very effective	37	19
quite effective	38	45
somewhat ineffective	11	20
do not do this	14	16
	100	100
Presiding over a meeting of a large group:		
very effective	32	40
quite effective	54	49
somewhat ineffective	6	6
do not do this	8	5
	100	100

	Percentage	
	W	M
Crisis ministry:		
very effective	44	41
quite effective	44	49
somewhat ineffective	9	8
do not do this	3	2
	100	100
Pastoral counseling:		
very effective	32	31
quite effective	54	55
somewhat ineffective	10	12
do not do this	4	2
	100	100
Parish home and hospital visitation:		
very effective	43	40
quite effective	46	49
somewhat ineffective	9	11
do not do this	2	0
	100	100
Organizing and motivating paid staff and volunteers to do the work of the parish:		
very effective	22	17
quite effective	51	53
somewhat ineffective	23	22
do not do this	4	8
	100	100
Stimulating parishioners to engage in service to others outside the parish:		
very effective	11	9
quite effective	47	51
somewhat ineffective	36	37
do not do this	6	3
	100	100
Recruiting new members for the church:		
very effective	14	15
quite effective	47	53
somewhat ineffective	27	29
do not do this	12	3
	100	100

2. *Some pastors are more directive in their ministerial leadership style, preferring to make decisions on their own, typically. Others are more democratic, typically seeking the opinion of a number of others in the church on decisions to be made. On a ten-point scale —going from 1 "directive" to 10 "democratic"—on*

	Percentage	
	W	*M*

leadership style, what number would you give your-self?

	W	M
1	0	0
2	1	1
3	3	6
4	10	12
5	11	16
6	13	10
7	19	19
8	27	26
9	12	7
10	4	3
	100	100

3. *Have you ever worked as an associate or assistant minister?*

yes	61	56
no	39	44
	100	100

If yes, to what extent was each of the following true of your relationship with the senior minister?
The senior minister and I spent an hour or so discussing the ministry of the parish:

often	62	·53
sometimes	17	26
rarely	15	17
never	6	4
	100	100
(N)	(381)	(409)

The senior minister was overly critical of my work:

often	7	6
sometimes	13	15
rarely	34	41
never	46	38
	100	100

The senior minister was overly protective of me, not giving me sufficient critical feedback:

often	12	5
sometimes	25	22
rarely	29	39
never	34	34
	100	100

	Percentage	
	W	M
very well	42	
satisfactorily	50	
not very well	8	
	100	

8. *For any conflicts or continuing difficulties you may have had with laypersons in your congregation, how important were/are each of the following as factors in this conflict or difficulty?*

Differences in theology, attitudes, or values:

	W	M
important	53	40
somewhat important	31	40
unimportant	16	20
	100	100

Misconceptions about your intentions or actions:

	W	M
important	34	38
somewhat important	38	45
unimportant	28	17
	100	100

If ever associate/assistant, the fact that you were not the senior pastor:

	W	M
important	17	10
somewhat important	28	31
unimportant	55	59
	100	100
(N)	(430)	(372)

The fact that you are a woman (this question not asked of clergymen):

	W	M
important	27	
somewhat important	35	
unimportant	38	
	100	

Part V: Support—Professional, Personal, and Monetary

PROFESSIONAL SUPPORT

1. *How many years have you been an official member, or on the rolls of, this judicatory?*

	W	M
1	11	5
2	15	6
3	14	5
4	15	6
5–9	28	26
10–18	10	27

	Percentage	
	W	M
19 plus	7	25
	100	100

2. *Approximately how many clergy are members of this judicatory?*

	W	M
1–50	11	16
51–75	8	11
76–100	11	12
101–150	9	10
151–200	13	11
200–300	16	15
301–400	10	9
401–600	13	8
601–800	4	4
800 plus	5	4
	100	100

3. *Of these, approximately how many are fully ordained women?*

	W	M
0–1	6	12
2–3	16	22
4–6	18	21
7–10	20	18
11–15	12	9
16–20	10	7
21 plus	18	11
	100	100
Have no idea (percent checking this)	5%	15%

4. *About how many clergy do you talk with regularly (at least once a month) in total?*

	W	M
1	3	2
2	3	5
3–5	15	18
6–10	23	32
11–15	20	17
16–24	14	12
25 plus	22	14
	100	100

Of these, how many are women clergy?

	W	M
1	32	47
2	22	29
3–5	27	18
6–10	14	5
11–15	4	1
16–24	1	0
	100	100

	Percentage	
	W	*M*

5. *Are you a member of any support/colleague/study group(s) of clergy?*

	W	M
yes	75	66
no	25	34
	100	100

If yes, what? (Categories not mutually exclusive.)

	W	M
clergy colleague/study group in local area	64	57
your denomination only	42	33
ecumenical	38	38
a national clergy group	12	8
your denomination only	10	7
ecumenical	5	3
some other type of clergy group	20	12

6. *Are you a member of any interest, social, or political group(s) composed of secular professionals and academics as well as clergy (which is not just for people in your parish)?*

	W	M
yes	48	47
no	52	53
	100	100

7. *How many different ongoing groups do you belong to—with which you meet at least once a year?*

	W	M
2 or less	21	23
3–4	31	31
5–6	22	21
7–10	15	11
11 or more	11	14
	100	100

8. *Are you a member of any colleague, professional, or interest group composed only of, or predominantly of, women?* (This question not asked of clergymen.)

	W
yes	57
no	43
	100

If yes, how many such groups?

	W
1	64
2	25
3	7
4	4
	100
(N)	(302)

	Percentage	
	W	M
If yes, is this group (categories not mutually exclusive):		
a local group?	25	
a regional group?	20	
a national group?	20	
composed only of clergy?	24	
composed of lay and clergy?	34	
only of your denomination?	29	
ecumenical?	28	

Do you think an all-woman professional support and/or interest group is something that clergywomen should seek to join or to establish?

	W	M
yes	61	
perhaps	28	
no	11	
	100	

9. *How frequently have you talked with the executive of your judicatory (bishop, synod president, conference minister, executive presbyter, district superintendent, area minister, etc.) during the last two months (approximately)?*

	W	M
not at all	15	15
1 or 2 times	38	38
3 or 4 times	22	26
5 or more times	25	21
	100	100

10. *About how well do you know this executive?*

	W	M
very well	34	30
quite well	22	33
fairly well	28	26
not very well	16	11
	100	100

11. *How supportive or helpful to you has this executive or a member of his staff been in each of the following areas?*
Professional or ministerial career concerns of yours:

	W	M
quite helpful	58	41
somewhat helpful	21	23
of little help	13	11
help not asked/needed	18	25
	100	100

	Percentage	
	W	*M*
Problems in/with your church:		
quite helpful	37	30
somewhat helpful	20	21
of little help	9	13
help not asked/needed	34	36
	100	100
Personal matters:		
quite helpful	21	23
somewhat helpful	14	14
of little help	10	10
help not asked/needed	55	53
	100	100
Other help from executive:	23	13

12. *Are you a member of any judicatory commissions or committees?*

	W	*M*
yes, presently	76	73
no, but have been	13	19
no, have never been	11	8
	100	100

13. *If you are or have been a member of a commission or committee, what generally has been the response of any laywomen members of this committee to you?* (This question not asked of clergymen.)

	W	*M*
good	82	
fair	9	
poor	2	
no laywomen on the committee	7	
	100	

14. *Would you be willing to be a clergy supervisor to a woman seminarian or intern in your church next year?*

	W	*M*
yes	89	80
maybe	7	13
no	4	7
	100	100

MINISTERIAL AND PERSONAL SUPPORT

1. *In handling conflicts among/with parishioners, how likely are you to turn to each of the following for assistance and/or advice?*

   One or more parishioners in your church:

	W	*M*
quite likely	47	59
somewhat likely	32	30

	Percentage	
	W	*M*
unlikely	21	11
	100	100
One or more staff in your church:		
quite likely	55	46
somewhat likely	15	23
unlikely	30	31
	100	100
Your spouse, other family member, or housemate:		
quite likely	57	62
somewhat likely	11	23
unlikely	32	15
	100	100
One or more clergy persons at other churches:		
quite likely	42	32
somewhat likely	34	41
unlikely	24	27
	100	100
close friend or friends outside this church, not in ministry:		
quite likely	26	17
somewhat likely	23	24
unlikely	51	59
	100	100
your denominational executive of your area:		
quite likely	29	33
somewhat likely	38	40
unlikely	33	27
	100	100
other:		
quite likely	69	63
somewhat likely	24	19
unlikely	7	18
	100	100
Who?		
seminary professor	14	7
counselor, clinical pastoral education supervisor	33	52
close friends from seminary or in ministry but far away	34	24
former pastor, pastoral mentor	10	17
clergywomen	9	0
	100	100
(N)	(70)	(29)

	Percentage	
	W	*M*
2. What is your present marital status?		
married	55	94
single, never married	32	4
widowed	3	0
divorced/separated	10	2
	100	100

3. If presently married, please answer the following question.

How long have you been married to your present spouse?

1–3 years	17	4
4–6 years	23	6
7–10 years	20	11
11–19 years	23	25
more than 20 years	17	54
	100	100
(N)	(342)	(677)

Overall, how resentful is your spouse of the time and energy you invest in your ministerial work?

never or rarely	68	48
sometimes resentful	29	48
frequently resentful	3	4
	100	100
(N)	(342)	(675)

Is your spouse employed?

no	12	35
yes, full-time	66	40
yes, part-time	22	25
	100	100
(N)	(342)	(675)

Is your spouse also ordained?

yes	60	4
no	40	96
	100	100
(N)	(342)	(675)

If yes, is your spouse:

a minister in your church?	57	48
a minister in another church?	32	19
working in a nonchurch setting?	11	33
	100	100
(N)	(173)	(21)

If no, what is the occupation of your spouse?

church work, not ordained	2	0
top professional	21	2

	Percentage	
	W	M
business executive, banker, large-business owner	5	1
school teacher, social worker, social service worker, pilot, engineer, librarian, newspaper editor, military officer, musician, artist	22	51
small-business owner, administrative personnel, insurance agent, semiprofessional, paraprofessional, reporter, sheriff, actor, mortician, computer programmer, lab technician, photographer, travel agent	26	26
clerical worker, sales worker, owner of little business (self-employed), postal worker, police officer, salesman, military personnel (nonofficer)	3	15
farmer (owner)	2	0
skilled manual laborer, fireman, machinists, hair stylist, carpenter	6	2
unemployed, homemaker, not in labor force, student	12	4
	100	100
(N)	(131)	(404)

As far as you can gather, how does your spouse's occupation affect your parishioners' opinion of you? In the majority they:

respect me more	56	35
respect me less	2	0
feel sorry for me	2	2
do not care	33	60
other	7	3
	100	100
(N)	(320)	(462)

Whose career goals actually seem to take priority when either of you considering a position(s)?

my own	12	76
my spouse's	18	2
both equally	70	22
	100	100
(N)	(325)	(470)

How active is your spouse in your church?

very active	54	66
somewhat active	19	30
rather inactive	27	4
	100	100
(N)	(331)	(675)

	Percentage	
	W	M
How do the majority of your parishioners feel about this degree of your spouse's participation in your church?		
very satisfied	54	57
satisfied	30	35
mixed in response or ambivalent	14	7
dissatisfied	2	1
	100	100
4. *Do you have any natural or adopted children?*		
yes	46	89
no	54	11
	100	100
If yes, how many children do you have?		
1	26	11
2	39	34
3	19	28
4 or more	16	27
	100	100
(N)	(276)	(639)
How many of these are (or is this child) under age 18?		
1	42	36
2	42	40
3 or more	16	24
	100	100
(N)	(213)	(403)
Were any of your children under the age of ten while you had a full-time ministerial position?		
yes	58	96
no	40	4
(part-time position)	2	0
	100	100
(N)	(262)	(629)
If yes to the above, how difficult was it for you to carry on a full-time ministry when your children were this young?		
very difficult	31	3
somewhat difficult	40	33
relatively easy	29	64
	100	100
(N)	(160)	(610)

	Percentage	
	W	*M*
5. *Have you ever been divorced?*		
yes	17	12
no	83	88
	100	100
	(90)	(79)
If yes, has (or did) your divorced status affect your ability to get parish positions?		
yes	31	32
no	63	53
have not tried since divorce to get a parish	6	15
	100	100
(N)	(78)	(73)
To what extent was this divorce caused by the conflicts over the time taken by (or the nature of) your ministerial work?		
to a great extent	7	19
to some extent	20	27
not related at all	73	51
do not know	0	3
	100	100
(N)	(89)	(73)
If presently single, widowed, or divorced, are there any adults who live with you?		
yes	21	15
no	79	85
	100	100
(N)	(274)	(48)
If yes, are they (or is this person):		
relative(s)?	40	29
nonrelative(s)?	60	43
both?	0	28
	100	100
(N)	(53)	(7)
Is this person (or persons) a source of support to you?		
yes, a source of great support	68	28
yes, some support	21	29
of little or no support	11	43
	100	100
(N)	(53)	(7)

FINANCIAL SUPPORT AND OTHER RESOURCES

1. *Do you live in a house provided by the church?*

	Percentage	
	W	*M*
yes	49	57
no	51	43
	100	100

2. *Do you own your own house or vacation home?*

yes	44	54
no	56	46
	100	100

3. *What is the cash salary paid you by the parish per year?*

$10,000 or under	39	10
$10,000–$15,000	47	39
$16,000–$20,000	11	28
$21,000 or over	3	23
	100	100

4. *Do you earn income from sources other than this parish?*

yes	37	26
no	63	74
	100	100

5. *What is your total family income before taxes per year?*

$15,000 or under	35	17
$15,000–$24,000	37	44
$25,000–$34,000	18	26
$35,000 or over	10	13
	100	100

6. *How likely is it that you will have sufficient income after you retire to live comfortably?*

very likely	26	25
somewhat likely	40	51
somewhat unlikely	21	18
very unlikely	13	6
	100	100

Part VI: Attitudes About Clergy, the Church, and Ministry

There are a number of possible ways in which a local congregation may respond to public issues involving matters of morality and social justice. For each of the following, would you please indicate whether you agree, have mixed feelings or opinions, or disagree:

1. My congregation should not involve itself with social and political matters; rather, it should concentrate on bringing people to Christ:

	Percentage	
	W	M
agree	2	4
mixed	10	25
disagree	88	71
	100	100

2. My congregation should organize itself into study-action groups to deal with issues that affect:

Personal morality and human sexuality:

agree	65	57
mixed	25	35
disagree	10	8
	100	100

Who should be elected to political office:

agree	35	25
mixed	30	40
disagree	35	35
	100	100

Equal rights for women:

agree	69	60
mixed	22	30
disagree	9	10
	100	100

Equal rights for blacks and other minorities:

agree	77	65
mixed	17	28
disagree	6	7
	100	100

Please now indicate whether you agree with, have mixed feelings about, or disagree with each of the following statements about clergy and the church.

1. I would be pleased if I had a son who wanted to be a parish minister:

agree	76	72
mixed	19	26
disagree	5	2
	100	100

2. I would be pleased if I had a daughter who wanted to be a parish minister:

agree	78	61
mixed	19	32
disagree	3	7
	100	100

	Percentage	
	W	M
3. More women should be ordained to full ministerial status in my denomination:		
agree	81	59
mixed	17	30
disagree	2	11
	100	100
4. My congregation should appoint/elect an equal number of laywomen to laymen on the parish governing board:		
agree	75	58
mixed	14	23
disagree	11	19
	100	100
5. If a ministerial vacancy should occur in my congregation (or finances permit an additional minister to be hired), the search committee should actively seek a woman candidate:		
agree	34	40
mixed	32	38
disagree	34	22
	100	100
6. Women, whether lay or clergy, do not hold positions or influence in this area (region) comparable to lay and clergy men of my denomination:		
agree	61	53
mixed	10	16
disagree	29	31
	100	100
7. Inclusive language should be used in church publications and services:		
agree	87	53
mixed	9	31
disagree	4	16
	100	100
8. There should be more women in executive staff positions in regional and national offices of my denomination:		
agree	85	49
mixed	10	37
disagree	5	14
	100	100

9. I think I have a promising future in my denomination:

agree	72	71
mixed	22	24
disagree	6	5
	100	100

10. The ordained ministry still carries prestige and dignity which no other profession shares:

agree	27	28
mixed	29	49
disagree	44	23
	100	100

Notes

Chapter 1

1. E. Wilbur Bock, "The Female Clergy: A Case of Professional Marginality," *American Journal of Sociology* 72 (March 1967), p. 539.
2. Martin E. Marty, *A Nation of Behavers* (Chicago: University of Chicago Press, 1976), p. 53.
3. *Perspectives on Working Women: A Databook* (Washington, D.C.: U.S. Department of Labor, Bureau of Labor Statistics), Bulletin 2080, October 1980, p. 3.
4. Richard B. Freeman, *The Over-educated American* (New York: Academic Press, 1976), pp. 123 ff.
5. Disciples include in their annual count of clergy both ordained and licensed ministers. The latter group of ministers change significantly from year to year and make difficult a true picture of trends among fully ordained Disciples clergy.
6. Marvin J. Taylor, ed., *Fact Book on Theological Education, 1980–1981* (Vandalia, Ohio: Association of Theological Schools, 1981), pp. 8–9.
7. Hartford *Courant*, January 30, 1982.
8. For a fuller treatment several of these factors, see Freeman, *The Over-educated American*, pp. 165 ff.
9. Daniel Yankelovich, *New Rules* (New York: Random House, 1981), p. 103.
10. Freeman, *The Over-educated American*, p. 176.
11. Jackson W. Carroll and Robert L. Wilson, *The Clergy Job Market: Oversupply and/or Opportunity* (Hartford, CT: The Hartford Seminary Foundation, 1978), p. 87.
12. Carole R. Bohn, "The Changing Scene: Women Come to Seminary" (paper presented at the meeting of the American Academy of Religion, Dallas, Texas, 1980), p. 7.
13. Bock, "The Female Clergy," p. 531.
14. Everett C. Hughes, "Dilemmas and Contradictions of Status," *The American Journal of Sociology* 50 (March 1945), pp. 353–59. The article has been reprinted in Everett C. Hughes, *Men and Their Work* (Glencoe, IL: The Free Press, 1958).
15. Cited in Bohn, "The Changing Scene," p. 7.
16. For a discussion of ambivalence over conflicting statuses, see Elinor Barber and Robert K. Merton, "Sociological Ambivalence," in *Sociological Theory, Values and Sociocultural Change*, ed. Edward A. Tyriakian (New York: The Free Press of Glencoe, 1963), pp. 91–120. We might add that another stereotype of the minister—male or female—is of the "holy" person, that is one who represents moral purity. Such a stereotype causes ambivalence both for the minister and others when he or she is in a group of "good old boys" or when he or she acts out of character. The point is that stereotypes, status contradictions, and ambivalence are not exclusive to clergywomen, but to men as well.
17. Rosabeth Moss Kanter, *Men and Women of the Corporation* (New York: Basic Books, 1977), pp. 207 ff.

18. Joy Charlton, "Women Entering the Ordained Ministry: Contradictions and Dilemmas of Status "(paper presented at the meeting of the Society for the Scientific Study of Religion, Hartford, Connecticut, October 26–29, 1978), p. 22.

19. These included Bock, "The Female Clergy"; Charlton, "Women Entering the Ordained Ministry"; Marjorie Garhart, "Women in the Ordained Ministry," Lutheran Church in America, 1976, mimeographed; Harry Hale, Jr., Morton King, and Doris M. Jones, *New Witness, United Methodist Clergywomen* (Nashville: United Methodist Board of Higher Education and Ministry, 1980); Arthur R. Jones, Jr., and Lee Taylor, "Differential Recruitment of Female Professionals," in *Professional Women*, ed. Athena Theodore (Cambridge: Schenkman Publishing Company, 1971), pp. 355–362; Kanter, *Men and Women of the Corporation;* Edward C. Lehman, *Project S.W.I.M.: A Study of Women in Ministry* (Valley Forge, PA: Task Force on Women in Ministry of the American Baptist Churches, 1979); G. Lloyd Rediger, "The Feminine Mystique and the Ministry," *The Christian Century*, July 4–11, 1979, pp. 699–702; "Research Report of the 1978 Women in Ordained Ministry Questionnaire," Lutheran-Northwestern Theological Seminaries, St. Paul, Minnesota, duplicated; "Report of the Advisory Commission on Women in Church and Society to the Twelfth General Synod of the United Church of Christ," United Church of Christ Executive Offices, New York, 1979, duplicated; "Seminary Selection Study, Research Division of the Support Agency, "United Presbyterian Church, New York, 1977, duplicated; Gay H. Tennis, "Clergywomen in the United Presbyterian Church, U.S.A." (paper presented at the meeting of the Religious Research Association, San Antonio, Texas, October 19, 1979).

20. The responses to the layleader questionnaire can be obtained from the Center for Social and Religious Research, Hartford Seminary, 77 Sherman Street, Hartford, CT 06105 for the cost of reproduction and postage.

Chapter 2

1. Barbara Brown Zikmund, "The Feminist Thrust of Sectarian Christianity," in *Women of Spirit*, ed. Rosemary R. Ruether and Eleanor McLaughlin (New York: Simon and Schuster, 1979), pp. 209–220.

2. Harry Leon McBeth, "The Role of Women in Southern Baptist History," *Baptist History and Heritage* 12, no. 1, pp. 3–25.

3. Charles H. Barfoot and Gerald T. Sheppard, "Prophetic vs. Priestly Religion: The Changing Role of Women Clergy in Pentecostal Churches," *Review of Religious Research* 22, no. (September 1980), pp. 2–17.

4. Ibid., p. 4.

5. See, for example, Josephine Massingbyrde Ford, *Which Way for Catholic Pentecostals?* (New York: Haper & Row, 1977).

6. Barbara Welter, "The Feminization of American Religion: 1800 to 1860," in *Clio's Consciousness Raised: New Perspective on the History of Women*, ed. Mary Hartman and Lois W. Banner (New York: Harper & Row, 1974), pp. 137–57.

7. William Bean Kennedy, *The Shaping of Protestant Education* (New York: Association Press, 1966), p. 63.

8. Elaine Magalis, *Conduct Becoming to a Woman* (Women's Division, Board of Global Ministries, United Methodist Church, 1973), p. 38.

9. See, for example, Lorraine Lollis, *The Shape of Adam's Rib* (St. Louis: Bethany Press, 1970), pp. 22–28.

10. Magalis, *Conduct*, p. 38.

11. McBeth, *Role of Women*, p. 7.

12. Lester G. McAllister, "Women Became Involved through the Christian Woman's Board of Missions," *Discipliana* 33, no. 1 (Winter 1973), p. 6.

13. Katherine Schutze, "Women and Ministry," *The Disciple* 1, no. 13 (June 23, 1974), p. 4.

14. Report on Project 368: Lay Professional Development and Support," Division for Professional Leadership, the Lutheran Church in America, March 27–29, 1980.

15. Mary O. Evans, "Removing the Veil: The Liberated American Nun," in Reuther and McLaughlin, *Women of Spirit*, pp. 255–78.

16. Frederick S. Weiser, *United to Serve* (Gladwyne, PA: LCA Deaconness Community, 1966), p. 3.

16 Norene Carter, "The Episcopalian Story," in Ruether and McLaughlin, *Women of Spirit*, p. 357.

18. Virginia Lieson Brereton and Christa Ressmeyer Klein, "American Women in Ministry: A History of Protestant Beginning Points," in Ruether and McLaughlin, *Women of Spirit*, p. 311.

19. McBeth, *Role of Women*, pp. 12–14.

20. Elizabeth Gray Vining, "Women in the Society of Friends," Ward Lecture, Guilford College, November 11, 1955.

21. Brochure from the Society of the Companions of the Holy Cross, by Mrs. Joan Russell, General Secretary of the Society.

22. Peter Berger, Brigitte Berger, and Hansfried Kellner, *The Homeless Mind* (New York: Random House, 1973).

23. Elizabeth Howells Verdesi, *In But Still Out: Women in the Church* (Philadelphia: Westminster Press, 1976), "The Women That Publish the Tidings Are a Great Host," pp. 55–78.

24. Lollis, *Shape*, p. 68.

25. Max Weber, *Economy and Society*, ed. Gunther Roth and Claus Wittich (New York: Bedminster Press 1968), p. 212.

26. Private correspondence, Mary Sudman Donovan, January 5, 1981.

27. Private correspondence, Suzanne Hiatt, 1982.

28. *The Discipline of the Methodist Church* (Nashville: Methodist Publishing House, 1964).

29. "More about Deaconesses," *The Deaconess* 8, no. 2 (Fall 1978), p. 3.

30. Charles E. Raven, *Women and the Ministry* (Garden City, NJ: Doubleday, Doran & Co., 1929), p. 67.

31. "Professional *and* Pastoral," *The Deaconess* 8, no 2 (Fall 1978), p. 4.

32. Janet Harbison Penfield, "Women in the Presbyterian Church: An Historical Overview," *Journal of Presbyterian History* 55, no. 2 (1977), p. 155.

33. "Bishop's Address Read Before the General Conference at Its First Session, Wednesday Morning, May 4, 1910," *Journal of the Sixteenth General Conference of the Methodist Episcopal Church, South*, 1910, p. 26.

34. Raven, *Women*, pp. 23–29.

35. Verdesi, *In But Still Out*, pp. 120–32.

36. As quoted in ibid., pp. 151–52.

37. See ibid., Chapter 6, for a discussion of the way this occurred among religious educators.

38. Our thanks to the Rev. Susan Robinson for this information.

39. Carter Heyward, *A Priest Forever* (New York: Harper & Row, 1976), pp. 32–33.

40. Fran Ferder, *Called to Break Bread?* (Mt. Ranier, MD: The Quixote Center, 1978), p. 53.

41. Rt. Rev. Stanley Atkins, "The Theological Case Against Women's Ordination,"

in *The Ordination of Women: Pro and Con,* ed. Michael Plock Hamilton and Nancy S. Montgomery (New York: Morehouse-Barlow, 1975), p. 27.

42. "Report of the Division for Missions in North America, Consulting Committee on Women in Church and Society," Lutheran Church in America, 1980, pp. 45–46.

43. Barbara Brown Zikmund, "Attacking the Male Power Structure in American Protestantism" (paper presented at the meeting of the American Academy of Religion, New Orleans, November 1978).

Chapter 3

1. Carole R. Bohn, "The Changing Scene: Women Come to Seminary" (paper presented at the American Academy of Religion Meeting, Dallas, Texas, 1980), p. 6. More specifically, she indicates: "A large percentage of respondents said that their fathers were important role models. Although there were not frequently named as role models, mothers seemed to provide considerable more emotional support than decisive, suggesting a sex difference in the manner in which parents and significant others effect vocational development" (p. 8).

2. Good discussions, reviews, and articles on the determinants and correlates of social class may be found in Reinhard Bendix and Seymour Martin Lipset, eds., *Class, Status and Power,* 2nd ed. (New York: The Free Press, 1966); Ely Chinoy, *Society: An Introduction to Sociology* (New York: Random House, 1961), pp. 130–166; and William J. Goode, ed., *The Dynamics of Modern Society* (New York: Atherton Press, 1966), pp. 63–108.

3. While clergy was a choice of only 2 percent of the college students surveyed by Gallup in 1973–74, between three-fifths and three-fourths of these came from families where the father had a high school education or less, or were employed in clerical, sales, or blue collar occupations. Gallup Opinion Index, Religion in America, Report no. 114 (1975), pp. 34–37.

4. The tendency for lower socioeconomic classes to be members of fundamentalist denominations or sects, or doctrinally orthodox wings of mainline Protestant denominations has been documented in numerous studies. For example, see Wade Clark Roof, "Traditional Religion in Contemporary Society," *American Sociological Review* 41 (April 1976), pp. 195–208. Also, lower parental socioeconomic status has been shown to be associated with clergy who hold doctrinally orthodox beliefs. See Jackson W. Carroll, "Structural Effects of Professional Schools on Professional Socialization: The Case of Protestant Clergymen," *Social Forces* 50 (Summer 1971), pp. 61–74; also Yoshio Fukuyama, *The Ministry in Transition* (University Park, Pennsylvania: Pennsylvania State University Press, 1972), pp. 5, 26–27.

5. Gideon Sjoberg and James Otis Smith, "Origin and Career Patterns of Leading Protestant Clergymen," *Social Forces* 39 (May 1961), pp. 290–96. The authors indicate a very high level of involvement in nonparish ministries among those in *Who's Who* listings, most of whom came from leading families.

6. N. J. Demerath III, *Social Class in American Protestanism* (Chicago: Rand McNalley, 1965); S. Goldstein, "Socioeconomic Differentials Among Religious Groups in the United States," *American Journal of Sociology* 74 1969), pp. 612–31; B. Lazerwitz, "Religion and the Social Structure of the United States," in *Religion, Culture and Society,* ed., Louis Schneider (New York: Wiley, 1964).

7. Lehman also reports in a recent study of American Baptist seminary graduates that the women were significantly more likely to come from higher social class families. Edward C. Lehman, Jr., "Placement of Men and Women in the Ministry," *Review of Religious Research* 22 (September 1980), pp. 18–40.

8. Cynthia Fuchs Epstein, *Women in Law* (New York: Basic Books, 1981), pp. 24–31, quote p. 31.

9. Personal communication from The Reverend Dr. Roger Fjeld, Field Director, Office of Support Ministries of the American Lutheran Church.

10. See for example, Eli Ginsberg, et al., *Occupational Choice: An Approach to General Theory* (New York: Columbia University Press, 1959), p. 141; also Arthur R. Jones and Lee Taylor, "Differential Recruitment of Female Professionals: A Case Study of Clergywomen," in *The Professional Woman*, ed. Athena Theodore (Cambridge, Massachusetts: Schenkman Publishing Company 1971), pp. 355–62.

11. The Reverend Dr. Diane Tennis, Staff Associate, Professional Development, of the Presbyterian Church in the United States, suggests in personal correspondence that the reason "more PCUS women are in religious colleges probably has to do with their being in private colleges which is probably a lingering phase of delayed urbanization."

12. The Reverend Susan Robinson, Director of Developing Ministries of the Christian Church-Disciples of Christ comments in personal correspondence that "The high percentage [of clergy attending denominational colleges] may be due to the strong recruiting efforts of our denominational colleges and their offering of work in preministerial degrees. Also, affluence and geography may have played a part. Our population is sparse in the Northeast, where the private secular colleges are located." She also suggests that, "The Disciples would have a larger number of clergy who attended secular colleges if the clergy were divided between those who attended college "pre- and post-1950.""

13. Burton R. Clark, et al., *Students and Colleges: Interaction and Change* (Berkeley, California: Center for Research and Development in Higher Education, University of California, Berkeley, 1972), pp. 300–16.

14. Allen H. Barton, "The Religious Factor in the 1968 Student Demonstrations at Columbia," mimeographed paper, March 1973. Barton found the higher the parental social class, the less likely college men were to espouse religious values.

15. Wagner Thielens, Jr., "Some Comparisons of Entrants to Medical and Law School," *The Student Physician*, ed. Patricia L. Kendall, Robert K. Merton, and George C. Reader (Cambridge, Massachusetts: Harvard University Press, 1957), pp. 131–52. For example, Wagner Thielens argues that one reason medical students made an earlier decision than law students to attend their respective graduate professional schools is the higher standing of medicine than law in society, hence making it more attractive to youth.

16. Orville Brim, Jr., "Adult Socialization," in *Socialization and Society*, ed. John A. Clausen (Boston: Little, Brown and Company, 1968), pp. 183–226, quote p. 187.

17. Ronald M. Pavalko, *Sociology of Occupations and Professions* (Ithaca, Illinois: F. E. Peacock Publishers, Inc., 1971), pp. 80–109.

Chapter 4

1. Marvin J. Taylor, ed., *Fact Book on Theological Education, 1974–75* (Vandalia, Ohio: Association of Theological Schools, 1975), pp. 5–6.

2. The Cornwall Collective, *Your Daughters Shall Prophesy: Feminist Alternatives in Theological Education* (New York: The Pilgrim Press, 1980).

3. See George Lindbeck (in consultation with Karl Deutsch and Nathan Glazer), *University Divinity Schools: A Report on Ecclesiastically Independent Theological Education* (New York: The Rockefeller Foundation, 1976).

4. This point has been emphasized in two articles in *Theological Education* 18 (Au-

tumn, 1981): Leon Pacala, "Reflection on the State of Theological Education in the 1980s," pp. 32–33; and Jackson W. Carroll, "Project Transition: An Assessment of ATS Programs and Services," pp. 69–70.

5. Lindbeck, *"University Divinity Schools,"* p. 32, reports that for a "fair number" of students who attend these interdenominational university seminaries (Harvard, Union-New York, University of Chicago, Vanderbilt, and Yale) "divinity school represents the last serious involvement with organized religion, and this holds also for some who go on and teach religion in colleges, universities, or even seminaries. In contrast, it is a rare denominational seminary which does not initially send eighty—and usually over ninety—percent of its M.Div. graduates into parish work."

6. Walter Robert Strobel, "Personal and Academic Problems of Bachelor of Divinity Degree Candidates at a Large Metropolitan Theological Seminary" (Ed.D. dissertation, Teacher's College of Columbia University, 1966); Adair T. Lummis, "Especially Union? Educational Policy and Socialization in an Elite Boundary Professional School" (Ph.D. dissertation, Columbia University, 1978).

7. "Seminary Selection Study," Research Division of the Support Agency, United Presbyterian Church in the U.S.A., pp. 50–51.

8. Donald E. Edgar, "The Institutional Context," in *The Competent Teacher,* ed. Donald E. Edgar (Sydney, Australia: Angus and Robertson, 1974), p. 19.

9. Donald Ploch, *Faculty as Professionalization and Change Agents,* final report (USHEW Project 0-0355), p. 1972.

10. "Research Report of the Advisory Commission on Women in Church and Society to the Twelfth General Synod of the United Church of Christ," United Church of Christ Execution Offices, New York, 1979, duplicated; "Research Report of the 1978 Women in Ordained Ministry Questionnaire," Lutheran-Northwestern Theological Seminaries, St. Paul, MN. duplicated; Gay Tennis, "Clergywomen in the United Presbyterian Church, U.S.A." (paper presented at the meeting of the Religious Research Association, San Antonio, TX, October 19, 1979).

11. Marjorie Garhart, "Women in the Ordained Ministry" (a report to the Division for Professional Leadership, Lutheran Church in America, 1976).

12. Lummis, "Especially Union?" pp. 315–519.

13. This is suggested or directly indicated by Lindbeck, *University Divinity Schools,* and Lummis, "Especially Union?" dealing with faculty goals and preferences in university seminaries; the Ploch study of fifteen seminaries (many of which were at least university associated if not interdenominational), and a study comparing goal emphases in different types of seminaries for the kinds of student products produced: Jackson W. Carroll, "Structural Effects of Professional Schools on Professional Socialization: the Case of Protestant Clergymen," *Social Forces* (September 1971), pp. 61–74.

14. Edward C. Lehman Jr., *Project S.W.I.M.: A Study of Women in Ministry* (Valley Forge, PA: Task Force on Women in Ministry of the American Baptist Churches, 1979).

15. Rosabeth Moss Kanter, "Some Effects of Proportions on Group Life: Skewed Sex Ratios and Responses to Token Women," *American Journal of Sociology* 82 (March 1977), pp. 965–90.

16. For a good theoretical discussion of this process of how professions acquire the power to certify, see William J. Goode, "The Theoretical Limits of Professionalization," in *The Semi-Professions and Their Organization,* ed. Amitai Etzioni (New York: Free Press, 1969), pp. 266–313.

17. "Report of the Advisory Commission on Women," 1979, duplicated; and Harry Hale, Jr., Morton King, and Doris Moreland Jones, *New Witnesses, United Methodist Clergywomen* (Nashville, TN: Division of Ordained Ministry, United Methodist Church, 1980), especially pp. 51–53.
18. Jackson W. Carroll and Robert L. Wilson, *Too Many Pastors?* (New York: The Pilgrim Press, 1980), pp. 76–77.
19. Elizabeth Rodgers Dobell, "God and Woman: The Hidden History," *Redbook Magazine*, March 1978, pp. 37–44.
20. Beverly Wildung Harrison, "Sexism and the Contemporary Church: When Evasion Becomes Complicity," in *Sexist Religion and Women in the Church: No More Silence!*, ed. Alice L. Hageman (New York: Association Press, 1974), pp. 195–216.
21. Beverly Wildung Harrison, "The Early Feminists and the Clergy: A Case Study in the Dynamics of Secularization," *Reivew and Expositor* 72 (Winter 1975), p. 51.
22. Laurie Davidson and Laura Gordon, *The Sociology of Gender* (Chicago: Rand McNally Publishing Company, 1979), pp. 190–99.
23. Ibid., pp. 191–95.
24. The Cornwall Collective, *Your Daughters Shall Prophesy*.
25. Barbara Brown Zikmund, "Attacking the Male Power Structure in American Protestantism" (paper presented at the meeting of the American Academy of Religion, New Orleans, November 1978).
26. Davidson and Gordon, *Sociology of Gender*, p. 199.
27. The *alpha* coefficient, indicating the relative homogeneity of the four items, is .77.

Chapter 5

1. Both studies were undertaken by Edward C. Lehman, Jr. The first, Project S.W.I.M.: *A Study of Women in Ministry* (Valley Forge, PA: Task Force on Women in Ministry of the American Baptist Churches, 1979), involved a comparative study of American Baptist clergymen and women, and included data from laity and denominational officials. An article based on the study, "Placement of Men and Women in the Ministry," was published in the *Review of Religious Research* 22 (September 1980), pp. 18–40. The second is a forthcoming study of United Presbyterian clergywomen, a portion of which was presented as "Correlates of Placement of Women in Ministry: Half a Replication," at the 1981 meeting of the Association of the Sociology of Religion.
2. Jackson W. Carroll and Robert L. Wilson, *Too Many Pastors? The Clergy Job Market* (New York: Pilgrim Press, 1980), pp. 33–35. For another, slightly different classification, see William C. Bonifield and Edgar W. Mills, "The Clergy Labor Markets and Wage Determination," *Journal for the Scientific Study of Religion* 19 (June 1980), pp. 146–58.
3. Carroll and Wilson, *Too Many Pastors*, p. 35.
4. The actual question wording asked, "How long after you were ordained did it take for you to obtain a parish position?" This was not a good question, since many denominations require a call to a position as a prerequisite for ordination. In spite of the question wording, to which some respondents called attention, most understood it as in inquiry to the difficulty or ease of first placement.
5. Carroll and Wilson, *Too Many Pastors*, pp. 33–48.
6. Ibid., pp 31–2.
7. Lehman, "Correlates of Placement of Women in Ministry," pp. 24–6.

8. Lehman, "Placement of Men and Women in Ministry," pp. 35–8.
9. Lehman, "Correlates of Placement of Women in Ministry."
10. Ibid., pp. 24–6.
11. Edward C. Lehman, Jr., "Organizational Resistance to Women in Ministry" (paper presented at the Association for the Sociology of Religion, New York, New York, August 24–26, 1980).
12. Denominational differences exist in salaries paid to men and women, but to control for both salary and denominational differences for men and women creates too few cases in many categories for meaningful analysis. Suffice to say that salary differentials appear to exist for women and men in all denominations, with women receiving lower salaries than men.
13. Bonifield and Mills, "The Clergy Labor Markets," pp. 154–55.
14. Lehman, "Correlates of Placement of Women in Ministry," p. 26.
15. Joy Charlton, "Women Entering the Ordained Ministry: Contradictions and Dilemmas of Status" (paper presented at the annual meeting of the society for the Scientific Study of Religion, Hartford, Connecticut, October 26–29, 1978).
16. Cynthia Fuchs Epstein, *Women in Law* (New York: Basic Books, 1981), pp. 268–69.
17. Edward C. Lehman, Jr., personal correspondence.
18. For a discussion of reference groups and relative deprivation, see Robert K. Merton, *Social Theory & Social Structure* (London: The Free Press of Glencoe, 1957), pp. 225 ff; and Peter M. Blau, *Exchange & Power in Social Life* (New York: John Wiley & Sons, 1964), pp. 151–60.

Chapter 6

1. Edward C. Lehman, "Organizational Resistance to Women in Ministry" (paper presented at the annual meeting of the Association for the Sociology of Religion, New York City, August 24–25, 1980).
2. Ibid.
3. Philip Selznick, *Leadership in Administration* (New York: Harper & Row, 1957), pp. 120–27, argues that for many members of an organization, organizational survival is identical with maintaining the organization as a distinctive or particular kind of organization.
4. Donald E. Edgar, "Socialization Theory," in *The Competent Teacher*, ed. D. E. Edgar (Sydney, Australia: Angus and Robertson, 1974), pp. 1–13.
5. See for example, the following studies: Mary Jean Huntington, "The Development of a Professional Self-Image," in *The Student Physician*, ed. S. Patricia L. Kendall, Robert K. Merton, George C. Reader (Cambridge, Mass.: Harvard University Press, 1957), pp. 179–97; Charles Kadushin, "The Professional Self-Concept of Music Students," *American Journal of Sociology*, 75 (November, 1969), pp. 389–404; Wagner P. Thielens, Jr., *The Socialization of Law Students* (Ph.D. dissertation, Columbia University, 1965), pp. 282–84.
6. Gerald J. Jud, Edgar W. Mills, Jr., and Genevieve Walters Burch, *Ex-Pastors: Why Men Leave the Parish Ministry* (Philadelphia: Pilgrim Press, 1970), p. 91 and p. 107.
7. See studies cited in footnote 5 above, as well as: Ronald M. Pavalko, *Sociology of Occupations and Professions* (Itasca, Illinois: F. E. Peacock Publishers, Inc., 1971), pp. 87–88, 98.
8. Clergywomen on Church Staff in Last Ten Years:

	Laymen	*Laywomen*
None	30%	25%
	(108)	(92)
1 to 2	70%	75%
	(247)	(281)
	100%	100%
	(355)	(373)

9. Edward C. Lehman, *Project S.W.I.M.: A Study of Women in Ministry* (Valley Forge, PA: Task Force on Women in Ministry of the American Baptist Churches 1979).
10. Edward C. Lehman, Jr., "The Minister-At-Large Program: An Evaluation," report issued by the Vocation Agency, the United Presbyterian Church in the USA, May 1981.
11. Mitchell found that the discrepancy between social class backgrounds of pastors and their parishioners made it more difficult for the pastor to minister effectively to them. Robert Edward Mitchell, "When Ministers and Their Parishioners Have Different Social Class Positions," *Review of Religious Research* 7 (Fall 1965), pp. 28–41.

Chapter 7

1. For a discussion of the role-set concept, see Robert K. Merton, *Social Theory & Social Structure* (London: The Free Press of Glencoe, 1957), pp. 368–80. For a discussion of the concept in relation to the ordained ministry, see Gerald J. Jud, Edgar W. Mills, Jr. and Genevieve Walters Burch, *Ex-Pastors, Why Men Leave the Parish Ministry* (Philadelphia: Pilgrim Press, 1970), pp. 80 ff.
2. See, for example, Phillip E. Hammond, et al., "Clergy Authority and Friendship Patterns," *Pacific Sociological Review* (April 1972), pp. 185–201.
3. Marjorie Garhart, "Women in the Ordained Ministry," a report to the Division for Professional Church Leadership, Lutheran Church in America, 1976; Harry Hale, Jr., Morton King, and Doris M. Jones, *New Witnesses, United Methodist Church Clergywomen* (Nashville: United Methodist Board of Higher Education & Ministry, 1980), pp. 59–60; Edward C. Lehman, *Project S.W.I.M.: A Study of Women in Ministry* (Valley Forge, PA: Task Force on Women in Ministry of the American Baptist Churches, 1979), pp. 18–19; and Report of the Advisory Commission on Women in Church and Society to the Twelfth Annual Synod of the United Church of Christ, 1979, duplicated.
4. Joseph Bensman and Arthur J. Vidich, *Small Town in Mass Society* (Garden City, N.Y.: Doubleday Anchor Books, 1958), p. 244.
5. Jackson W. Carroll, "Some Issues in Clergy Authority," *Review of Religious Research* 23 (December 1981), pp. 99–117. See also Phillip E. Hammond, Lois Salinas, and Douglas Sloane, "Types of Clergy Authority: Their Measurement, Location, and Effects," *Journal for the Scientific Study of Religion* 17 (September 1978), pp. 241–53.
6. Hammond et al., "Types of Clergy Authority," pp. 247–50.
7. Joy Charlton, "Women Entering the Ordained Ministry: Contradictions and Dilemmas of Status" (paper presented at the annual meeting of the Society for the Scientific Study of Religion, Hartford, Connecticut, October 26–29, 1979), p. 23.

8. Jeffrey K. Hadden, *The Gathering Storm in the Churches* (Garden City, NY: Doubleday, 1969).

9. The Rev. LaVonne Althouse, personal correspondence.

10. Discussion and illustration of appropriate clerical dresses for women appears in Garhart, "Women in the Ordained Ministry."

11. Hedwig Jemison, "Clothing Men of the Cloth," *Ministry: A Magazine for Clergy* (July 1980), pp. 5–6.

12. For a general discussion of the importance of normative consistency in the three components of "front" (setting, appearance, and manner), see Erving Goffman, *The Presentation of Self in Everyday Life* (Garden City, NY: Doubleday, 1959), pp. 22–30.

13. For a review of equity theory and research, see William J. Goode, *The Celebration of Heroes, Prestige as a Social Control System* (Berkeley: University of California Press, 1978), pp. 376–94.

14. Jud et al., *Ex-Pastors*, pp. 81–83.

15. Overall differences in our study between men and women in how they get along with other clergy are smaller than reported in other studies. See "Research Report of the 1978 Women in Ordained Ministry Questionnaire," Luther-Northwestern Theological Seminaries (duplicated), pp. 7–10; and Lehman, *S.W.I.M.*, pp. 18–19.

16. Jackson W. Carroll and Robert L. Wilson suggest that "the degree of competition and tension between men clergy and women clergy will be in direct ratio to the scarcity of available positions in the church" (*The Clergy Job Market* [New York: Pilgrim Press, 1980], p. 85).

17. See Merton, *Social Theory & Social Structure*, pp. 225–386.

18. Lehman (*S.W.I.M.*, pp. 19–20) reports that male ministers were accepted much better by other ministers' spouses in the community than were women clergy.

19. Bishops are also usually well aware of the potential role conflict in their job of being judge, counselor, friend, and conflict manager to clergy and their congregations. They are also aware that the role of judge must take precedence; therefore, they often delegate the counseling role to others in the diocese. See "Bishops and Diocesan Councils View the Episcopate: A Study in Church Leadership," a report by the Commission of Pastoral Development, House of Bishops of the Episcopal Church, pamphlet dated October 1, 1979. Also see Jud et al, *Ex-Pastors*, p. 85.

Chapter 8

1. Conflict can occur, as Merton describes, not only between demands made on one individual by members of his or her role set attached to his or her occupational status, but as easily or more easily because of conflicting demands on the individual occasioned by people he or she associates with in private life contrasted to demands made on the individual by people he or she associates within occupational life. Robert K. Merton, *Social Theory and Social Structure* (London: The Free Press of Glencoe: 1957), pp. 368–84.

2. Various ways individuals can reduce role strain are described in: William J. Goode, "A Theory of Role Strain," *American Sociological Review* 25 (August 1960): pp. 483–96.

3. E. Wilbur Bock, "The Female Clergy: A Case Study of Professional Marginality," *American Journal of Sociology* 72 (1967): pp. 331–39.

4. Elizabeth M. Havens, "Women, Work, and Wedlock: A Note on Female Mari-

tal Patterns in the United States," in *Changing Women in A Changing Society*, ed. Joan Huber (Chicago, University of Chicago Press, 1973), pp. 213–19

5. Cynthia Fuchs Epstein, *Women in Law* (New York: Basic Books, 1981), pp. 340–41.

6. Michael P. Fogarty, Rhona Rapoport, and Robert N. Rapoport, *Sex, Career and Family* (Beverly Hills, California: Sage Publications, 1971), pp. 334–82.

7. Harry Hale, Jr., Morton King, Doris Moreland Jones, *New Witnesses: United Methodist Clergywomen* (Nashville, Tennessee: Board of Higher Education and Ministry, the United Methodist Church, 1980), p. 76.

8. Erving Goffman, *The Presentation of Self in Everyday Life* (Garden City, New York: Doubleday and Company, Inc., 1959).

9. Rosabeth Moss Kanter, "Some Effects of Proportions on Group Life: Skewed Sex Ratios and Responses to Token Women," *American Journal of Sociology* 82 (March 1977), pp. 965–90, pp. 966, 972 especially.

10. Epstein, *Women in Law*, p. 194.

11. An earlier study of UCC clergy dropouts from the parish ministry also indicated that clergy who experience role conflicts between what parishioners expected of them, and what they wanted and expected of, and for, themselves, led to dissatisfaction with their present position and eventual withdrawal from the parish ministry altogether. See Gerald J. Jud, Edgar W. Mills, Jr., and Genevieve Walters Burch, *Ex-Pastors: Why Men Leave the Parish Ministry* (Philadelphia: Pilgrim Press, 1970).

12. Dean R. Hoge, John E. Dyble, and David T. Polk, "Organizational and Situational Influences on Vocational Commitment of Protestant Ministers," *Review of Religious Research* 23 (December 1981), pp. 133–149, quote p. 147.

Chapter 9

1. See F. Ross Kinsler, *The Extension Movement in Theological Education, A Call to the Renewal of Ministry* (S. Pasadena, CA: William Carey Library, 1978), pp. 12–14.

2. See *Perspectives on Working Women: A Databook* (Washington, D.C.: U.S. Department of Labor Statistics, Bulletin 2080, October 1980), pp. 48 ff.

3. This definition is an adaptation of that of racism in Robert W. Terry, *For Whites Only* (Grand Rapids, MI: Eerdmans, 1970), p. 41.

4. See Jackson W. Carroll and Robert L. Wilson, *Too Many Pastors? The Clergy Job Market* (New York: Pilgrim Press, 1980), Loyde Hartley, "Economics of American Protestant Congregations," mimeographed (Hartford Seminary Foundation Research Report, 1980); and Dean R. Hoge and David A. Roozen, *Understanding Church Growth and Decline* (New York: Pilgrim Press, 1979).

5. This discussion is influenced by Cynthia Fuchs Epstein's, "Encountering the Male Establishment: Sex-Status Limits on Women's Careers in the Professions," *American Journal of Sociology* 75 (May 1970), pp. 965–82.

6. See Jackson W. Carroll, "Some Issues in Clergy Authority," *Reivew of Religious Research* 23 (December 1981), pp. 111–14.

7. Paul Tillich, *Systematic Theology*, Vol. 3 (Chicago: University of Chicago Press, 1963), pp. 212–13.

Index

Address (clerical titles), clergy's attitutes toward, 173–74

Affirmative action, opinions about, 124, 147

Age: of clergywomen, 206; differences in, between senior and junior ministers, 178–79; and loneliness, 198; of parishioners, and relations with clergy, 164–65; and perceptions of career development, 116–17; of women seminarians, 103

ALC. See American Lutheran Church

American Baptist Churches in the U.S.A.: career advancement in, 117; church activity of college students in, 65–66; clergywomen in, 6 table; deployment of pastors in, 110, 119, 120 table; denominational switching in, 58 table; faculty support among, 90; family support among, 66; the job market in, 115; lay attitudes toward women clergy in, 142, 143 table, 144; motivations for seeking ordination in, 95, 96; number of clergywomen in, 43; regional officials of, 121; responses from, for study, 15 table, 17 table; second careers in, 71; seminary enrollment in, 7 table; social class of clergy in, 53, 54 table, 55 table; status of clergywomen in, 125; study of (Lehman), 124, 125, 142, 144; supportive friends and, 67

American Lutheran Church (ALC): age of parishioners and attitudes toward clergy, 164–65, businessmen's relations with clergy in, 163, 164; church activity of college students in, 65–66; clerical dress in, 173; clerical support groups in, 183; clergy's perceptions of helpfulness in the judicatory, 185; denominational switching in, 57, 58 table, 59; deployment of pastors in, 110–11, 119, 120 table; faculty support and, 90; jobs in, 117; lay attitudes toward women clergy in, 143 table; professional peer relationships among, 180; regional officials in, 121; responses from for study, 15 table, 17 table; seminaries, women in, 7 table, 77, 80, 82; social class of clergy in, 53, 54 table, 55 table, status of clergywomen in, 125; supportive friends in, 67; women clergy in, 5, 6 table

Authority, pastoral: exercise of, 170–72, 174–75; symmetry and asymmetry in, 169–70; types of, 33

Baptist. See American Baptist Churches in the U.S.A.

Baptist churches: deaconesses in, 28; women in, 22

Barfoot, Charles H., 22–23

Bensman, Joseph, 169

Berger, Peter, 31

Birthrate, decline of, 8

Bock, E. Wilbur, 1, 8, 190

Bohn, Carole R., 50

Bonifield, William, 132

Boston Theological Institute, 50

Brim, Orville, 73–74

Burch, Genevieve W., 141

Businessmen, relations of, with clergywomen, 162–64

Careers: attitudes of women toward, 133–35; differences in progression of, by sex, 128–30; help from church executives and, 185–86. See also Deployment; Jobs; Status

Carroll, Jackson W., 110, 169
Civil Rights Act, Title VII (1964), 8
Change, social, the church and, 211–12
Charlton, Joy, 12–13, 132, 170
Christian Church. *See* Disciples of Christ
Christian Science (Church of Christ Scientist), 21
Christian Woman's Board of Missions, 27
Church, the: attitudes of, toward the role of women, 21, 22–23, 24, 29–31, 32, 38, 53; modernization of, 31–33, 47, 111; participation in, of college students, 60, 61–62; rural, isolation of clergy in, 182–83, 199; tradition of "sacred masculinity" in, 9–12, 210; types of, and clergy couples, 137
Church of England, 34–35
Church of the Nazarene, 21
Church Feminism Scale. *See* Organizational Church Feminism Index
Class, social: and clergy, 59; of clergywomen, 51–56
Clearinghouse for clerical jobs, 111
Clergy: degrees of feminism among, 100–101, 102 *table;* role of the, 38–39; personal attributes of, 123
Clergywomen: assessment of the current job market by, 113–15; career advancement for, 115–18; education of, 60–61; fathers of, 51–56; as an institutional threat, 140; mothers of, 56; numbers of, 3, 4 *table;* perceived as incongruous, 142, 144; role models of, 50; sampling of, 14–15; single, private life of, 191; social class of, 51–56
Clergy couples, jobs for, 135–37, 205
College: attendance at, 60–67; religious, 61–62, 63–66; types of, 60–61
Competence: clergy's self-assessment of, 141; of clergywomen, 204
Competition, and relations with professional peers, 180–81
Conflict between clergy and parishioners, 165–69
Congregations, and deployment of pastors, 112, 122–24
Congregational churches, deaconesses in, 28
Congregational Yearbook (1927), 38
Co-pastorship, 195–96

Cornwall Collective, the, 77
Cumberland Presbyterians, 38

Data, source and design of, 13–19
Deaconesses, role of, 28, 34–37
Denomination, change of, by clergy, 57–59
Deployment, practices of, 110–12, 118–21. *See also* Jobs
Diaconate, the, 34, 35
Disciples of Christ (Christian Church): age of parishioners and attitude to clergy, 164, 165; career advancement in, 117; church activity of college students in, 64–65; clergywomen in, 5, 6 *table,* 38, 43; clerical dress in, 173; clerical support groups in, 182; denominational switching in, 58 *table;* deployment in, 110, 119, 120 *table;* family support and, 66; the job market in, 114, 115; lay attitudes toward clergywomen in, 143 *table;* regional officials in, 121; responses from, for study, 15 *table,* 17 *table;* second careers in, 71; seminary enrollment in, 7 *table;* social class of clergy in, 53, 54 *table,* 55 *table;* status of clergywomen in, 125; supportive friends in, 67; types of college attended, 61, 64–65; women as decision makers in, 26
Divorce, 194
Dress, clerical, 172–73
Dual-career marriages, clergywomen and, 192–93
Dyble, John E., 201

Eddy, Mary Baker, 21
Education, religious, 39
Edwards, the Reverend Phyllis, 35
Episcopal Church; age of parishioners and relationships with clergy, 164, 165; Anglo-Catholic, 149; bishops and deployment practices, 121; career advancement in, 117; clergy's perceptions of helpfulness in the judicatory, 185; clergywomen in, 5, 6 *table;* clerical dress in, 172, 173; deaconesses in, 28, 34, 35, 37; denominational switching in, 56–57, 58 *table,* 59; deployment in, 110–11, 119, 120 *table;* effect of women clergy in, 43–44; faculty support and, 90; family support and,

66; the job market in, 114, 115; lay attitudes toward women clergy in, 143 *table;* motives for seeking ordination in, 95–96; nuns in, 34; ordination of women in, 1–2, 42; professional peer relationships in, 179–80; regional officials in, 121; responses from, for study, 15 *table,* 17 *table,* second careers in, 71; seminaries, women in, 7 *table,* 77; social class of clergy in, 53, 54 *table,* 55 *table;* status of clergywomen in, 125, 126; supportive friends and, 66–67; types of colleges attended by, 61; women's movements in, 30

Episcopal Society of the Companions of the Holy Cross, 30

Epstein, Cynthia F., 56–57, 132, 191, 198

Evaluation, difficulty of, in the church, 210–11

Evangelical congregations, deaconesses in, 28

Evangelical and Reformed congregations, deaconesses in, 28

Executives. *See* Businessmen

Faculty: attitudes of, toward women seminarians, 86–91, 103–106; influence of, 86; sampling of, 18–19; support from, 89–91; women, in seminaries, 78–79, 89

Family, support from, 66, 67

Father: background of, and choice of seminary, 81 *table;* influence of, on clergywomen, 51–56

Feminism: and the church, 98–102; and clergy's relations with senior ministers, 177–78; and conflict between clergy and laity, 166–67; laity and, 147–52; and ordination of women, 45; and women seminarians, 97–98, 104–106, 107–108

Friends, support from, 66–67

Friendship with parishioners, 167–69

General Convention (Episcopal), 28

General Council of the Assemblies of God, 23

Goffman, Erving, 197

Harrison, Beverly, 98

Havens, Elizabeth M., 190

Hiatt, Suzanne, 34–35

Hoge, Dean R., 201

Hughes, Everett C., 10–11

International Church of the Foursquare Gospel, 21, 23

Job market: for clergywomen, 204–205, 206–207; perceptions of, by sex, 113–15

Jobs, clerical, finding, 113, 116, 118–24, 132. *See also* Deployment

Joel, 21

Jud, Gerald J., 141

Judicatory, attitudes among, toward clergywomen, 207; and deployment of pastors, 111–12; women in, 150, 183–86

Kanter, Rosabeth Moss, 12, 93, 198

Kelley, Dean, 140

Laity: attitudes of, toward clergywomen, 139–41, 205, 207; clergy's relationships with, 161–69; feminism among, 100–102; perceptions of clerical leadership by, 171–72, 174–75; sampling of, 16, 18

Lambeth Conference, the, 28, 35

Language, inclusive, 149–50, 209

Lawyers, women, 3–4, 56–57, 133–34, 191

Lay leaders, assessments of clergy by, 141–47

Lay professionals, women as, 39–40

LCA. *See* Lutheran Church in America

Leadership, ministerial style of, 169–72

Lee, Mother Ann, 21

Lehman, Edward C., Jr., 90, 118, 124, 125, 132, 140, 141, 142, 144, 152, 157

Loneliness, for clergywomen, 197–200, 207

Lutheran church, the: clergy's relations with the judicatory, 184; expectations of clerical dress in, 172, motives for seeking ordination in, 95–96; pastoral style and the laity of, 163–64; role of deaconesses in, 28; study on women in seminary in, 86, 88. *See also* American Lutheran Church; Lutheran Church in America

Lutheran Church in America (LCA): age of parishioners and attitudes toward clergy, 164–65; career advancement in, 117; clergy relations with businessmen in, 163; clergywomen in, 6 *table;* clerical dress in, 172, 173; deaconesses in, 36; denominational switching in, 57, 58 *table,* 59; deployment in, 110–11, 119, 120 *table;* faculty support and, 90; family support and, 66; the job market in, 115; lay attitudes toward clergywomen in, 143 *table;* motives for seeking ordination in, 96; regional officials in, 121; responses from, for study, 15 *table,* 17 *table;* seminary enrollment in, 7 *table,* 77; social class of clergy in, 53, 54 *table,* 55 *table;* status of clergywomen in, 125; support from pastors and, 66; supportive friends in, 67; women as decision makers in, 27

Lutheran Deaconess Association, 36, 37

McPherson, Aimee Semple, 21, 23

Marginality, professional, of clergywomen, 12–13

Marital status, and loneliness, 198–99, 207

Marriage: advantages of, to clergymen, 190; between clergy, and deployment, 135–37; clergywomen and, 190–97

Marty, Martin, 2

Marx, Karl, 31

Methodist. *See* United Methodist Church

Methodist Episcopal Church, 28, 38

Methodist Episcopal Church South, 28

Methodist Protestant Church, 28

Mills, Edgar W., Jr., 132, 141

Ministry, the. *See* Parish ministry

Missionaries, women ordained as, 37–38

Missionary movement, women and, 25–27

Missionary societies, organization of, 32–33

Morgan, Emily M., 30

Motherhood: lay perceptions of effect of, on clergywomen, 145; strains of, for clergywomen, 192–93

Mothers, influence of, on clergywomen, 53, 55 *table,* 56

National Council of Churches, 140

Networks, informal, in clerical job market, 112

Nuns, 27–28, 30, 34

Oberlin Theological School, 11

Occupation, before ordination, 70 *table*

Officials, regional, and career advancement, 121–22

Orders, religious, women in, 34

Ordination: as an expression of vocation, 96; faculty support in decisions about, 90–91; missionary work and, 25–26, 37–38; motives for seeking, 7–9, 40–41, 44–45, 46, 47, 93–98, 107; as professional status, 94–95; social movements and, 43–44, 96–98; of women, denominational differences in, 42–43

Organizational Church Feminism Index (Church Feminism Scale), 100–101, 102, 107, 151, 177

Palmer, Phoebe, 21

Parents, influence of, on clergywomen, 45–57, 59, 60

Parish, types of, and differences by sex, 127–28

Parish government, lay opinions on women in, 149

Parish ministry: as a career, 115–18; commitment to, 200–201; motivations for seeking, 84–85; orientations of clergywomen toward, 95–98; seminary training and, 79; women's aspirations for, 107

Parishioners, relationships with, 205

Part-time work. *See* Work, part-time

Pastor: influence of, on choice of seminary, 82; support from, for decision to enter seminary, 66; wife of, and the church, 30–31, 83–84, 137, 182

Paul, Saint, 10, 22

PCUS. *See* Presbyterian Church in the United States

Peers, relations with professional, 179, 205–206

Pentecostalism, women and, 22–23

Pike, Bishop James, 35

Pilgrim Holiness Church, 21

Pillar of Fire Church, 21

Ploch, Daniel, 85–86

Polk, David T., 201
Position in the ministry, 178; differences, by gender, 125–27; satisfaction with, 199–201
Presbyterian church, ordination of women in, 42
Presbyterian Church in the United Status (PCUS): attitude toward clergy and age of parishioners, 164, 165; career advancement in 117; clerical support groups in, 182; clergy's relations with judicatory in, 184–85; clergywomen in, 6 table; denominational switching in, 58 table; deployment in, 110–11, 119, 120 table; job market in, 113, 115; lay attitudes toward clergywomen in, 143 table, 144, 145; regional officials in, 121; responses from, for study, 15 table, 17 table; second careers in, 71; seminary enrollment in, 7 table; social class of clergy in, 53, 54 table, 55 table; status of women clergy in, 125, 126; study of (Lehman), 124; support from pastors of, 66; supportive friends among, 67; types of college attended, 61. See also United Presbyterian Church
Princeton Theological Seminary, 78
Pritchard, Harriet, 39–40
Private life, balancing of, with professional duties, 189–97
Professionalism, as a motive for ordination, 44–45
Professionalization of women in the church, 33–46
Project S.W.I.M.: A Study of Women in Ministry (Lehman), 142
Protestantism: decline of, and lay attitudes to clergywomen, 209–10; institutionalization of, 23
Protestants, 44
Puritanism, 22

Quakers, the, 21, 30

Reform movements, and women in the church, 29–30
Regular Baptists, 22
Religion, life-cycle of, in America, 20–27; charismatic stage, 20–21, 24, 25, 47; consolidation, 22–23, 26, 47; institutionalization, 23, 47; social mobility and, 27–29

Religious socialization, 57–60
Roman Catholic church, 42–44; nuns in, 27–28, 30, 34
Role models: for clergywomen, 50–51, 56–57; women as, 91–93

Salary: of clergy couples, 137; discrepancies in, between sexes, 130–32, 207, 209
Second careers: and decisions to enter seminary, 69–72; the ministry as, 9, 45; for women seminarians, 103–104
Self-assessment, by clergywomen, 205
Self-concept, professional, of clergy, 141, 155–58
Senior minister: clergy's relations with, 175–79; lay preferences in, 145–46, 148
Separate Baptists, 22
Seventh-Day Adventist Church, 21
Seminary: age, and decision to enter, 67–72; atmosphere in, for women, 204; choice of, 79–82; decision to enter, 62–66; denominational, 77–78, 89; effect of women students on, 77–78; enrollment in, 5–7, 76–78, 88–89, 92 table, 106–107; experiences of women in, 85–93; influence of, on women, 107; interdenominational, women in, 77–78, 88–89; motivations for attending, 82–85; support for decision to enter, 66–67; women faculty in, 89
Sexism in the church, 96–102, 106, 207, 208–209. See also Feminism
Shakers, the, 21
Sheppard, Gerald T., 22–23
Sisterhood of the Good Shepherd, 34, 35
Social change, and the ordination of women, 45–46
Social concerns, and feminism, 151–152
Southern Baptist Convention, 2
Status: of deaconesses, 36–37; effect of women on, 41–42; of lay professionals, 39–40; of the ministry as a profession, 68; ordination of women and, 47; of women as clergy, 9–13, 210
Stereotype: of the clergy, 142–43; of women, 11
Success, and perceptions of career advancement, 118
Sunday school, women and, 24
Sunday School Union, 24